Searchable Talk

ALSO AVAILABLE FROM BLOOMSBURY

Discourse of Twitter and Social Media, Michele Zappavigna
Writing on the Wall, Tom Standage
Discourse and Identity on Facebook, Mariza Georgalou
A Critical Hypertext Analysis of Social Media, Volker Eisenlauer
The Discourse of Blogs and Wikis, Greg Myers

Searchable Talk

Hashtags and Social Media Metadiscourse

MICHELE ZAPPAVIGNA

BLOOMSBURY ACADEMIC

LONDON · NEW YORK · OXFORD · NEW DELHI · SYDNEY

BLOOMSBURY ACADEMIC
Bloomsbury Publishing Plc
50 Bedford Square, London, WC1B 3DP, UK

BLOOMSBURY, BLOOMSBURY ACADEMIC and the Diana logo are trademarks of
Bloomsbury Publishing Plc

First published in Great Britain 2018

Cover design by Holly Bell

A catalogue record for this book is available from the British Library.

A catalog record for this book is available from the Library of Congress.

ISBN: PB: 978-1-4742-9237-5
        HB: 978-1-4742-9236-8
       ePDF: 978-1-4742-9235-1
      eBook: 978-1-4742-9234-4

Typeset by Integra Software Services Pvt. Ltd.
Printed and bound in Great Britain

To find out more about our authors and books visit www.bloomsbury.com
and sign up for our newsletters.

For my mentor, Jim Martin, who led me up the garden path
and over the cliff of knowledge, and for my friend and colleague,
Sumin Zhao, who helped me during the fall.

Contents

Figures

Tables

Acknowledgements

I would like to thank Jim Martin, Sumin Zhao, and Shooshi Dreyfus for their comments and suggestions on this work. Thanks also go to Kit Wong for photographing hashtags 'in the wild'. I would also like to acknowledge my husband, Mark Assad, for his technical help and ever-generous support, as well as my parents, Joe and Jill Zappavigna, and my parents-in-law, Joe and Sue Assad, for their help in babysitting my two children so that I could write in peace.

Note on Text

Extracts from social media texts are shown in Courier New font. Authors of social media posts are referred to as 'users' in order to indicate that they are simultaneously a social media user (i.e. someone who makes use of a social media service) and a language user (someone who construes meaning with language). All usernames, with the exception of those pertaining to institutions or public figures, are anonymized as @user.

Linguistic features are annotated in **bold**.

Ideation-attitude couplings are shown as:

[ideation: X/attitude: Y]

1

Introduction

Background

I began writing this book in 2016 when two seismic political events occurred: 'Brexit',[1] the UK vote to leave the European Union, and Donald Trump's victory in the US presidential election. These events spawned significant volumes of social media communication. For example consider the following post to the microblogging service Twitter:

> **#brexit: #trump:**
> "I think we've had enough of experts, don't you?"
>
> Welcome to the post-factual age of the idiot. Protect yourselves.

This tweet contains two examples of hashtags, a form of social tagging[2] featuring the # symbol followed by a word or phrase. *Hashtag* was voted 'Word of the Year' by the American Dialect Society in 2012[3] (Zimmer & Carson, 2013). The # symbol has become a charged emblem representing 'a way of thinking that has deeply penetrated cultural consciousness' (Scheible, 2015, p. 91). Hashtags remain a popular means of coordinating social media discussion, referencing ideas, cracking jokes, and producing metacommentary. Having captured public imagination, the practice of tagging, once an act of classification, has emerged as a means of forging and contesting social bonds. It is this emergent function that is the focus of this book.

Social media services, such as Twitter, are currently a popular platform for communicating views about public affairs (Vaccari et al., 2015). The political hashtags *#Brexit, #Trump*, and *#Election2016* featured in the top trending hashtags of 2016 (Berland, 2016). Throughout 2016 and into 2017, there was highly visible, polarized political debate between social media users[4] from opposing ends of the political spectrum. In parallel there was self-affirming discourse inside 'social media bubbles' (Berghel, 2017), where users were saturated with like-minded opinions. At the time of writing, a particular complex of interpersonal bonds was very visible, threading its way across multiple discursive regions, traversing communities and sub-communities, and adopted by various types of personae: shared ridicule of Trump and his administration. Lampooning Trump has become a worldwide pastime with people who were, and continue to be, disgruntled, disturbed, shocked, or horrified expressing their reactions to his words and actions. Parallel to this discourse is exultant 'alt-right'[5] adoration of Trump and his attitudes, but that is a topic for another book.

We know from work on gossip that complaining, teasing, ridiculing, condemning, and generally negatively appraising a third party is a highly aligning activity (Bosson, Johnson, Niederhoffer, & Swann, 2006; Dunbar, 2004; Eggins & Slade, 1997/2005). This kind of language is also involved in the establishment of in-group/out-group boundaries (Gagnon & Bourhis, 1996; Jaworski & Coupland, 2005; Tajfel, 1970; Wert & Salovey, 2004). For example, consider the shared values construed in the following tweets, featuring the hashtag *#OrangeCheeto*. This hashtag combines a reference to Donald Trump's overuse of fake tan with the brand name of a popular snack, both of which are class markers[6]:

> Why does Canada get the handsome @JustinTrudeau and we get an **#orangecheeto** for president?

> "ALT-Right - Delete!" ☺ #AltRight #NoBannonPresident #RESIST #ResistTrump #SoCalledPresident **#OrangeCheeto**

> **#OrangeCheeto** needs vacation already? Sad! #NoStamina! #RESIST #NotMyPresident

> We will not obey and we will not go away. #TheResistance. #Resist #Protest #Misbehave #Disobey #FuckTrump **#OrangeCheeto** #NotMyPresident

> Make America Great Again and resign from office. **#Orangecheeto**

#OrangeCheeto functions, as we will see in Chapter 2, as both metadata and metadiscourse. On the one hand, the tag operates as metadata, in the sense that a particular instance of a tag is associated with all other instances of the same tag in the social stream.[7] On the other hand, it functions as metadiscourse, in the sense that it encapsulates, at a higher order of

abstraction, the interpersonal meaning being made in the tweet (in this case an assessment of Trump). As Chapter 3 will explain by drawing on Halliday's (1973) notion of linguistic metafunctions, the meanings that might be made by using a particular hashtag can enact a range of functions. They can be both ideational (e.g. a tag indicating that a post is about #Trump) and interpersonal (as in the above examples). The function is always also textual, since the # symbol organizes the post as a communicative unit. The # separates the tag from the body of the post, as well linking it to the meanings made in other texts using the same hashtag.

Hashtags and social tagging as a form of searchable talk

Hashtags are a special form of user-generated metadata that has achieved global prominence. Metadata has a long history in the domain of information management. However, this is the first historical period where we see it so closely tied to enacting social relations, having extended its semiotic reach as an information-organizing tool to a social resource for building relationships and communities through the practice of social tagging (Zappavigna, 2015). While we might be used to thinking about 'tags' as labelling things, social tags, as we will see in this book, can have a function well beyond classification. Some scholars have suggested that hashtags are 'performative' (Papacharissi, 2015), acting as an 'interpretative frame' (Bonilla & Rosa, 2015, p. 5). In this way they provide insight into what a user's communication is '"really about," thereby enabling users to indicate a meaning that might not be otherwise apparent' (Bonilla & Rosa, 2015, p. 5).

Social tagging has only recently begun to be studied by discourse analysts (e.g. a forthcoming issue of the journal *Discourse, Context and Media* is devoted to linguistic studies of social tagging (Lee, in press)). As a practice, social tagging involves 'publicly labelling or categorizing resources in a shared, on-line environment' (Trant, 2009, p. 1). It has also been termed 'collaborative tagging', 'conversational tagging', 'social classification', 'social indexing', 'mob indexing', and 'folk categorization' (Baca, 2008). All of these terms reference the act of annotating a digital text with user-generated (as opposed to predefined) tags so that other users can find it. Merholz (2004) analogizes with 'desire lines' – the trails worn in a landscape as people choose certain paths repeatedly over time – to suggest the emergent nature of the kind of 'ethnoclassification' produced through 'free-form' tagging.

Examples of early social tags include freely chosen tags used on social bookmarking sites such as *del.icio.us,* where the main function was to index and collate interesting media. 'Folksonomic' tags were also used on photo-sharing sites such as Flickr, where the main function was to describe an image. The use of tags in both of these cases is aimed at enabling particular resources to be found by other users, and in this sense, is a form of social 'sharing'. Because these tags are user-defined, they do not necessarily conform to a predictable taxonomic structure. Instead social tagging systems have tended to draw on 'shared and emergent social structures and behaviours, as well as related conceptual and linguistic structures of the user community' (Marlow, Naaman, boyd, & Davis, 2006, p. 31). This kind of collaborative tagging, that evolves with community use, is often referred to as a practice of 'folksonomy' (Vander Wal, 2007). Folksonomies, unlike taxonomies, are non-hierarchical, and different tags will wax and wane depending on contextual factors. Folksonomic tagging is different to the top-down hierarchical approaches of traditional document classification since it is a 'decentralized practice by which individuals and groups create, manage, and share terms, names, and so on (called tags), to annotate and categorize digital resources in an online "social" environment' (Baca, 2008).

More recent and widespread social tagging has occurred with the development of social media services such as Twitter, Facebook, and Instagram where it fulfils both a similar function to social indexing, and, as we will see, a range of additional discursive functions. Hashtags are the most prominent and ubiquitous form of social tag used in social media and are used across a range of services aside from Twitter, for example, Facebook, Tumblr, Instagram, Google+, and Pinterest. They are words or phrases marked with the # symbol (sometimes referred to as a *hash* or *pound* sign, *octothorpe, hex*, or as the *number symbol* on a keypad) to indicate their special status as a tag. As we will see in Chapter 2, the # symbol 'has been promoted from a rather peripheral typographic resource to an emblem of social media linguistic practice' (Heyd & Puschmann, in press).

An example of a tag marked with # is shown in Figure 1.1. Here the hashtag, *#sysfunc,* indicates that the post is part of ongoing discourse about

Michele Zappavigna
@SMLinguist

Presenting on social tagging at Sydney Uni
linguistics department #sysfunc

7:00 PM - 15 Oct 2015

FIGURE 1.1 *An example of a tweet containing a hashtag.*

issues relating to Systemic Functional Linguistics, the model of language used in this book. The #sysfunc tag allows users to be part of unfolding discussion about relevant topics (which may also be indicated with further hashtags). This coordinating function means that tags have often been seen as conversational in nature (Huang, Hornton, & Efthimiadis, 2010) and social media services themselves as conversation networks (Bruns, 2012; Honeycutt & Herring, 2009).

Most accounts of the origins of the Twitter hashtag identify Chris Messina as coining the term, citing the following tweet that he posted in 2007:

```
How do you feel about using # (pound) for groups. As
in #barcamp [msg]?
```

However, while this post does appear to contain the first use of a hashtag, it was another user, Stowe Boyd, who coined the term. He did this as a way of referring to the tag in Messina's original post:

```
I support the hash tag convention: http://tinyurl.
com/2qttlb #hashtag #factoryjoe #twitter
```

This is an example of 'how even very new terms are prey to faulty or incomplete memories about their origins' (Zimmer & Carson, 2013, p. 83). Boyd went on to suggest in a blog post that hashtags could facilitate 'groupings' by being used to 'define shared experience of some kind'. He argued 'tags imply communities' even though their use on social bookmarking sites and blogs had conditioned users and developers to think about these tags imply as metadata for retrieving bookmarks or posts (Boyd, 2007).

Like other highly visible, novel digital practices such as taking 'selfies' (self-portraits taken with the front camera of a smartphone), hashtags have been subject to criticism and offered as evidence of the narcissistic self-involvement of digital practices. For example, the following description of hashtag activism (using a hashtag to contribute to an online campaign supporting a social issue) is characteristic of this kind of discourse:

Hash tagging fits neatly in the social media world. It thrives on the superficial. While hashtag activism presents the appearance of benevolence and altruism, it is merely another form of narcissism. By hash-tagging, we feel a sense of satisfaction that we've contributed something good, however hollow, to the world's problems. It's a self appeasing exercise, laden with feel-good mentality that does nothing to address the actual issue. (Hughes, 2015)

For instance, the hashtags accompanying an image of a woman participating in the *2017 March for Science* (held globally as a reaction to Trump's climate change denial and his links to anti-science, anti-expert worldviews) might be interpreted as an over-specification of meaning symptomatic of such self-involvement:

```
#girlsjustwannahavefunding #sciencemarch
#marchforscienceboston #MarchforScience #factsmatter
#knowledgeispower #stem #steminist #factsmatter #resist
#resisttrump #scientists #scienceisreal #sciencefunding
#americarunsonscience #womeninscience #womeninstem
#igerscambridge #igersboston
```

However, as we will see in Chapter 8, the kinds of image-tag relations that these hashtags establish are part of the political views being expressed. Tagging patterns of this kind have little to do with narcissism. As with other forms of social media practice that foreground point of view, these tags are 'an act of political engagement rather than disengagement' (Zhao & Zappavigna, in press).

More personal uses of the hashtag have also been pathologized as a 'cultural epidemic' where 'people often overuse the practice or, worse, use it as a way of poking fun at themselves or others' (Costello, 2016, p. 9). However, even in these contexts, it is more productive to think of how these tags are functioning to expand semiotic meaning potential as a form of searchable talk.

Previous research on hashtags

Hashtags have received extensive attention in social media research, a broad and interdisciplinary field attracting researchers from media and communication studies, computing, linguistics, cultural theory, marketing and psychology, amongst other disciplines. This is because of the new communicative affordances hashtags offer users that make them interesting to fields involved in understanding how communication works. It is also because they provide a novel means of collecting discourse about a particular topic, person, or event that might be relevant to the concerns of a particular discipline. In fact most academic disciplines feature work on domain-relevant hashtags. This work is aimed at providing insight into the particular field[8] rather than into social media practices in their own right. Research domains have included political discourse (as we will consider below), crisis communication (Glasgow & Fink, 2013; Grasso et al., 2017; Lachlan, Spence, Lin, Najarian, & Greco, 2014; Mendoza, Poblete, & Castillo, 2010; Palen, Starbird, Vieweg, & Hughes, 2010; Wukich & Steinberg, 2013), public relations, particularly when public relation campaigns falter due to the public re-appropriating a hashtag (Fathi, 2009; Jackson & Foucault Welles, 2015; Sanderson, Barnes, Williamson, & Kian, 2016), and mental health (McCosker, 2017).

Within linguistics there has been a concentration of studies interested in exploring the different functions that hashtags can enact (Zappavigna, 2015). These studies have been undertaken across a wide range of contexts including translation (Carter, Tsagkias, & Weerkamp, 2011; Desjardins, 2016), inferential processes in reading (Scott, 2015), self-branding and microcelebrity (Page, 2012), bullying discourse (Calvin et al., 2015), digital libraries (Schlesselman-Tarango, 2013), and political memes (Zhu, 2016). They have included studies of the role of hashtags in codeswitching (Jurgens, Dimitrov, & Ruths, 2014), speech act theory (Wikström, 2014), and sarcasm detection and analysis (Kovaz, Kreuz, & Riordan, 2013; Kunneman, Liebrecht, van Mulken, & van den Bosch, 2015). There has also been interest within computational linguistics in using hashtags to improve emotion classification, sentiment analysis, and other semantic computational tasks (Mohammad & Kiritchenko, 2015; Qadir & Riloff, 2013).

In terms of research methods, creating social media corpora and text collections[9] by using a hashtag as a search term has become a popular strategy (Page, Barton, Unger, & Zappavigna, 2014). Because of the ease of collecting digital data, most studies tend to draw on quantitative methods or mixed methods (incorporating qualitative analysis of data collected via some quantitative selection criteria). Hashtags are often used as a means of sampling texts in specific domains of social life. For example, #funeral, used to sample Instagram images relating to funerals (Gibbs, Meese, Arnold, Nansen, & Carter, 2015), #ausvotes, used to sample posts relating to an Australian election (Bruns, 2017; Burgess & Bruns, 2012), or #auspol used to sample posts about Australian political discourse more broadly (Sauter & Bruns, 2015; Zappavigna, 2014d). A limitation of this hashtag-based sampling strategy is that it does not necessarily capture all relevant communication since there will be posts and replies about a topic that do not incorporate a hashtag (Zappavigna, 2017a).

In addition, hashtag-based sampling may not provide a corpus representative of broader public discourse on a particular issue due to the self-selecting nature of hashtag use, and because the Twitter Application Programming Interface (API)[10] places restrictions on researchers that make it difficult to trace contextual information relating to particular texts and interactions (Burgess & Bruns, 2015). Exhaustive or representative corpora are very difficult to create. Since 2010 Twitter has not made the 'firehose' of all tweets available at an affordable price for most research projects and instead many researchers rely on the 'garden hose' feed (Bruns & Burgess, 2012b). This is a selection of the more comprehensive feed that has been 'randomized' via an algorithm that Twitter does not disclose. Using the smaller subset of data that the garden hose feed generates makes retrieving entire threads of activity difficult, particularly since these may range across many users, across long periods of time, and overlap in ways that other kinds of 'conversational' data do not.

Hashtags have been seen as a way of increasing the communicative reach of a social media text by attracting a greater audience who might 'engage' (to use social media marketing parlance) with a post. This has, meant that entities wishing to use Twitter for commercial purposes have been interested in issues such as the optimal location in a post at which a hashtag will increase engagement.[11] Work of this kind relies on computational approaches to understanding how hashtags spread through social media networks in terms of propagation and diffusion (Bastos, Raimundo, & Travitzki, 2013; Tsur & Rappoport, 2012). Computational approaches to hashtags have also been considered useful for contributing to particular natural language processing goals such as topic modelling (Wang, Liu, Huang, & Feng, 2016). There has also been interest in automatic hashtag recommendation aimed at helping users find material relevant to their interests (Godin, Slavkovikj, De Neve, Schrauwen, & Van de Walle, 2013; Mahajan et al., 2016; She & Chen, 2014).

A concentration of computational work has focused on the issue of hashtag diffusion and popularity. Some tags will have short life cycles, while others may endure for long periods, and particular hashtags will tend to co-occur (Wang, Liu, & Gao, 2016). For instance, an early study found that short hashtags were more successful in propagating than longer tags, contrasting examples such as #music with #fatpeoplearesexier (Cunha et al., 2011). Romero, Meeder, and Kleinberg (2011) analysed the persistence of hashtags by comparing information diffusion across different topics. This study found that hashtag persistence varied and that different 'activity dynamics' were associated with different 'social semantics'. There has also been work aimed at understanding 'spikes of collective attention' by investigating peaks in the activity of hashtags and categorising hashtags based on their evolution profile (Lehmann, Gonçalves, Ramasco, & Cattuto, 2012, p. 251). Complementary to this is interest are studies of the co-occurrence patterns of 'viral' hashtags (Wang, Wang et al., 2016, p. 851).

The aim of this computational work is usually not only to model how tags spread but to predict which hashtags will become popular (Kong, Mei,

Feng, Ye, & Zhao, 2014; Ma, Sun, & Cong, 2012). This is part of an ongoing focus in this field in unpacking the mechanisms for achieving popularity in terms of 'the properties of collective attention and the principles underlying the diffusion of novel items' (Zhang, Zhao, & Xu, 2016). Some of this work has thought about the spread of tags as a diffusion of linguistic innovation (Paradowski & Jonak, 2012).There has also been interest in applying techniques for modelling infectious disease to characterize how hashtags spread (Skaza & Blais, 2017).

Hashtags as 'conversation'

The most obvious metaphor that has been used to describe how hashtags function in social media research is the idea of a 'conversation'. The use is metaphorical since the ways in which social steaming discourses unfold is different to traditional conversation, in both the folk and linguistic senses of this term. Social tagging has been described as 'conversational tagging' (Huang et al., 2010) since, in microblogging environments at least, tags can facilitate forms of mass communication. This might be about a particular ideational target (e.g. an event) or an interpersonal value (e.g. a political issue). Because microblogging services are generally global and public by default, they have been amendable 'to the development of means for automatically organising discussions of specific topics through shared conversation markers' (Bruns, 2012, p. 1324). Some studies have considered the role of non-human actors in these conversations, for instance, considering how 'bots' (software programs that send out automated social media posts) using hashtags influence 'conversational networks' in the political domain (Murthy et al., 2016, p. 4952).

Tags can be conversational in the sense that they help users to engage with topics receiving broad interest. More locally, they can be conversational by affording forms of interpersonal metacommentary and linguistic play, as we will see later in this book. Most approaches to understanding hashtags take a priori this notion that hashtags facilitate conversation and discussion (Bruns, 2012; Bruns & Burgess, 2011b; Rossi & Magnani, 2012), particularly in the political domain (Highfield, 2016). However, what might seem dialogic in nature is actually 'multilogic' (Zappavigna, forthcoming). For instance, microblogging exchanges are more like 'interchanges' involving cacophonies of different voices, as we will see in Chapter 5. The relationship that social media exchanges might have to existing forms of dialogic exchange that have been studied in linguistics remains to be specified. It likely will require renovating key concepts such as turn-taking or 'exchange structure' that have been useful in characterizing in offline conversation (Berry, 1981; Martin, 1992).

One area of consolidated interest is in practices of live-tweeting in real time. This is sometimes termed 'two screen' or 'second screen' viewing. Users view some primary form of live media at the same time as engaging with social media on a secondary device (Highfield, 2013; Kroon, 2017; Lochrie & Coulton, 2012; Zappavigna, 2017a). For instance, this might involve live-tweeting a TV show using hashtags to contribute to unfolding commentary produced by other user watching at the same time (Deller, 2011; Harrington, 2013; Rossi & Giglietto, 2016; Sauter & Bruns, 2014; Schirra, Sun, & Bentley, 2014; Zappavigna, 2017a). It might also involve other kinds of live events such as sport (e.g. the Tour De France (Harrington, 2013)). This Live-tweeting of this kind has been characterized as a form of 'backchannel' communication (McNely, 2009).

Research into how hashtags coordinate political debate is one of the main areas to use this notion of hashtagging as a form of conversation. Social media communication is itself often equated with public opinion by political journalists (Anstead & O'Loughlin, 2015). There are, however, problems with this assumption, since not all sectors of the public in all countries use social media. Like many other kinds of social media research, studies often select a domain-relevant hashtag and then use this as a keyword for creating a text collection to analyse (Larsson & Moe, 2012). This analysis has included content analysis of political communication in particular countries (e.g. Canadian politics (Small, 2011)), as well as work on how different kinds of political actors use hashtags (e.g. comparing how journalists and politicians use hashtags (Enli & Simonsen, 2017)). There has also been interest in how hashtags, and social media more broadly, impact agenda-setting by traditional media (Conway, Kenski, & Wang, 2015).

Many studies have focused on the role of hashtags during elections (Burgess & Bruns, 2012; Jungherr, Schoen, & Jürgens, 2016). There has also been work on political controversies (Callison & Hermida, 2015; Garimella, Morales, Gionis, & Mathioudakis, 2016; Maireder & Schlögl, 2014). While most studies sample texts during a particular political moment, or across a unit of time such as the course of an election, there has been some longitudinal work (e.g. a longitudinal dataset of *#agchatoz* tweets, a tag relating to the Australian agricultural industry) (Burgess, Galloway, & Sauter, 2015).

The use of hashtags as part of protest or social movements has received a lot of attention in the media. This is perhaps due to popular 'mythologies' suggesting that hashtags engender social movements 'by some kind of social media magic' (Gerbaudo, 2012, p. 102). There has thus been a lot of work on what has been termed 'hashtag activism'[12] (Chiluwa & Ifukor, 2015; Kuo, 2016; Lindgren & Lundström, 2011; Potts, Simm, Whittle, &

Unger, 2014; Stache, 2015; Vats, 2015). Hashtags such as *#Libya* and *#Egypt* used during the Arab Spring uprisings of 2011 have received attention (Bruns, Highfield, & Burgess, 2013) as part of broader interest in whether Twitter can be used to promote social progress in Saudi Arabia (Chaudhry, 2014). There has also been a concentration of work on 'hashtag feminism' (a form of feminist activism) (Clark, 2016; Drüeke & Zobl, 2015; Horeck, 2014; Jackson, 2016; Kim, 2017; Scott, 2017; Williams, 2015) as well as work on the role of hashtags in the social construction of gender and race (Pham, 2015; Rightler-McDaniels & Hendrickson, 2014).

A social semiotic approach to analysing hashtags

Hashtags are an interesting object of study since they can be approached both from the perspective of their *affordances* as metadata and from the perspective of their *function* as meaning-making resources. In this way they operate as a 'semiotic technology' (Zhao, Djonov, & van Leeuwen, 2014)[13]. This is because they provide users with both a technical means for annotating their posts as well as with a resource for making a range of meanings. Hashtags render communication more readily searchable and visible within the social stream. At the same time they render social media communication more open to processes of 'ambient affiliation' whereby users share and contest social bonds (Zappavigna, 2011, 2012b).

This book adopts a social semiotic approach to how hashtags, as social tags, are used for making meaning. The premise is that investigating how these tags operate in their functional context[14] will illuminate their role as a semiotic resource. This perspective is grounded in Halliday's (1978) ideas regarding language as social semiotic, and the model of language, known as Systemic Function Linguistics (SFL) that has grown out of his work. SFL posits language as a meaning-making resource. It has been viewed as distinct amongst linguistic theories because it develops theory regarding social processes as well as applying an 'analytical methodology which permits the detailed and systematic description of language patterns' (Eggins, 1994, p. 23). Since social media environments incorporate a range of semiotic modes, and hashtags are often used to annotate multimedia artefacts such as images, the work undertaken also draws on a related field, Multimodal Discourse Analysis. MDA is a perspective that argues that semiotic modes other than language can be modelled in a manner analogous to, or inspired by, the accounts developed for systematizing linguistic meaning.

The structure of this book

Hashtags are very complicated objects of study by virtue of being a semiotic technology. As just noted, this necessitates accounting for both their technical and semiotic aspects. This book approaches the hashtag from multiple perspectives, as befitting a phenomenon that has high dimensionality. We begin in Chapter 2 by considering how hashtags function as 'searchable talk', an interplay of their role as metadata and as metadiscourse. This involves unpacking what 'meta' means both in terms of data about data and in terms of orders of meaning.

Chapter 3 applies Halliday's (1973) concept of linguistic metafunctions to hashtags, demonstrating how they can construe an ideational function (indicating a topic), an interpersonal function (construing relationship), and a textual function (aggregating and organizing discourse). This chapter also notes emerging spoken and gestured hashtags which have yet to stabilize as a resource. Chapter 4 focuses in more detail on one metafunctional dimension, the interpersonal, investigating the important and novel function that hashtags have accrued in construing evaluative metacommentary. This chapter introduces the Appraisal framework (Martin & White, 2005), the model of evaluative language used to analyse opinion and sentiment in social media texts throughout this book.

Hashtags are inherently heteroglossic (Bakhtin, 1986). They are an explicit way of linking a social media text to other potential perspectives construed by other texts in the social stream. Chapter 5 investigates the concepts of metaperspective and intersubjectivity. It explores how hashtags enable voices and perspectives to be referenced and evaluated in new ways. The particular focus is on the quoted voice: I introduce a model for exploring quoted social media voices that extends White's (1998) work on vocalization developed for understanding journalistic voice.

In order to understand how a voice construes a social value, we need to understand how ideation and attitude come together as 'couplings' of meaning. Chapter 6 explains the concept of coupling as introduced by Martin (2000, p. 164) and developed by other discourse analysts. This chapter considers how hashtags can be used to mark, and make more alignable, couplings in social media texts. These couplings can be negotiated in discourse as social bonds that are shared or contested. This is the focus of Chapter 7, which aims to extend the approach to ambient affiliation introduced in my previous book on the discourse of Twitter (Zappavigna, 2012b). Chapter 7 develops affiliation theory by exploring how hashtags are involved in construing different kinds of orientations towards a coupling. These orientations are instantiated through the discursive systems, *convoking*, *finessing*, and *promoting* It also provides a more comprehensive model of affiliation, building on Knight (2010).

Since an account of hashtags that does not consider their intermodal relations would not fully capture their multimodal meaning potential, Chapter 8 introduces the notion of intermodal coupling. This chapter investigates ideational and interpersonal image-tag relations, and intertextual relations in social media more generally. It considers the function of these relations in internet memes, a form of shareable media where users contribute iterations on a theme or template, mostly as displays of wit.

The hasthags explored across these chapters are examples of mockery of current US president Donald Trump. This choice was made in order to provide a functional context for analysis in accord with the social semiotic approach to language. This context-aware approach was designed to avoid the problem of approaching new technologies as a genre, rather than a multimodal resource involved in enacting different kinds of genres. Just as early studies of computer-mediated communication focused heavily on characterizing 'the language of email' or 'the language of instant messaging', early studies of social media have tended to think of channels or platforms as genres (or entire languages), rather than as resources involved in creating different types of texts within different social contexts. The problem is analogous to that identified by Androutsopoulos (2006, p. 421): 'Rather than identifying e-mail, chat or weblogs as new genres per se, the question is how these communications technologies are locally appropriated to enact a variety of discourse genres.'

A note on sampling

The method for collecting the texts analysed throughout this book relied on a fusion of grounded theory sampling (Strauss & Corbin, 1994) with inspection of concordance lines. The latter is an approach derived from corpus linguistics. Rather than constructing a local corpus on my host computer, I instead relied on hashtag searches (as made available by various services such as Twitter and Instagram) to generate these concordance lines. This is perhaps analogous to 'web as corpus' approaches that have been advocated as a means of exploring electronic discourse more broadly (Hundt, Nesselhauf, & Biewer, 2007; Kilgarriff & Grefenstette, 2003). This involved searching for hashtags in relation to a particular analytical dimension until saturation of description was reached. Saturation was defined as the point at which collecting additional data did not appear to modify the description (i.e. the description of a feature was exhausted). It might be argued that the databases underlying social media services are not properly balanced linguistic corpora, However, the aim of this book is to characterize the explosion of meaning potential seen with hashtag use, rather than to make any claims about exhaustive representation of every possible function that they might enact as searchable talk.

2

Hashtags as a Semiotic Technology

Introduction

Many researchers have characterized hashtags as 'discourse that recognizes itself as such' (Rambukkana, 2015b, p. 2). They have also been recognized as metadata (data about data). Hashtags are both *technical resources*, in the sense of being metadata with particular affordances, and *semiotic resources*, in the sense of being metadiscourse with particular functions. This chapter considers both these dimensions of hashtags as a semiotic technology (a technology for making meaning). It begins by investigating their affordances as metadata, and then considers some of the textual functions hashtags can enact as metadiscourse.

Metadata is a core dimension of social media services as digital technologies. For example, social media services automatically generate metadata when a user adds contacts to their friend/follower lists, posts updates/statuses, adds comments, or re-shares other users' posts. In addition, there are forms of metadata that a user can more[1] directly generate such as likes/favourites[2] and hashtags. 'Social metadata' is the label given to metadata associated with social media services. This kind of metadata is social in the sense that it operates in the service of the main goal of social media: creating different kinds of connections or social relations, via making use of 'interpersonally important and socially linking information' appended to a media object (Skågeby, 2009, p. 60).

What makes the hashtag a particularly interesting form of metadata is the way it is integrated into the linguistic structure of the texts it annotates. Traditionally, metadata was separated from an information object (e.g. hidden from the view of users of an information system, or separated from the main body of a text). However, hashtags are assimilated into their host texts, and can perform particular functional roles in those texts. They make meaning seamlessly in these texts, even as they point, as multimodal discourse markers, to the presence of other texts in the social stream. In this sense they are both inward and outward facing metadiscourse.

This chapter is primarily concerned with the textual function of hashtags in terms of discourse organization both within and across posts. We will also focus on how the # symbol acts as a graphologically realized discourse marker indicating 'metadata follows me'. In terms of Hjelmselv's (1943/1961) content/expression distinction for semiotic systems, the analysis is predominately located on the expression plane. This is often a useful place to start when beginning to analyse complex semiosis. Following on from this expression plane analysis, we will consider the content plane in Chapter 3. This chapter will focus on the ideational (topic-construing) and evaluative (comment-construing) functions that hashtags can enact.

What is a semiotic technology?

Because hashtags have both technical affordances and semiotic functions, we term them a 'semiotic technology'. In so doing we draw upon Zhao et al.'s (2014, p.72) suggestion that semiotic technology is 'technology that is designed for meaning making and has meaning-making potentials built … [into it] through various semiotic modes (e.g. layout, texture, colour, sound, etc.) on its interface'. In other words, semiotic technologies are configurations of technical affordances interacting with the discursive functions of multimodal resources. For example, the presentation program, PowerPoint, has been explored from a multimodal perspective aimed at understanding how different semiotic modes and technical dimensions work together (Zhao et al., 2014). While hashtags have largely emerged organically rather than being designed, they nevertheless have developed in order to meet particular social and communicative needs.

Approaching hashtags as a semiotic technology means that we need to account for both their discursive functions and their technical affordances (Figure 2.1). In order to do this, the approach adopted in this book integrates the social semiotic lens offered by SFL with analysis of how hashtags operate as a technological resource. The notion of a linguistic *function* is concerned with what people use language to do in a particular context. SFL focuses on 'meaning in context'[3], perspective that arose out of the 'functional tradition' of Firthian systemics (John Rupert Firth, 1957) and the Prague school of linguistics (Jakobson, 1971).

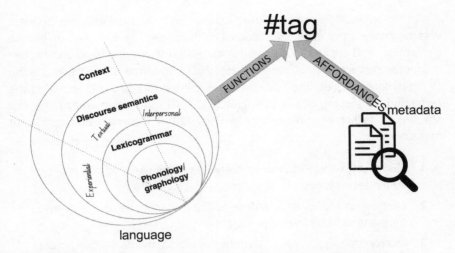

FIGURE 2.1 *Approaching the hashtag as both language (with functions) and metadata (with affordances).*

One of the main insights that we will draw on is Halliday's idea that language enacts three main functions (termed *metafunctions* in the sense that linguistics is *metalanguage* because it uses language to investigate language). These are an *ideational* function of construing experience, an *interpersonal* function of enacting relationships, and a *textual* function of organizing itself into coherent communication. The co-tangential circles in Figure 2.1 represent these three dimensions of meaning, traversing four linguistic strata. Each stratum is related to the other via a realization relationship: discourse semantics is realized by lexicogrammar, which is realized by phonology/graphology.

As a technology, hashtags have emerged out of the history of resources for managing how we read/traverse texts, and how we group texts together. In other words they have arisen from a history of technologies that support text navigation (e.g. headings and tables of contents) and classification (e.g. library subject indexes). This is not necessarily a linear history, but instead the result of cultural development in which technology and social processes are in a constant 'feedback loop' with each other. This feedback loop is the sense that technological changes are influenced by people's communicative needs; and how people use that technology changes culture itself. For example, developers produce new software tools to meet particular requirements, and communities of users find new ways to use existing tools. How these new technological resources are used in society in turn influences, and often expands, communicative meaning potential – for instance, the expanded range of meanings that can be made using a hashtag.

An 'affordance' is what a user can do with technology. The concept was originally introduced by Gibson (1979) as part of a theory of human perception, and applied to areas such as design (Norman, 1988) and human computer interaction (McGrenere & Ho, 2000). In terms of its use in relation to digital technologies, the term has been central to interest in exploring the technological shaping of sociality (Hutchby, 2001), in tandem with the social shaping of technology. According to Riley (2017) the main affordances of metadata are:

1 *Discovery*, where structured metadata helps users to find an information object.

2 *Display*, where visual reference to the metadata helps the user to understand the information object.

3 *Interoperability*, where metadata describing an information object means that it can be transferred from one system to another, despite these systems having different structures.

4 *Digital object management*, where metadata assists in presenting the correct version, or rendering, of an information object to a user.

5 *Preservation*, where metadata helps ensure that an information object is transferred with integrity (i.e. without data corruption) if migrating across systems/platforms.

6 *Navigation*, where metadata enables the user to traverse an information object, both in terms of the various parts of the object (e.g. within a page or section) and across different versions.

Before exploring which of these affordances can be enacted with a hashtag, it is necessary to be more specific about exactly what kind of technology hashtags are.

A note on the prefix *meta-*

The prefix *meta-* originated in the ancient Greek sense of 'after' or 'beyond' 'though in Greek it mainly has to do with change and sharing and following' (Sinclair, 2005, p. 164). It was only much later, perhaps due to misinterpretation of the title of Aristotle's work, *Metaphysics,* that the modern sense of abstraction via transcendence or encapsulation developed (e.g. in *meta-data, meta-economics,* and *meta-philosophy*). This sense may have arisen due to mischaracterization of metaphysics as a science of physical transcendence. This led to 'a prodigious erroneous extension in modern usage, with meta- affixed to the names of other sciences and disciplines, especially in the academic jargon of literary criticism' (Harper, 2001).

Distillation of some 'essence' (or first principles of something) is another common sense in which the prefix is used. For example, within Logic and Linguistics as disciplinary fields, *meta-* can act as prefix 'to various terms to denote something of a second-order or more fundamental kind, *esp.* a construct, method, classification, etc., which is concerned with the underlying principles of a system, or applies to the whole of a system' (e.g. in *metacondition* or *metagrammar*) (Oxford English Dictionary). *Meta* can also have functions beyond prefixing. For example this is seen in modern US reference (originating in the 1980s) to creative works that self-reference themselves or the conventions of their genre.

Meta can also function as a noun in slang, particularly in social media discourse, perhaps due to awareness of the kinds of layering of meanings that digital communication accommodates, for instance:

You're the sidekick in your own story! That's very **meta**, Tara.

The "basicbitch" hashtag is suuuuuper **meta** right now …

Memes have become so **meta** we are now making a meme of making a Spotify playlist with the titles making a meme.

Instances such as these indicate that for users, orders of meaning are important, and that something being 'meta' has significance in terms of their semiotic practices.

What is metadata?

The archetypal form of metadata is information at some higher order of abstraction appended to a primary artefact, typically for the purposes of classification. Metadata schemas, as classificatory systems, predate digital computing. They may be traced to the origins of subject categorization in the first ancient libraries. For example, the ancient Library of Ashurbanipal, established during his 668–627 BC reign, is thought to have hung inscriptions above stone tablets. The Great Library of Alexandria, established around the third century BC, employed *tituli* (Latin inscriptions), hung from the end of scrolls, so that each scroll did not need to be unwound in order to find a particular text.

The ongoing development of written text, that occurred with the advent of the printing press in the fifteenth century, saw the emergence of resources for aiding navigation within a text, for example, headings, numberings, tables of contents, and indexes. These conventions further developed within institutional and disciplinary contexts, for example, the use of numbering in rules, regulations, and legislation, and in logical positivist tracts such as Wittgenstein's *Tractatus*. Skipping over many centuries of development, a period of growth in analogue metadata occurred around the time of the advent of photography, due to the need to track dimensions such as who was in a particular photograph.

It was not until the 1960s, with the development of Machine-Readable Cataloguing in libraries, that digital metadata, of the kind we are familiar with today, began to proliferate. Modern coinage of the term 'metadata' arose around the same time, with Bagley's (1968) definition from the programming domain:

> Metadata. As important as being able to combine data elements to make composite data elements is the ability to associate explicitly with a data element a second data element which represents data 'about' the first data element. This second data element we might term a 'metadata element' ... (Bagley, 1968, p. 26)

This is usually glossed as 'data about data'. Bagley's definition figures metadata as a type of abstraction used to describe another data instance, for example, the contents of a cell in a table, or the parameters of the cell itself. This is a distinction between descriptive metadata (about content), and structural metadata (about form). Since this period, an abundance of metadata standards have been produced for managing different types of resources across disciplines. For instance, hundreds of standards have developed within the cultural heritage sector (Riley & Shepherd, 2009).

Metadata has been crucial to the development of the World Wide Web. It is used throughout the web to describe the attributes of web pages so that they can be located by search engines that use particular algorithms to decide which pages appear first in their search results. A simple example is the title tag that appears in the HTML (Hyptertext Markup Language) source code for a user's Twitter profile page, for example:

```
Donald J. Trump (@realDonaldTrump) | Twitter
```

In the above, the tags are shown with angled brackets. <title> is the start tag, and the slash indicates that </title> is the end tag. The material in between is the content, often referred to as the 'body'. Search engines will use this tag to find this profile page when, for instance, someone searches for 'Donald Trump'. HTML tags are also used to specify how the page is displayed by the web browser in terms of colour, layout, font etc. These tags are not directly displayed to the user, who instead sees the output as a properly formatted web page.

It is generally agreed that there are three main types of digital metadata: *descriptive* metadata (e.g. used for classification), *structural* metadata (e.g. used for determining the sequence of elements in an object), and *administrative* metadata (e.g. used for resource management). Within the domain of digital libraries, for example, metadata has been defined as 'information about objects and collections' (Group, 2007, p. 2). Baca (2008, p. 2) suggests that all information objects involve three dimensions that should be represented via metadata: content (what the object is about or contains), context (information about how the content was created), and structure (sets of relations within or between objects).

Once the purview of technologists and librarians, metadata has now become part of popular consciousness. This is in part due to concern about new forms of computer-mediated surveillance. It is also in part because of the widespread use of hashtags and the visibility of other social media metadata (e.g. timestamps and location information). These factors have meant that more people are aware of the concept of tagging. Social media services featuring metadata have been enthusiastically and pervasively embraced across sociocultural groups. The resultant social media communication, and 'big data' about the public more generally, is currently being 'mined' by software companies, governments, and other bodies for what it might reveal about public behaviour and opinion. This has obvious privacy implications (Andrejevic, 2014; Crawford & Schultz, 2014). Social metadata such as user connections, activity patterns, likes/favourites, location information, and hashtags are often considered by these bodies 'to be more valuable than the content itself' (Kennedy & Moss, 2015, p. 1). Ascribing such a privileged position to social metadata an interesting turn in the history of metadata.

A technical definition of the Twitter hashtag

Hashtags have a very specific definition in terms of their technical instantiation. The following is an extract of the specification (in Java) defining what Twitter accepts as a valid hashtag:

```
VALID_HASHTAG = Pattern.compile("(^|[^&" + HASHTAG_LETTERS_
NUMERALS + "])(#|\uFF03)(?!\uFE0F|\u20E3)(" + HASHTAG_LETTERS_
NUMERALS_SET + "*" + HASHTAG_LETTERS_SET + HASHTAG_LETTERS_
NUMERALS_SET + "*)", Pattern.CASE_INSENSITIVE);
(Twitter, 2016)
```

TABLE 2.1 Special characters that can appear as part of a hashtag

Name	Form
Zero width non-joiner (ZWNJ)	[non-printing character]
Zero width joiner (ZWJ)	[non-printing character]
Cyrillic kavyka	˘
Hebrew punctuation maqaf	־
Hebrew punctuation geresh	׳
Hebrew punctuation gershayim	״
Fullwidth tilde	～
Wave dash	〜
Katakana-hiragana voiced sound mark ``	゛
Katakana-hiragana semi-voiced sound mark	゜
Katakana-hiragana double hyphen	゠
Katakana middle dot	・
Ditto mark	〃
Tibetan mark intersyllabic tsheg	་
Tibetan mark delimiter tsheg bstar	༌
Middle dot	·

This roughly translates as a hashtag being valid if all of the following criteria are satisfied:

1 The hash symbol occurs at the start of a tweet, or immediately after a character that is not a letter or number:

   e.g. f#Trump and 4#Trump are not valid hashtags.

2 The tag begins with a hash symbol, or a 'fullwidth number sign' (a wider version of the hash symbol):

   e.g. #Trump or ＃Trump

3 It consists of a string that is made up of letters, numbers, and symbols, but must contain at least one letter. These characters are made up of symbols from many languages.

Hashtags are case insensitive, which means that they can include either lower or uppercase letters, or both. The symbols (special characters) that are allowed as part of a hashtag are shown in Table 2.1. All other symbols (%, &, * etc.) are not allowed as part of a valid hashtag. The marker for the end of a hashtag is the first non-letter, number, or special symbol that does not meet the above criteria.

Other social media services such as Instagram may have different hashtag specifications but are likely similar to the above.

The history of the # symbol

Hashtags are marked by the # symbol (referred to variously as the pound symbol, octothorpe, hex etc.). The # has an interesting semiotic history deserving of its own book-length treatment. Houston's (2013) cleverly titled, *Shady Characters: The Secret Life of Punctuation, Symbols, and Other Typographical Marks*, devotes a chapter to the #, providing a detailed account of its origins and development. According to this study, the symbol may have originated in the Latin *libra pondo,* the Roman pound weight. This was abbreviated to '*lb*' in the late fourteenth century when *libra* entered English and 'was transformed into the # by the carelessly rushing pens of successive scribes' (Houston, 2013, p. 43). At the same time, *pondo* was transformed into 'pound' in modern usage. Finally, the two trajectories of meaning were reunited in the 'pound sign', displayed as #. This is a symbol which is now used so widely that its meaning depends on context: it has been used as a sign for weight and ordinal numbers, to signify checkmate in a game of chess, to distinguish between code and commentary in programming, and as a proofreading mark. It also has developed other more obscure uses, such as indicating the end of a press release with ### (Houston, 2013).

Since the nineteenth century, the history of the # symbol seems to have involved two main trajectories

- use within technical, mathematical, and mediated contexts
- use that supports semantic aspects of enumerating/systematizing information. (Heyd & Puschmann, in press)

In terms of its use in computer-mediated communication, the # symbol is thought to have first established itself as marker in Internet Relay Chat (IRC), an early protocol for real-time chat sessions. Here the # was used to indicate a channel. Users, employing a client program designed for use with IRC, logged into a particular IRC server in order to chat with other users on that server. An example of an IRC channel operating in the 1990s, when this form of communication was popular, is *#india*. This channel featured expatriate South Asians 'using Hindi codeswitching together with more widespread features of IRC language' (Paolillo, 2001, p. 181). Most IRC channels could be joined by typing the following command, featuring the # symbol as the channel marker:

```
/join #channel_name [CHANNEL PASSWORD]⁴
```

A notification would appear in the chat log visible to everyone in the channel as follows:

```
User1 has joined #channel_name
```

In the above the # functions as a special character with a particular meaning in terms of both the technology and relevant social protocols.

Special characters are a tool used in computing (referred to as 'escape characters' or 'metacharacters') where the use of the character invokes an alternative interpretation of the sequence of characters that follow it. For instance, there is 'a history among computer programmers of prefacing specialized words with punctuation marks, such as $ and * for variables and pointers, or the # sign itself for identifying HTML anchor points' (boyd, Golder, & Lotan, 2010, p. 2). For example, if we wanted to create a link to a particular location in a webpage using HTML, we would create an anchor using the <a> tag to indicate where the link should be directed:

```
<a name="section1"></a>
```

A link pointing to this anchor could then be made as follows, where putting the # in front of section1 indicates it is the anchor:

```
Click <a href="#section1">here</a> to read section 1.
```

Returning to more recent usage, employing the # symbol as a marker to indicate a hashtag originated with microblogging. In this context, the symbol indicates that the material that follows it is a tag (in the special sense introduced in section 5). The presence of the # symbol in a social media post thus has the technical function of indicating the beginning of a unit of metadata. Before Twitter hashtags became 'clickable', a user would need

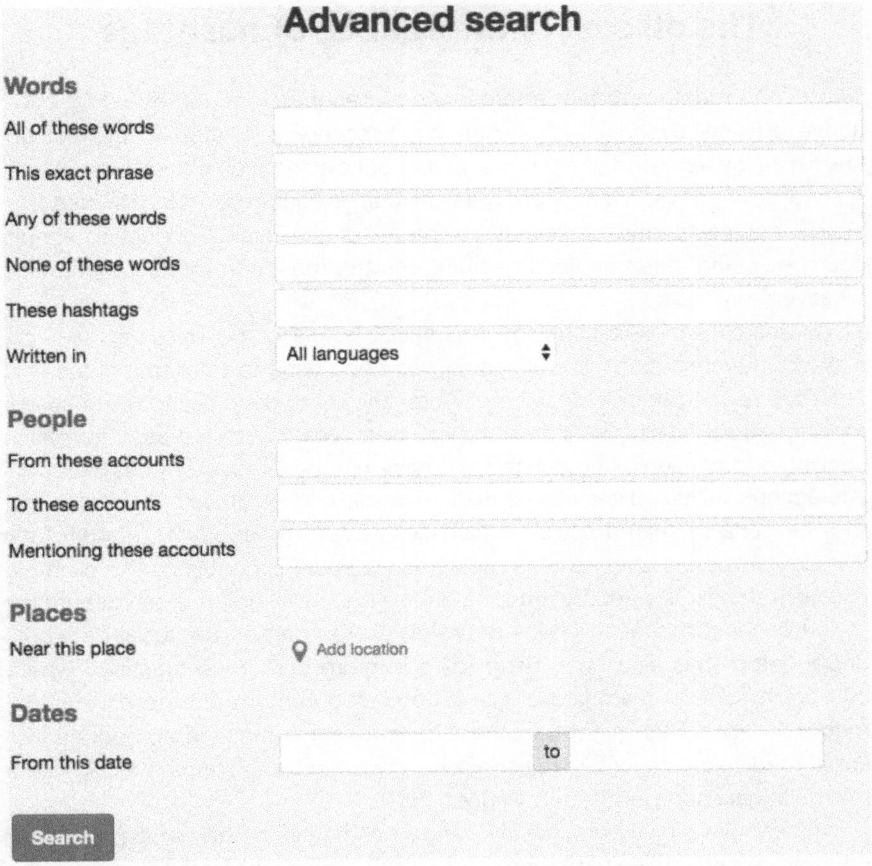

Advanced search

Words

All of these words

This exact phrase

Any of these words

None of these words

These hashtags

Written in   All languages   ⏷

People

From these accounts

To these accounts

Mentioning these accounts

Places

Near this place   ⭘ Add location

Dates

From this date   to

Search

FIGURE 2.2 *Twitter's interface for conducting an 'advanced' search.*

to search for the hashtag via the social media service's search interface. This would allow them to find other instances of posts containing the same tag. In the case of Twitter, they could do this by typing the hashtag into the standard search bar, or by typing it into the hashtag field in the 'advanced search' interface (Figure 2.2).

Use of the # has since spread from microblogging to other forms of social media communication. It has also converged with other mediated contexts such a television and advertising. Hashtags function across all social media platforms where the # symbol is a special character. Their current ubiquity ensures that 'words and phrases [marked with the #] can be identified anywhere as tags' (Barton, 2015, p. 63). In this way the # has achieved a kind of symbolic power and has become 'part of a quotidian discourse the basic grammar of which is understood even by nontwitterers' (van Dijck, 2013, p. 86).

The discovery affordance of hashtags

Two of the most important affordances of hashtags defined by Riley (2017) above are 'discovery' and 'navigation'. Discovery is related to the activity known as 'search', one of main the drivers of how the web currently operates. As we saw above, web pages can include embedded metadata used by search engine to retrieve relevant content for the user. Conducting simple searches using these engines has become the most common kind of online discovery practice.

As search engine technology and social media communication have co-evolved, the concept of 'social search' has been used to refer to a number of practices relating both to social metadata, and more generally to using search to meet social goals. Social search has been broadly defined as 'information seeking and sensemaking habits that make use of a range of possible social interactions: including searches that utilize social and expertise networks or that may be done in shared social workspaces' (Evans & Chi, 2008, p. 485). This includes online discovery that is mediated via social connections. An example is search that is assisted by information from a social graph (a representation of the connections/relationships between users in an online social network). Social search has also been used to refer more broadly to practices where by people retrieve material from user-generated content produced via social media services. This might be achieved via a search function embedded in a social media service, or via a user asking a question as a status message on a microblogging service (Efron & Winget, 2010).

An example of social search involving a hashtag is the following post about the pink knitted 'pussy hat'[5] worn at the 2017 Women's March:

```
So is there a place where I can buy a pussy hat
online? #WomensMarch
```

This hashtag here directs the question to people who are interested in the Women's March and may hold the relevant answer. As Efron and Winget (2010) note, this kind of practice does not necessarily require the post to be formulated as a question, for instance:

```
if anyone went to a #WomensMarch and is willing to sell
a pink pussy hat you got i'll buy it I want one so bad
```

Social search on Twitter is sometimes explicitly indicated with hashtags such as *#lazyweb* or *#twoogle* (a portmanteau of 'Twitter' and 'Google') (Rzeszotarski, Spiro, Matias, Monroy-Hernández, & Morris, 2014), for example:

Where's the video of the 60 Minutes episode with Trump
and Putin? **#lazyweb**

Dear **#lazyweb,** send me the best takes on the Trump
meeting with Silicon Valley CEOs.

What happens for Trump's cabinet in terms of their day
jobs? Do they stand down from those? TIA **#lazyweb**

When is Trump's inauguration? **#Twoogle**

Did I hear shit right? Is Donald Trump banning the export
of Oreos to South Afrika? I was too lazy to read **#twoogle**

Is there a way to block to everything related to
Donald Trump on twitter? **#Twoogle**

Zappavigna (2012b, p. 6) terms one of the main tendencies of social search
'interpersonal search'. What is typically retrieved, in contrast to the explicitly
tagged *#lazyweb* posts above, is opinion and sentiment about some issue,
rather than just information about a topic. An example of interpersonal search
would be searching for *#WomensMarch* together with a tag such as *#resist* or
#ImpeachTrump. This would return posts such as the following where people
are expressing their negative assessment of Trump's administration:

100 days in, @realDonaldTrump, and we're just getting
started **#WomensMarch #NotMyPresident #ImpeachTrump
#Resist**

If you attended **#TaxMarch** or the #WomensMarch you
need to also attend the **#ScienceMarch.** If you haven't
marched yet, GO TO THIS ONE #Resist

This is the rebirth of the women's movement!
#womensmarch #resist #werise [URL]

Ideational and interpersonal hashtags may have different kinds of
relationship to social search. On the one hand, hashtags such as *#Trump*
aggregate posts that conform to this topic. On the other hand, hashtags
such as *#TrumpIsEvil* enact metacommentary. 'TrumpIsEvil' is unlikely to be
used as a search query by another microblogger, yet invokes the possibility
of an 'imagined audience' (Litt & Hargittai, 2016; Marwick & boyd, 2011) who
share the same opinion. Interestingly, as social media platforms mature in
age, interpersonal tags will accrue more and more instances in the ongoing
social stream. Thus tags that would once have been unlikely to return any
results will return many search results

Sometimes of idiosyncratic tags will achieve the social status of an internet meme. This happens when iterations on a theme are widely shared (as we will see in Chapter 9). For instance *#ManyPeopleAreSaying* became a meme used to mock Trump's frequent use of the phrase 'many people are saying' as a preface to his controversial claims:

> **#ManyPeopleAreSaying** I play more fucking golf than a 70-year-old retiree who moves to Florida to play golf full time *[link to article from The Washington Post titled 'Trump's cake and gold presidency']*

> **#ManyPeopleAreSaying** that Trump's next milliary action is to drop great tasting chocolate cakes on Assad – not me – but many say this

> **#manypeoplearesaying** The new health care bill will be called the SAA (Screw Americans Act).

As we will see in Chapter 4, and in more detail in Chapter 5, instead of only 'tagging for findability, users now tag social media posts with words and phrases that are not necessarily intended to appear in a standard data search', and which are instead a form of 'metacommunication' (Daer, Hoffman, & Goodman, 2014, p. 1). However, as interpersonal communication and interpersonal tagging proliferate on social media, an ideational versus interpersonal criterion for distinguishing whether something is intended to be marked as searchable will likely break down.

The navigation affordance of hashtags

Intersecting with the discovery affordance is the affordance of navigation. Since 2009 Twitter has made hashtags 'clickable', meaning that they appear as blue links within posts (Figure 2.3). When a user clicks on a particular hashtag via the web interface, they are presented with a page displaying a feed of other posts using the same tag. For instance, clicking on the *#ManyPeopleAresSaying* hashtag (via the Twitter web interface) will return a feed of posts containing this tag. The relevant part of the HTML source code, that defines the hashtag as a clickable link, is shown below:

<a href="/hashtag/ManyPeopleAreSaying?src=hash" data-query-source= "hashtag_click" class="twitter-hashtag pretty-link js-nav" dir="ltr" >
<s>#</s>
   ManyPeopleAreSaying
   <a>

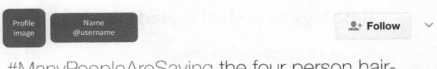

#ManyPeopleAreSaying the four person hair-
care team that failed to cover the hairpin when
Trump was in Mexico have been replaced for
debate

RETWEETS   LIKE
2   1

4:40 AM - 26 Sep 2016

FIGURE 2.3 *An example of a clickable Twitter hashtag appearing in blue on Twitter.com.*

Clickable hashtags are seen across different social media services. For example, they were introduced for Facebook hashtags in 2013. The clickability affordance of hashtags is related to other resources seen in digital media for managing reading paths through a document. For example, most word processing applications allow users to generate tables of contents. These usually allow the user to click on a heading or page number to jump to that section of the document. Similarly, academic citations can be rendered as links to the relevant reference in the bibliography.

The kinds of post that are returned to a user when they click on a hashtag may be filtered by the social media service. This largely depends on how the service manages other kinds of metadata about the user, such as their location and preferences. In this way, social media services have a high degree of control over the symbolic power of tagging, even as the # acts as an emblem of free expression (since a tag can be whatever the user chooses). Twitter currently filters the search results that they return to users. Tabs group results as 'top' (grouped by popularity, as defined by Twitter), 'latest' (grouped by time of posting), 'people' (grouped by accounts), 'photos' (grouped by media attribute), 'video' (grouped by media attribute), 'news' (grouped by account type), and 'broadcast' (grouped by media attribute). As we will see later, this type of organization influences how attention, as an important currency in social media, is regulated and distributed.

Hashtags as textual metadiscourse

Having considered the affordances of hashtags as metadata, we now turn to their linguistic functions, in particular their 'textual' function. The textual function of language is concerned with how discourse is organized so that it has 'the status of a communicative event' (Halliday, 1994, p. 37). Hashtags can include a word, initialism, concatenated phrase,[6] or an entire clause, as shown in the following examples:

> 45 calls North Korean leader "pretty smart cookie" but he calls Pres Obama "sick and bad." We officially live in the twilight zone. **#trump**

> Hypocrisy at its finest. Who's paying for that wall again? **#maga #tinytrump**

> The more all this goes on, day by day, the more disgusted & disconnected I'm becoming from anyone who voted for and supported **#pussygrabber**

> Sets up National Loyalty Day – just like every good dictator should. **#FuckTrump**

> Deport Trump to federal prison! **#TrumpCrimeFamily #DonTheCon #TrumpIsEvil #TrumpRussia #TrumpRussianCollusion #TrumpImpeachmentParty**

> Reading this NPR piece on Trump's immigration execut Excellent reporting. **#TrumpIsEvil**

Each of the hashtags above perform a different type of meaning: from indicating the semantic domain of the post (e.g. *#Trump*), linking the post to a meme (e.g. *#TinyTrump*), re-appropriating a political slogan (*#maga*), to making an emotionally charged metacomment (e.g. *#FuckTrump, #TrumpIsEvil*). In each of these examples the hash symbol acts as a kind of multimodal discourse marker, indicating the special status of the material following the #. As mentioned earlier, when used as a marker in this way, # means 'metadata follows me'. At the level of graphology, the # symbol indicates the beginning of the tag, as well as invoking its special status with regard to the information flow.

Hashtags are metadiscursive in the sense that this tagged material has special textual status in the post, drawing on the affordances of the # symbol as a metadata marker. A post containing a hashtag incorporates two orders of meaning: it can incorporate both untagged (shown underlined) and tagged (shown in bold) language:

#ManyPeopleAreSaying the four person hair-care team that failed to cover the hairpin when Trump was in Mexico have been replaced for debate

This is a novel phenomenon because, despite visually indicating the presence of these two orders of meaning, hashtags can be seamlessly integrated into the linguistic structure of the post. For example, in the following examples, the tag acts as a Classifier in a nominal group in a clause, rather than being structurally separated from the main content (as is the case with other navigational resources such as tables of contents, indexes, or headings):

#Trump speech at his so-called rally is a disgrace & embarrassment to America. As the world loses respect for USA & the ignorant cheer.

Soon at a **#Trump** rally near you:
Trump: Former President O-Bammma …
Crowd: LOCK HIM UP! LOCK HIM UP!
Trump: We're gonna look into that.

Hashtags are very flexible syntactically. They can occur as an adjunct to the lexis, clause, or clause complex constituting the main body of a post. Alternatively they can integrate themselves seamlessly into that content. In terms of positioning within the syntactic structure, the hash symbol can mark tags at any point within a post,. However hashtags are most commonly found at either the beginning or end of a post (Tsur & Rappoport, 2012, p. 2).

Tsur and Rappoport (2012) term these three possible locations *infix* (beginning), *prefix* (middle), and *suffix* (end) positions. Successive hash symbols may mark hashtags in a sequence at each of these locations, without any intervening content between the tags. In terms of the information flow of a text, we can interpret these positions as *initial, integrated*, and *culminative*:

initial:
#Trump is on record, confessing to such crime. Should he remain in the highest office in the land? Is this a role model or a hypocrite?

integrated:
See what all this praise for bombing **#syria** has done. Now **#madman #Trump** has sent warships to Korean Peninsula. Seeking praise risking lives

culminative:
Every single day I think that I can't hate him more than I do, and every single day I'm proven wrong. **#NotMyPresident**

When in initial or integrated position, the tags take on functional roles in the clause. In culminative position, while the hashtag can construe any number of functional roles on its own (e.g. experientially construing the 'topic' of a post), it is typically not integrated into the clause. Instead it is appended at the end of the post.

This ability for hashtags to work seamlessly inside social media texts is a novel property for metadata. It subverts the traditional role of metadata: separating meta-information from primary content (e.g. form from content in HTML). For example consider the hashtags in the following post:

@realDonaldTrump @nytimes Anyone who says something that doesn't fit trumps current agenda gets the **#fakenews** seal of disapproval! **#dictator**

On the one hand the #fakenews tag is involved in how the evaluative language in this post unfolds. For instance, i the negative attitude that saturates the post. At the same time, by virtue of being metadata, this tag explicitly marks its intertextual relationship to other posts with the same tag. It also enters into a relationship with other hashtags that co-occur with this tag, both in the original post, and in other posts in the Twitter stream (and across social media platforms that incorporate social tagging such as Instagram and YouTube). We might think of this integration of a social tag into the linguistic structure of the body of a post as a product of grammaticalization, specifically of lexicalization. In other words, as a shift from closed-class to open-class functionality; from being realized only as a marker at the end of a post, to being realized as lexis anywhere in the post. Grammaticalization is a framework for considering the dynamic (diachronic and synchronic) relationship of lexical, constructional, and grammatical dimensions of language (Hopper & Traugott, 2003).

The textual metafunction also organizes texts into 'waves' of information (Halliday & Matthiessen, 2004). There are little waves at the level of clause, which are organized into bigger waves in longer texts at the level of paragraph, and into even bigger waves at the level of whole texts (Martin & Stenglin, 2007). Given that tweets are very small texts, these waves are micro-waves of Theme and New information – where Theme relates to information at the beginning of a clause, and New relates to information about what is contained in the Theme. A hashtag can function as either Theme or New, depending on whether it has a topic marking function or not. For example, when a hashtag has a topic marking function, it typically functions as the Theme about which some New information is given in the rest of the clause. For example (Theme shown in bold; New shown underlined):

#Trump <u>is so disgusting and such hypocrite</u>

Here the Theme is *#Trump* and the rest of the post is the New information provided. When the tag has the evaluative function, the Theme may be found in the tweet and the hashtag may contain the New, for instance:

Sensible, moderate Republicans you have Trump to thank for destroying your party. <u>#Sad</u>

In the above, *#Sad* is the New. To summarize, the salience of the tweet may be to indicate two types of meaning – the interpersonal and the experiential. The hashtag may orient the reader towards the experiential meaning (the topic e.g. *#Trump*), or the interpersonal meaning, when the hashtag is evaluative (e.g. *#Sad*).

Are hashtags punctuation?

The structural and functional flexibility noted thus far might be related to the co-occurring evolution of graphological systems such as punctuation beyond boundary marking. For example, Knox (2009) argues that emoticons, another interesting feature prevalent in social media discourse, are part of an ongoing evolution in punctuation to support the ever-more complex demands placed on language in electronic environments. Knox explains this progression in terms of the way systems of punctuation have developed to perform more interpersonal functions, evolving from their original textual (organizing discourse) function:

> The trajectory for interpersonal punctuation … begins with boundary marking, moves to punctuating speech function, and then to punctuating attitude and identity. At the same time, the prosody of punctuation spans (potentially) longer stretches of text, with the punctuation of attitude and identity through emoticons now able to spread over entire messages. Knox (2009, p. 162)

This is based on Halliday's (1985/1989/1990, p. 35) ideas about how punctuation relates to grammar and phonology, and on the functions of punctuation that he proposes. Halliday attributes three main functions to the several 'special purpose symbols' that have entered language:

1   *Boundary marking* – indicating the borders of different constituent
    grammatical units (e.g. space, comma, semicolon, and full stop)
2   *Status marking* – indicating speech function and projection (e.g. full
    stop, question mark, exclamation mark, and single/double quotes)
3   *Relation marking* – indicating different kinds of relations between units
    (e.g. dash, parenthesis, hyphen, and apostrophe)

Punctuation is somewhat of a fraught concept when applied to computer-
mediated communication. In part this is because, as we have seen, special
characters and symbols can have particular affordances in online media
beyond what is achieved in other written modes. Also, there seems to be
an essential indeterminacy in what is actually meant by punctuation in a
technical sense. Just as we will see with the term 'metadiscourse' later
in this chapter, there are two dual functions that punctuation appears
to realize: a textual function of separating elements in sentences, and a
more interpersonal function of augmenting meaning by 'intruding' into the
discourse. Depending on your definition of punctuation, you may recognize
one but not the other. If we are to see hashtags as a form of punctuation, we
will need to recognize both.

One interesting additional problem is when something stops being a
marker (e.g. in the sense of a boundary marker) and becomes a symbol of the
thing that is being marked. For example, some studies refer to emoticons as a
new form of punctuation. However, emoticons have the added complication of
being iconic, in the sense of visually representing facial expression (amongst
other possibilities). They also 'straddle the boundaries of image and language'
Knox (2009). For instance, consider the following posts:

```
I am like why is president Trump's twitter showing up
on my feed. Just realizing cause I follow @POTUS:(Not
Barack anymore

My son is gay and when this dick trump revokes his
rights I am going to lose my fucking mind:(Nothing
will stop me then, I will never tire

@BarackObama look at us now:-(Trump is going to ruin
the U.S. and I am terrified! Miss you so much!!!
```

In these posts, the 'sad face' emoticon does seem quite similar to a full stop.
In each case it is followed by a capital letter, as we would expect in standard
usage. However, it is also part of construing the negative assessment of the
various situations identified, coordinating with the evaluative language. This

kind of functional fuzziness is a symptom that the system has yet to stabilize, or that punctuation is inherently hybrid in nature:

> In the digital mediascape, traditional conceptualizations of the parameters of punctuation as a category of typographic symbols no longer seems adequate to characterize the range of signification practices at play in textual exchanges ... identifying such as mark [as the hashtag] as punctuation, when it has not traditionally been used in writing, productively alerts us to shifts in the ways language and image relate to each other via contemporary textual practices. (Scheible, 2015, p. 9)

Some scholars have viewed the # symbol as having emerged as new punctuation because it was needed to meet the complex communicative goals emerging with social media environments. To a certain extent this appears to be true: the # seems to have stabilized as very recognizable graphology and is involved in the segmentation of experience (as we will see later). We might think of the # symbol as following a trajectory where punctuation has evolved from boundary marking to indicating the voice being realized (Chapter 5), and finally to marking the bond at stake (Chapter 7) (Figure 2.4). However, I have chosen to refer to the hash symbol as a graphologically realized discourse marker rather than as punctuation because of the way it points both to itself,

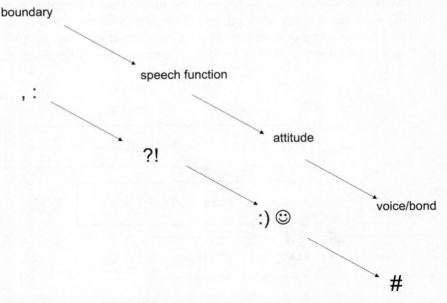

FIGURE 2.4 *Evolution of punctuation, based on Knox (2009).*

locally in the individual text, and to other texts, more globally in the social stream. As we will see later in this book, the # has also expanded in meaning potential to indicate the presence of other potential voices in the social stream, and at a higher order of abstraction, other potential bonds.

Hashtags as inward and outward facing metadiscourse

Hashtags are also textual metadiscourse in the sense that they draw on the affordances of metadata to make meanings about the rest of the body of the post[7] (i.e. the untagged parts of the post), as well as about other potential posts in the social stream that might use the same tag (Figure 2.5). In this way they are both 'inward' and 'outward' facing discourse (Figure 2.5). Hashtags make meanings not only about themselves (in the 'discourse about discourse' sense) but also about the potential co-presence of other texts in the social stream. Some scholars have interpreted this duality as a kind of hybridity:

> In the taxonomy of information types, hashtags are hybrids. They are both text and metatext, information and tag, pragmatic and metapragmatic speech. They are deictic, indexical – yet unlike other such signs that point elsewhere, hashtags point to themselves, to their own dual role in ongoing discourse. (Rambukanna, 2015, p. 161)

The intertextual relation might be between the text and other potential texts containing the same tag by other authors. It might also be with other posts produced by the same user as part of a 'multi-tweet story' (Dayter, 2015, p. 19). In this case it might coordinate with other resources to provide cohesion.

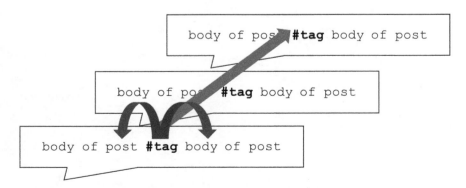

FIGURE 2.5 *Hashtags as inward and outward facing discourse.*

It should be noted at this point, that I am utilizing a definition of metadiscourse very different to how it has traditionally been used in linguistics where it remains an ambiguous term, particularly in terms of its scope.[8] On the one hand, metadiscourse has been used in the sense of 'discourse about discourse' to indicate moments where a text calls attention to its status and organization as a semiotic artefact (e.g. *This book is structured as follows ...*) (Crismore, 1989; Vande Kopple, 1985; Williams, 1981). On the other hand, it has been used to refer to the whole gamut of interpersonal resources available for managing how a text positions itself in relation to its real or potential audience. For example, metadiscourse has been seen as encompassing interpersonal meanings through which texts manage interactive and interactional resources: in other words, resources through which 'propositional content is made coherent, intelligible, and persuasive to a particular audience' (Hyland, 2005, p. 39).

Neither of these perspectives on metadiscourse are particularly satisfactory in terms of accounting for the second order meaning that hashtags introduce into a text. Most likely because the concept of metadiscourse has been aimed at accounting for meaning in only one modality, and not the intertextual dimension of texts linked via metadata. As free form text, limited only by the character constraints of posts and the technical specifications defined earlier in this chapter, hashtags can enact all of the functions of language proposed by Halliday. In this sense they do not conform to the different restricted definitions of metadiscourse that have been proposed in linguistics.

Garnering ambient attention

Linguistics has mostly theorized information flow and reading paths in terms of textual organization. Within social media environments, information flow is important, not only within a particular text, in terms of how it is organized, but also across multiple texts, linked via social tags. Textual organization can thus also be approached from the perspective of how the text is organized to attract attention, where achieving 'influence' is an important social goal (Romero, Galuba, Asur, & Huberman, 2011). The rhetorical function of textual meaning realized by hashtags is in the service of garnering this social attention. Messages without a hashtag have been seen as 'broadcast' messages aimed at followers (Kwak, Lee, Park, & Moon, 2010), whereas messages with a hashtag expand the potential audience beyond these linked accounts. Pavalanathan and Eisenstein (2015, p. 205) suggest that hashtags play an 'audience-selecting role'. This study found that posts containing hashtags had less local, non-standard lexical variables than posts without these tags, suggesting that the former are aimed at wider audiences.

Related to the notion of attracting attention in the social stream, is the concept of 'engagement' or 'influence'. These terms variables used in marketing to assess the extent to which a post has received click-throughs, likes, and other kinds of social recognition. Hashtags direct attention, both to themselves as visible metadata and to the texts they annotate. They render this text more visible in a social stream because, by virtue of being a tag, they can be aggregated by a social media service. This means that a post will appear in unfolding feeds of content visible to audiences beyond an individual's network of associates. Posts containing a hashtag are more likely to reach audiences outside a particular user's set of existing followers (Naaman, Becker, & Gravano, 2011). Indeed, hashtags may accumulate vast audiences 'under shared attention conditions' (Lin, Keegan, Margolin, & Lazer, 2014, p. 2). An example of this kind of attention condition is mass reaction to Donald Trump's controversial political campaign and election victory that we saw in 2016.

The discovery affordances (that we explored earlier in relation to search) also provide the hashtag with the symbolic power of an 'attention mobilizer', involved in construing new forms of social visibility (Wang, Liu et al., 2016, p. 852). The process of garnering attention with a hashtag is influenced by the tags that are popular at a particular time, in relation to contextual variables. For example, the rate of hashtag use doubles during media events (Lin et al., 2014), rendering competition for attention more intense:

> For example, in normal times, tweets on a particular topic are likely to appear on the screens of the small number of people who are paying attention to a particular hashtag at that time, but may stay visible in their feed for several minutes. During a media event about this topic, a tweet would go to a large number of people but be quickly replaced by tweets from others in a matter of seconds. (Lin et al., 2014, p. 2)

A given social media service will have particular ways in which they present popular hashtags to the social stream. These methods will change and evolve with the functionality of the service (Bruns, Moon, Paul, & Münch, 2016). Twitter has a predefined proprietary algorithm which specifies which 'trending' hashtags will dominate. Trending hashtags are tags that have experienced 'sudden bursts in activity volume' (Ferrara, Varol, Menczer, & Flammini, 2016, p. 563)[9]. They will be presented differently depending on particular user interests, follower networks, and locations.

Wu (2017) also suggests that patterns in our collective attention have become commodities bought and sold by 'attention merchants' who have found ways to commercialize how and where we spend our time online. This has meant that 'the shape of our lives [has] yielded further and further to the logic of commerce – but gradually enough that we should now find nothing strange about it' (Wu, 2017). In addition the structure of our experiences has been altered:

> Hashtags, likes, favourites, location data, filters, and algorithms serve not only as a site's tools for managing or curating the flow of social media activity, but also build an array of segments around daily routines, events, spaces, places, interests, groups, relationships, networks, experiences and so on. As epistemic and ontologic devices, metrics and the site features that enable them are shaping our access to personal experiences, over-coding those experiences and hence circumscribing information flows. (McCosker, 2017)

The above affords the social media forms of discursive control, both in influencing the shape of our experience and in controlling what is brought to our attention and when.

We are used to thinking about metadata in terms of classification since classification of both material and semiotic objects into types is an ancient practice. As I flagged in the previous chapter, while metadata has a long history in the domain of information management, this is the first historical period where we see it so closely tied to enacting and organizing social relations. Metadata has extended its semiotic reach as an information-organizing tool to become a social resource for building relationships and communities. In other words, the affordances of metadata have expanded to include social roles not previously enacted. The next chapter considers in these social roles by examining in detail the different linguistic functions that hashtags can construe.

3

The Ideational and Interpersonal Functions of Hashtags

Introduction

Hashtags, once an emergent form of linguistic innovation (Cunha et al., 2011), appear to have stabilized. They have accumulated two main functions (in addition to the discourse organizing function we surveyed in the previous chapter). These are an experiential function (e.g. topic-marking), and an interpersonal function (e.g. evaluative metacommentary). Most linguistic studies of hashtags take as a basic distinction a difference in meaning between ideational hashtags, marking topics, and interpersonal hashtags, indicating attitudes or alignments (Caleffi, 2015; Page, 2012; Wikström, 2014; Zappavigna, 2015).

Compare, for example, the different roles that hashtags play in the following two posts:

Watch Donald Trump's full speech on economic policy *[link to YouTube video]* **#Economicpolicy**

"If you're not part of the solution, you're part of the problem." **#AmericanDisaster #TrumpIsDestroyingAmerica #DisgustedByHisRacism**

The tag in the first post indicates that it is 'about' economic policy, whereas the tags in the second post present attitudes about President Trump and his impact on the United States. Bourlai, Herring, and Abdul-mageed (2016) propose two further sub-types of hashtags. *Ambifunctional* tags both indicate 'aboutness' and add evaluation to a post. *Extracontextual* tags provide information or context not easily inferred in the post. This study found ambifunctional tags were often noun phrases incorporating evaluation of a target, for instance:

```
@realDonaldTrump @POTUS two weeks in to your big boy
job Donny! You're a disaster! #terriblepresident
```

Extracontextual hashtags were often nouns or noun phrases, and also verb phrases, for example:

```
So, I think the color orange may now be ruined for me
forever. #WatchingTrump
```

As we will see, these different meanings can be systematically explored in terms of their realization as different ideational and interpersonal patterns by using the metafunctional lens offered by SFL.

A metafunctional lens

Halliday's (1973, 1978) notion of linguistic metafunctions is one of the most useful analytical tools offered by the social semiotic perspective on discourse. It is a way of interpreting how language, as a complex semiotic system, is able to simultaneously enact an *experiential* function of construing experience, an *interpersonal* function of negotiating relationships, and a *textual* function of organizing information. This chapter draws on Halliday's metafunctional lens to interpret how hashtags can at once indicate the topic of a text, add emotion and opinion to a text, and provide a means of aggregating similar texts.

Metafunctional diversification can be said to span across all linguistic strata from context, through discourse semantics and lexicogrammar, to phonology and graphology (Matthiessen, 1995). In terms of structure, these three dimensions of meaning tend to be realized via different kinds of patterning: *experiential* meanings have a constituent structure (e.g. a 'topic' realized by a single hashtag), *textual* meanings are concerned with the order in which the text unfolds as a cohesive structure, and *interpersonal* meanings tend to be realized more prosodically, 'colouring' other meanings in the text (e.g. as evaluative language). Halliday and Matthiessen (2004, p. 328) note that these are very general tendencies, 'worked out differently in every language but probably discernible in all'.

If we adopt a metafunctional perspective, hashtags can be seen to realize the following linguistic functions that will be explored in detail in this chapter:

1. An *experiential* function of classifying the post as being of a particular experiential type. For instance, the tags in the following indicate that the post is about Trump's executive order temporarily banning immigration from certain Muslim majority countries. This topic-marking function is the

most commonly observed function of hashtags (Zappavigna, 2015). It is related to concept of subject classification used in information and library management:

> 🎉🎉BREAKING: 9th Circuit Court rejects Trump admin request to overturn Friday's ban by federal judge on its **#immigrationban #muslimban**🎉🎉

2. An *interpersonal* function of construing relationships, for example, by facilitating evaluative metacomment that resonates across an entire post to construe an evaluative stance:

> The fact that Trump was voted in as president just goes to show how sexual discrimination and racism is endorsed by many.**#HORRIFIC**!!

3. A *textual* function of organizing the post. For example, at the typographic level, the # symbol functions as a special character that acts as a form of punctuation, signalling that the tag is metadata. For instance, in the post in 1. above, it separates the tagged topic (*#immigrationban*; *#muslimban*) from the rest of the post. This kind of delineation is possible even where the tag is embedded in the linguistic structure, for instance:

> So the **#MuslimBan** was about 'National Security' … meanwhile, the National Security Advisor was actually compromising our National Security?

While it is useful to isolate these functions for the purpose of analysis, they are in fact enacted simultaneously in any linguistic performance, and are not mutually exclusive. As we will see in the rest of the chapters in this book, these linguistic functions are, in turn, used in the service of higher order rhetorical and social functions: construing values, positioning and mocking voices, and enacting ambient affiliation.

The cataloguing function of hashtags

As mentioned earlier, hashtags have been viewed as primarily having a classificatory function of indicating the 'aboutness' as a kind of keyword (Kehoe & Gee, 2011) or 'topic tag' (Wikström, 2014, p. 132). Scholars have noted that 'individual hashtags can be interpreted in terms of their general semantic field (such as politics, sport and so on)' (Page, 2012, p. 188). Many computational studies have used hashtags in tasks related to modelling topics (Mehrotra, Sanner, Buntine, & Xie, 2013). Hashtags appear to cluster 'around well-defined topics, such as health, entertainment and politics'[1] (Bastos et al., 2013, p. 164). Indicating the topic of a post has been seen as linking the post to ongoing 'conversation' (see section 'Hashtags as "conversation"', in Chapter 1). However, while users can engage in direct dialogic exchanges via most social media services, the unfolding is more often a 'multilogue' of simultaneous voices, particularly in the case of microblogging, as we will see in Chapter 5.

In the early phases of hashtag use, this experiential topic-marking function found a very practical application in managing mass emergencies, the earliest social context in which hashtags began to proliferate (Starbird & Stamberger, 2010). The first widely recognized hashtag, *#sandiegofire,* was used to coordinate communication about the San Diego forest fires in 2007. Examples include the following tweets from the time:

> **#sandiegofire:** Campo Road is now open West of Steele Canyon Road.
>
> Any word or updates on fallbrook fires? Have 2 very worried friends with me looking for updates **#sandiegofire**
>
> **#sandiegofire** Busload of 14 elderly patients were taken by a Camp Pendleton bus to El Centro.
>
> Mandatory evacuation: Del Rio Rd. East to Steele Canyon Rd., Fury Lane South to Millar Ranch Rd. and Millar Anita **#sandiegofire**

These kinds of tags tend to have an ideational function used for coordination. Other contexts in which these kinds of hashtags often occur is reaction to live performances or public events. For example, hashtags are necessary for coordination in live tweeting practices (introduced in Chapter 1), where social media communication acts as a backchannel to some other unfolding communication. For example, the following is backchannel communication produced on Twitter during Donald Trump's televised presidential inauguration:

> It feels like I'm watching a 70 yr old Joffrey Baratheon[2] **#InaugurationDay2017**
>
> **#InaugurationDay2017** I will not normalize a Muslim registry or ban. I will not normalize mocking a disable person.
>
> It's all just one big episode of #BlackMirror,[3] right? Right?! **#InaugurationDay2017**

The untagged parts of the tweets above do not contain a lexical item explicitly indicating that the post is about Trump's inauguration. Instead the hashtag provides this experiential context. This type of pattern has been seen as a contextualizing relation, necessitated by the character economy of the microblogging medium where 'there is often no space to provide contextual information explicitly' and so hashtags aid pragmatic inference (Scott, 2015, pp. 9–10).

In terms of experiential meaning at the level of lexicogrammar, hashtags can take up all of the experiential roles in clauses defined by Halliday and Matthiessen (2004). They can function as *participants* realized as nominal groups in a clause:

> Interesting fact: **#Trump** won't be able to get medical treatment under the "New & Improved Healthcare" because his "dementia" is pre-existing
>
> Yes! There is NO POINT in treating **#Trump** as just 'poor at his job'. Enough patience with this Patient. He needs REAL 'TREATMENT'. #Impeach
>
> An ethics lawyer needs to file suit against **#Trump** for subverting 1st Amendment rights. Trump is a shameless provocateur.

Experiential hashtags can also function as *processes* realized as verbal groups. For instance, *#resist* was a popular hashtag used by anti-Trump supporters as a 'call to arms':

> **#resist** FAKE NEWS!
>
> Trump's anti-science stance is a danger to the future of mankind. We must **#resist** alternative facts. #DumpTrump [URL]
>
> Is it possible there are gonna be economic repercussions on America for Trump continually meeting with dictators? Asking for America **#resist**

Hashtags can also function as *circumstances* in the clause, realized as adverbial groups or prepositional phrases:

> .@IvankaTrump @realDonaldTrump Anyone else notice the lack of diversity in this picture? #WhiteNationalism **#InTheWhiteHouse**
>
> **#AsPresident,** I will create a Department of Peace and pursue peace, rather than war. Add your ideas. #election2016 #AskTrump

An amusing kind of circumstantiation can be achieved with a novel *'because + noun'* construction that is often seen in internet communication to concisely realize a circumstance of cause, for example:

> ```
> "We're nerds, we're wet, we're really really upset"
> #marchforscience #saveourplanet #becausescience
> ```
>
> ```
> Wall not smart. #becausescience Hydrogeologist and
> geophysicist weigh in on Trump's border wall http://
> po.st/ DFAtfy via @SmithsonianMag [link to article
> titled 'What Geology has to say about building a
> 1,000-mile border wall]
> ```
>
> ```
> The "abortion" scenario that trump described is not
> how it works. Technically and surgically IMPOSSIBLE.
> #becausescience
> ```

Here the hashtag combines with the compacted construction to pack up the justification, achieving a playful or snarky tone.

The experiential meaning of a particular hashtag may remain relatively opaque to those who fall outside its community of use, since they often incorporate acronyms, abbreviation, and concatenation (Posch, Wagner, Singer, & Strohmaier, 2013). For example, the tag *#MAGA* (Make America Great Again), an acronym for Trump's campaign slogan, or *#CWW* (Concealed Carry Weapon), a pro-gun tag, are not transparent terms. They can only be unpacked with some contextual knowledge. From the perspective of the person searching for information, tags that are too specific or too idiosyncratic may not be discoverable. In addition, tags that are very general (e.g. *#politics*) will likely be too broad to return useful results.[4] Dimensions such as the level of generality, technicality, and abstraction of experiential meaning in a tag are also likely related to the level of popularity a given tag will garner. Here again linguistic function and the technological affordances of search are interwoven.

A note on cataloguing images

Hashtags may also be used to tag visual meaning-making. When a hashtag is used to tag an image, it can construe both ideational and interpersonal meaning. For example, the Instagram images of a placard used during the March for Science (held in Sydney as part of the global protest of the Trump administration's attitude to science (see #MarchForScience in 'Glossary')) was appended with the following respective captions (Figure 3.1):

FIGURE 3.1 *Examples of Instagram images annotated with hashtags.*

> One side of my **#marchforscience** placard. Using my
> **#handlettering** skills for good not evil! **#socialscience**
> **#socialscientist #sociology #linguistics #education**
>
> The other side of my **#marchforscience** placard. Using
> my **#handlettering** skills for good not evil! **#batgirl**
> **#dccomics #cape #academiclife** H/t to @User for
> inspiration

These hashtags construe a range of experiential meanings. They have the dual function of classifying the post and clarifying its contextual alignment by:

1. identifying the activity – e.g. #marchforscience
2. classifying the related academic discipline – e.g. #socialscience, #socialscientist, #sociology, #linguistics, #education
3. identifying the semiotic modality of the represented object – e.g. #handlettering
4. naming the represented participant in the image – e.g. #batgirl

We will return to hashtagged images in Chapter 8, since a model of image-tag coupling is needed to further interpret the intermodal meanings made with these kinds of tags.

Using an interpersonal lens: Hashtags as evaluative metacomment

While the experiential function explored above is very frequent, social media users do more than refer to 'topics'; they construe attitudes towards those topics, and enact relationships with the ambient audience. These are *interpersonal* functions, where interpersonal meaning is the region of meaning concerned with adopting stances and negotiating affiliations (Martin & White, 2005). Analogizing with spoken discourse, we may also think of interpersonal meaning as the social media user's 'ongoing intrusion into the speech situation … his [or her] perspective on the exchange, his [or her] assigning and acting out of speech roles' (Halliday, 1979, pp. 66–67). It is perhaps for this reason that interpersonal hashtags are sometimes likened to a muttered comment or 'playful aside' (Ford, Veletsianos, & Resta, 2014), removed from the main conversational move.

Hashtags can realize all the speech functions defined by Halliday and Matthiessen (2004). For example they can realize *statements* (giving information):

> How long before they propose "Camps" for gays
> to "pray" it away? Will they be mostly for
> "Concentration"? **#TrumpIsEvil**

> You can thank @POTUS when the Great Barrier Reef is
> destroyed due to Trump's attack on the environment
> **#ThisIsTheEnd** #EarthDay

> How about a good eviction from 1600 Penn[5]? That would
> be much better. **#notmypresident**

Pithy statements like *#notmypresident* often become iconized within social movements, especially in relation to 'controversies, conflicts, and crises' such as instances of racism (for instance, *#blacklivesmatter* condemning racist police violence in the United States since 2014) (Giglietto & Lee, 2017, p. 12).

Hashtags can also realize *questions* (demanding information). Note that, although many users will include a question mark, this will not appear as part of a valid hashtag due to the technical specification regarding the special characters that may form part of a valid hashtags (detailed in Chapter 2):

> Attorney General + perjury + Russia + Trump + all the
> things = head exploding **#whatishappening**

> @maddow you just drop some bombs tonight.. I didn't
> know all this was going on. **#WhatCanWeDo**? Trump
> changing the way we do things. 🤔

> .@realDonaldTrump I, and millions of Americans, want
> to see your TAX RETURNS Senior Pee Pee #TaxReturns
> **#WhereAreThey**

Hashtags can also be used to construe *offers* (giving goods and services). However, because the social media domain is electronic, rather than face-to-face, semiotic[6] rather than material goods and services are offered:

> Mad Trump won? Need to release some energy? Wanna find a reason to drink? **#HereYouGo** *[embedded image]*

> I'm a full blood mexican born in America, OIF, OND and OEF veteran. And i say, **#IwillBuildTheWall**

> Move to Canada http://15miles.info/move-to-canada/ via @onefivemiles #Trump #America **#ThisIsForYou**

Finally, hashtags can construe *commands* (demanding goods and services):

> Trump/Russia "story" IS real don't b distracted @ realDonaldTrump uses everything to deflect attention from investigation loves Putin **#resist**

> I keep waiting for someone to say, "This whole Trump thing, we're done. Back to usual buisness." **#makeitstop**

> Mike Pence is more dangerous than Trump. #mikepence **#goaway** #complicit

These interpersonal hashtags subvert the collectivizing function of hashtags. The main function of these interpersonally orientated tags has little to do with aggregating posts into searchable sets, and much more to do with adopting particular attitudinal dispositions, involved in enacting different kinds of identities (Zappavigna, 2014c). We will explore these evaluative meanings, at the level of discourse semantics, in the next chapter. This chapter will introduce Appraisal (Martin & White, 2005), a framework for interpreting how opinion and sentiment are construed at this stratum.

Offline hashtags

Due to their popularity and ability to concisely capture cultural moments, hashtags have expanded their reach to include offline urban environments. Meaning-making that is analogous to online hashtag use can be found across different semiotic modes. For example, the hash symbol can be represented in images. It can be articulated as the word 'hashtag' in spoken language. In addition it can be kinetically realized as a hand gesture in body language.

Hashtags can be found in advertising, street art, and graffiti, appearing on posters, billboards, chalkboards, shop windows, walls etc. (Figure 3.2). While the 'gradual appropriation of Twitter syntax across the Web and beyond – on T-shirts and magnets – signals its ubiquitous integration in online and offline social practices around the globe' (van Dijck, 2013, pp. 71–72), what is at stake is more than pervasiveness but iconization. In offline contexts, the technical affordances that we explored in Chapter 2 are no longer present, or at least less direct (e.g. requiring a person to search online for a hashtag they have encountered in the environment).

Iconization is the process whereby 'interpersonal meaning is foregrounded and the icon works to concentrate accumulated values (both ethical and aesthetic)' (Zappavigna, 2014d). Just as symbolic icons such as flags and memorabilia can function to 'rally visitors around communal ideals' within museum exhibitions (Martin & Stenglin, 2007, p. 216), or academic gowns and testamurs within a graduation ceremony (Stenglin, 2012), other kinds of symbols can forge feelings of shared value. In the case of the # symbol in offline contexts, exactly which value is being foregrounded can be difficult to determine. This is because offline hashtags are unlikely to have yet stabilized as a semiotic resource. The meaning most likely relevant is general positive assessment of social media communication and internet culture. This is in keeping with Heyd and Puschmann's (in press) observation that the # has become an 'emblem of social media linguistic practice'.

Offline hashtags are also subject to processes of commodification. Hashtags are widely used in advertising (Stathopoulou, Borel, Christodoulides, & West, 2017) and can be seen on billboards, posters, shop windows, and café chalkboards. They appear emblazoned on various kinds of commercial products such as clothing, décor, and mass-produced jewellery. It is possible

FIGURE 3.2 *Examples of hashtags in the urban environment (image 3 credit: @bonhomme69).*

to purchase hashtag earrings, balloons, ice cube moulds, and hashtag coffee tables (Figure 3.3). Products will also regularly incorporate hashtags into their packaging (e.g. Figure 3.4).

Offline hashtags span a wide variety of contexts, from the intimate/personal to the public/political. For example, they may occur as part of handwritten notes, or they may be worn on the body as handmade jewellery (Figure 3.5). They can also occur within pedagogic contexts, for instance, as resources used in learning vocabulary within a traditional school classroom (Figure 3.6). In contexts involving mass communication with the public, such as political campaigns and activist movements, offline hashtags have been viewed as having the textual function 'of emphasizing the message', with the # symbol functioning 'as a pre-positioned exclamation mark, possibly aiming at producing catchy formulations' (Caleffi, 2015, p. 66). Heyd and Puschmann (in press) have explored hashtags across different offline contexts found within urban environments. They observe what they describe as a 'functional shift' incorporating adaptation and appropriation. This involves four emerging dimensions of offline urban hashtags: the degree of commodification (e.g. hashtags working in the service of marketing on

FIGURE 3.3 *Examples of products featuring hashtags.*

FIGURE 3.4 *An example of packaging featuring hashtags (image 1 credit: Kit Wong).*

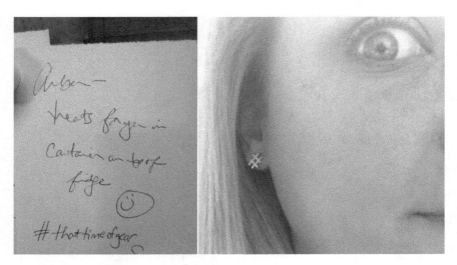

FIGURE 3.5 *An example of a handwritten note and an earring featuring a hashtag.*

advertising billboards or shop windows), the degree of professionalization (e.g. professionally printed material versus handwritten or hand-painted hashtags (e.g. graffiti, street art or paper notes)), and deictic status (e.g. whether these tags refer to existing tags in the digital domain).

Spoken and gestured hashtags have also been observed in face-to-face conversation and parody genres. For instance, a well-known example

FIGURE 3.6 *An example of hashtags used in the classroom.*

is a comedy sketch by Jimmy Fallon and Justin Timberlake on the Tonight Show (republished on YouTube with the description 'Jimmy Fallon & Justin Timberlake show you what a Twitter conversation sounds like in real life' (The Tonight Show Starring Jimmy Fallon, 2013)). This sketch mocks overuse of the spoken tag:

Jimmy Fallon: Hey, Justin what's up?

Justin Timberlake: Not much Jimmy, hashtag chilling. What's up with you?

Jimmy Fallon: It's been busy working, hashtag rise and grind! Hashtag is it Friday yet?

Justin Timberlake: Hey, check it out, I brought you some cookies. hashtag homemade, hashtag oatmeal raisin, hashtag show me the cookie.

Jimmy Fallon: Sweet. hashtag don't mind if I don't. Pretty good. Hashtag getting my cookie on. Hashtag I am the real cookie monster. Hashtag nomnomnomnomnom...

In this form of spoken/gestured tagging, the speaker says the word 'hashtag'. They also optionally make the gesture shown in Figure 3.7, where the finger position resembles a written # symbol. Hashtag gestures seem to be used mostly sarcastically, or 'ironically' to indicate intertextual awareness. Their use is sporadic in spoken discourse and most likely a fad (Caleffi, 2015).

While it is difficult to source examples of spoken hashtags from naturally occurring casual conversation, there are many examples of social media users reporting that they, or others, have used them in spoken conversations. Tweets noting this usage most commonly relay an instance that the user has found particularly amusing. These provide some evidence that spoken hashtags are considered a novel rather than prevalent resource:

"unfortunately a lot of people are **hashtag stupid**"
Words of my dad.

I just said "hashtag yolo" to my dad and he responded
with "hashtag dumb a**"' 😂😂

6: Seriously, Mommy. It was **hashtag ... stupid**!

Me:

6: Hashtag ... What?!

Me: 6: Hashtag ... For real.

Me: I just cannot even make this up.

FIGURE 3.7 *The hashtag gesture.*

My mom just said to me " **Hashtag dumb $?%"** wasn't even mad at her for calling me a name. Just mad at her about saying the word hashtag.

Just spilled some tea & said **"hashtag wow"** aloud unironically if you're wondering who it is that boomer prescriptivists are angry at.

Interestingly, some users spell out the hashtag in tweets, signalling playful awareness of use in both modalities:

Hashtag WOW, crispy potato balls, smashed avocado with poached eggs and watercress drizzle … *[image of a plate of food]*

> why I always post when none of the twins are online
> **hashtag stupid**
>
> how should i wake up my bf right now bc i wanna cuddle
> and make out but i dont wanna seem clingy and annoying
> **hashtag help**
>
> #AmexDell syncing my amex to my twitter account is
> stupid, but i'll do it for $100 off $300 purchase.
> **hashtag dumb.**

In addition to being a form of linguistic play that signals knowledge of the semiotic codes of both semiotic modes (i.e. electronic and spoken discourse), this kind of language may be mocking the use of hashtags in either mode.

Playful uses of offline hashtags are difficult to interpret since humour is notoriously difficult to analyse. Using the # symbol in the offline realm may signal that you know and appreciate online social media communication. A spoken hashtag may be used to suggest a kind of 'savviness'/'wittiness'/'pla

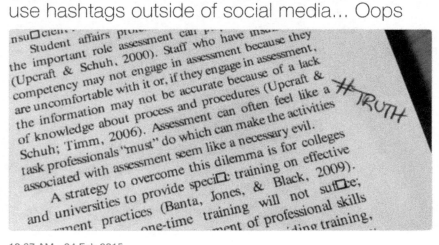

FIGURE 3.8 *An example of handwritten hashtag.*

yfulness' in being able to co-opt meanings across different semiotic modes. This metalinguistic play is itself sometimes the subject of posts. For example, Figure 3.8 is an example where the user humorously notes that they have violated a communicative norm by inserting a handwritten hashtag into the margin of a written document. However, Scott (in press) warns against reading offline hashtags merely as language games, arguing that '[s]peakers are adapting their use to fit with the affordances and constraints of the discourse context'.

There has been some very preliminary linguistic investigation of spoken and gestured hashtags. However, as mentioned earlier, obtaining naturally occurring examples is difficult. Spoken tags occur rarely. When they are used, this mainly happens within casual conversation, a challenging discourse situation to record because of its personal nature. Caleffi (2015) suggests that spoken hashtags tend to function as verbal exclamations, as in the following examples:

I'm hashtag confused!
Hashtag are you kidding me?
Hashtag, YOLO! (Caleffi, 2015, p. 66)

The tags identified by Scott (in press) have similar interpersonal functions, providing 'evaluative judgements on the rest of the utterance', and guiding 'inferences concerning the speaker's attitudinal stance' (e.g. 'hashtag blessed' or 'hashtag sarcasm'). This work draws on Pullum (2010)[7] and Curzan's (2013) commentary on punctuation transformed into spoken lexis. Scott (in press) notes that the main function of spoken hashtags, beyond their experiential function, is to offer higher order explicatures and implicatures. They can function as evaluative metacommentary which (in relation to online hashtags) is the focus of the next chapter.

4

#WhinyLittleBitch: Evaluative Metacommentary

Introduction

Firth's (1964, p. 112) insight that the 'promotion, establishment, and maintenance of communion of feeling is perhaps four-fifths of all talk' is as applicable to online communication as to offline conversation. Barton (2015, p. 64) has noted that there 'are many things going on in tagging spaces and it is not just about taxonomies, nor just about folksonomies'. For example, rather than indicating the topic of a post, the hashtag in the chapter title above is an example of a tag attacking Trump by prodding at his masculinity and status:

Trump: Being Pres is harder than I thought.

So call the Kremlin Complaint Dept at 1-800-Tuf-Shit. **#WhinyLittleBitch** *[link to a Reuters article titled 'Exclusive: Trump says he thought being president would be easier than his old life']*

A hashtag such as *#WhinyLittleBitch* construes an evaluative stance, as well as presenting a potential bond with which the ambient audience may or may not align (as we will see in Chapter 8). *#WhinyLittleBitch* is also an amusing hashtag, given Trump's propensity for braggadocio. Hashtags have become a vehicle for making such biting or pithy comments, and for participating in apparent cultural 'moments' incorporating humorous commentary on anything from the banal to the extraordinary. Social media networks tend to value humour and 'concise flippancy' (Highfield, 2016, p. 48), even as they reward expression of apparent 'authenticity' (Kytölä & Westinen, 2015), and hashtags enable succinct distillations of wit to be performed.

As we saw in the previous chapter, hashtags display a high degree of metafunctional flexibility, and are particularly useful in construing, as well as drawing attention to, an evaluative stance (Zappavigna, 2012b). The focus of this chapter is twofold: to introduce the model of evaluative language, known as the Appraisal framework (Martin & White, 2005), which informs the analysis undertaken throughout this book, as well as to explain how hashtags function as evaluative metacommentary, drawing on the description of metadiscourse undertaken in Chapter 2. We will explore how hashtags have taken on an important social function beyond classification, acting as a means of articulating short, evaluatively loaded, comments and observations.

Most linguistic studies have recognized that, beyond its most straightforward function as a topic-marker, the hashtag has 'been appropriated by users to perform other roles in the communicative process' (Scott, 2015). Evaluative hashtags are an example of 'metacommunicative tagging' with 'enough generic qualities … to warrant rhetorical analysis' (Daer et al., 2014, p. 2).These roles include contributing to 'conversational style' (Scott, 2015), with emotive and emphatic use linked to variations in illocutionary force. These are agnate to variations 'reminiscent of the work done by non-verbal cues in face-to-face conversation' (Wikström, 2014, p. 150). Hashtags have also been seen as facilitating dialogistic stance by functioning as what DuBois (2007) terms a 'stance follow'. This is a second subject's stance considered in relation to a first subject's stance, referred to as the 'stance lead' (Evans, 2016). Hashtags have also been argued to function as metapragmatic markers. For instance, they have been observed to play a role in negotiating levels of self-praise in practices of visual self-representation (e.g. via the tags, *#brag* and *#humblebrag* (Matley, in press)). In addition, they have been viewed as brief 'spontaneous interjections' with an increased emotive denotative power compared with the rest of a social media post (Cislaru, 2015, p. 466).

The Appraisal framework

Evaluation is a domain of interpersonal meaning where language is used to express attitudes, and to adopt stances regarding other texts and voices. For example, the following tweet by Donald Trump is loaded with attitudinal meaning aimed at undermining the credibility of people protesting against his administration:

```
The so-called angry crowds in home districts of some
Republicans are actually, in numerous cases, planned
out by liberal activists. Sad!
```

Similarly, the following reply to this tweet, construed as a series of hashtags is saturated with evaluation:

```
#WhinyLittleBitch #LOSER #CryBaby #WhinerInChief
#FuckTrump #Resist #theresistance
```

Here the evaluation is realized through a range of resources such as inscribed attitudinal lexis (e.g. *#LOSER*) construing negative opinion, and expletives (e.g. *#Fuck...*) expressing outbursts of underspecified negative emotion.

The model used in this book to interpret this type of attitudinal meaning is the Appraisal framework (Martin & White, 2005) (hereon Appraisal). This framework was developed within SFL to account for how evaluative language functions in situational and cultural contexts. It has been used in a number of social media studies, including studies of affiliation (Martin, Zappavigna, Dwyer, & Cléirigh, 2013; Page et al., 2014; Zappavigna, 2011, 2012b, 2014a, 2014c, 2014d, 2015), solidarity-building (Drasovean & Tagg, 2015), identity (Vásquez, 2014), narrative (Page, 2012), and social tagging (Chiluwa & Ifukor, 2015; Zappavigna, 2015).

Appraisal, influenced by Painter's (1984) work on infant protolanguage, developed out of a theory that the kinds of emotional reaction to the world seen in protolanguage matures into more complex systems of evaluation. This occurs as infants are socialized into a culture and into institutions. Feeling becomes institutionalized as *ethics and morality*, forming the judgement system, with which we construe rules and regulations regarding behaviour (top example, Figure 4.1). Feeling is also institutionalized as *aesthetics and value*, forming the appreciation system, with which we generate assessments based on our reactions to phenomena (bottom example, Figure 4.1).

The Appraisal framework defines three key dimensions of evaluative meaning: *attitude*, whereby a particular evaluation is construed, *graduation*, whereby that evaluation is modulated (e.g. scaling up or down in intensity), and *engagement*, whereby the evaluation enters into relationship with other potential stances (e.g. by endorsing or discrediting a viewpoint). Each of these systems is explained below using responses to Trump's tweet about protesters (from the beginning of the chapter) as examples. For further details on how to apply Appraisal the reader is directed to *The Language of Evaluation* (Martin & White, 2005) which provides extensive details on each of its discursive systems.

Appraisal models evaluation using system networks that represent meaning as choices between different potential resources. System networks are networks of interrelated options that are organized paradigmatically, in terms of 'what could go instead of what', rather than syntagmatically in terms of structure (Halliday & Matthiessen, 2004, p. 22).[1] They are an alternative to

Ethics/morality (rules & regulations)
Feelings institutionalised as proposals.

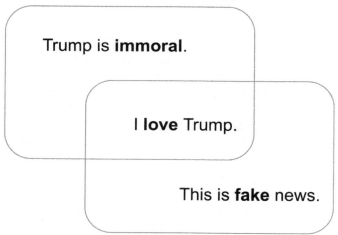

Aesthetics/values (criteria & assessment)
Feelings institutionalised as propositions.

FIGURE 4.1 *The institutionalization of affect, adapted from Martin and White (2005, p. 45).*

modelling language as a catalogue of structures. Figure 5.2 provides examples of each region of Appraisal (shown in bold) in the form of a system network as defined by Martin and White (2005). The network adopts the convention whereby capitalized labels in front of the arrows indicate different *systems* of meaning. Lowercase labels at the end of each path mark *features* within systems. A square bracket represents a choice between two options in a system (an 'or' relation), while a brace represents simultaneous choices (an 'and' relation). The example tweets appended to this network in the speech bubbles each illustrate a type of Appraisal. The network may be further specified to greater levels of delicacy depending on the kind of analysis for which it is being used.

As Figure 4.2 suggests, the Appraisal framework specifies three discursive regions of attitudinal meaning: AFFECT (expressing emotion, e.g. *love, disgust, and fear*), JUDGEMENT (assessing behaviour, e.g. *evil, ethical, and trustworthy*), and APPRECIATION (estimating value, e.g. *beautiful, treasured, and noteworthy*). Most of the attitude realized in reactions to Trump's tweets is of negative polarity. Tables 4.1, 4.2, and 4.3 show each of the subsystems of affect, judgement, and appreciation respectively.

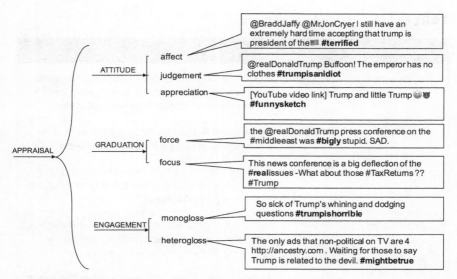

FIGURE 4.2 *The Appraisal system, adapted from Martin and White (2005, p. 38), with example tweets containing hashtags realizing evaluative metacommentary.*

TABLE 4.1 Types of affect

Affect	Tweet
(Un)Happiness	So heart broken that Trump won tonight. America will truly never be the same again.. #Election2016 #lgbtq **#sad**
In(Security)	@User Such a "Banana Republic" thing to say .... or does Trump believe that the as President, he can satisfy all his vendettas? #So**Frightening**
(Dis)Satisfaction	@SenWarren You could've been the Exec and now you're being told to shut up on the Senate floor. Trump is partly your fault! #IAMSO**MAD**

Evaluative meaning is clearly a complex semantic domain, and to a certain extent every utterance we make is tinged with evaluation and implicates particular value positions (cf. Voloshinov's (1929/1973/1986, p. 103) idea of the 'evaluative accent'). The Appraisal framework attempts to account for this complexity by distinguishing attitude which is 'inscribed', that is, realized via explicit evaluative choices, from attitude which is 'invoked', that is, suggested via ideational choices that imply evaluation. For example, consider the difference between the following posts about Trump falsely implying, during one of his rallies, that there had been some kind of terrorist attack in Sweden:

TABLE 4.2 Types of judgement

Judgement		Tweet
Social esteem	Normality	#swedenincident It's both hysterical & terrifying that Trump complains about fake news & then 2 minutes later he spews fake news **#insane**
	Capacity	It's so much fun to see #trump promise shit he will never be able to deliver #whata**moron**
	Tenacity	Questions about Trump's health begin to mount as he cancels multiple events during his overseas trip. #Trump #No**Stamina**
Social sanction	Veracity	Trump's health issues in Saudi Arabia are the first step towards a resignation without admitting guilt. Fits his (lack of) character. **#Liar**
	Propriety	@KellyannePolls Your comments defending Trump claiming he values women is like those who sold out Jews to the Nazi's. #youarea**disgrace**

TABLE 4.3 Types of appreciation

Appreciation	Tweet
Reaction	@TheTalkCBS That's what SNL does. The offense lies in demeaning Trump supporters. #itwas**hilarious**
Composition	Not a #FOX news regular I tuned in to see coverage of the #blackmail intel reports on #trump it was nonexistent **#balanced** news #laughable
Valuation	I swear to GOD, I am unfollowing the next person who tweets about Kanye at Trump Tower. #NOT**IMPORTANT**

> More **#raving** from the **#idiot #Putzident** #trump. #lastnightinsweden #WhatHasHeBeenSmoking? *[embedded link to a CBC post about an article titled "'What has he been smoking?: Swedes scratch heads at Trump's suggestion of major incident"]*
>
> Seriously, what has he been smoking? #LastNightInSweden

The first post contains explicit examples of lexicalized attitude (shown in bold), whereas the second post does not. However, the second post is clearly evaluative despite the absence of any particular instance of inscribed attitude. The idiomatic expression 'what has he been smoking' invokes negative judgement (capacity) by implying that Trump has taken a drug that has impaired his faculties.

Appraisal distinguishes between three systems of implied evaluation: *provoke, flag*, and *afford*. Attitude may be 'provoked' via lexical metaphors: for example, negatively appraising Trump by equating him to a *cheeto* (a brand of snackfood):

```
Hmm, Jesus before Trump? The #OrangeCheeto is not
gonna like that.;)
```

Alternatively attitude may be 'flagged' via graduation resources: for example, negatively appraising Trump by downscaling his size:

```
Tiny man, tiny man, tiny man with tiny hands! #tiny hand trump
```

Finally, attitude may be 'afforded' via ideation. For example, the Whitehouse is a shared positive symbol in American culture. Being invited to the Whitehouse invokes positive social esteem:

```
Given #trump's affinity for dictators, the recent
strongman tactics (killing protesters) assures #Maduro
an invitation to the #whitehouse
```

The negative Appraisal in the above tweet is achieved via the contrast of the afforded positive social esteem (*invitation to the #whitehouse*) with the inscribed negative propriety (e.g. *dictators*).

An interesting example of ideational meaning (in the form of a circumstance of time/location) affording attitude is the *#LastnightInSweden* hashtag. This tag was used to mock Donald Trump's suggestion that there had been a terrorist attack in Sweden in February 2017. Trump made the following statement during a rally in Florida on February 18, 2017:

Here's the bottom line. We've got to keep our country safe. You look at what's happening. We've got to keep our country safe. You look at what's happening in Germany. **You look at what's happening last night in Sweden. Sweden, who would believe this. Sweden. They took in large numbers. They're having problems like they never thought possible. You** look at what's happening in Brussels. You look at what's happening all over the world. Take a look at Nice. Take a look at Paris. We've allowed thousands and thousands of people into our country and there was no way to vet those people. There was no documentation. There was no nothing. So we're going to keep our country safe.

Tweets in response to this claim used the tag, #LasnightInSweden, to mock Trump's obviously bogus suggestion that there was an attack. The negative judgement of Trump's truthfulness is invoked via the ideational tag:

> Those evil fake terrorists. All those terrible fake deaths
> and injuries. Oh the fake humanities **#LastNightInSweden**
>
> Let's talk about what happened **#LastNightInSweden**.
>
> We need to work on our presidents sources!
> **#lastnightinsweden**
>
> **#lastnightinsweden** people were calm and pleasant there
> were not any "not my prime minister" protests as there
> was no reason.
>
> Never forget. #JeSuisIKEA **#lastnightinsweden**
> #swedenincident #Sweden #DonalTrump *[image of
> the Swedish flag, an allen key with the hashtag
> #swedenincident and the caption 'WE WILL REBUILD']*

The capacity of this tag to afford negative assessment is central to the kind of humour and sarcasm generated in these posts.

Evaluative metacommentary

As we saw in the previous chapter, hashtags are an important resource for construing what might be thought of as a kind of interpersonal 'aside' that adds a second layer of meaning to the post. This is sometimes likened to a *sotto voce* conversational aside in which a speaker reveals their true feelings. Hashtags that draw on Appraisal resources can be interpreted as a form of evaluative metacommentary. The comment can either be about the body of the post (e.g. *#CantbelieveIsaidThat*) or about the context (e.g. *#MoronsAreGoverningAmerica*):

> only song i like by mac miller is donald trump.
> **#truefact #cantbelieveisaidthat**
>
> If you are freaking out about impending war and
> you voted for Trump I have zero sympathy for you
> **#ThanksTrump #MoronsAreGoverningAmerica**

Where the comment is about the post body, there is some resolvable relationship between the tag and the post. For example, the tag

#cantbelieveisaidthat involves an anaphoric reference to the verbiage through 'that', and thus it is possible to co-textually abduce the relation. The tag might also refer to specific ideation or evaluation in the post body. In other cases, the hashtag appeals to something in the context. For example, an attitudinal stance adopted by others. This might involve a reference to a political slogan such as #MAGA (Make America Great Again) or some other form of shared knowledge. In this way we might make a distinction between evaluative metacommentary that involves intertextual commentary, and evaluative metacommentary that involves intra-textual commentary.

In terms of the different intra-textual (co-textual) relationships that can be instantiated between an evaluative hashtag and the rest of a post, there appear to be two main choices: the hashtag may *supply* attitude that is not directly inscribed in the body of a post, or *supplement* existing attitude through introducing new instances of Appraisal. These new instances may *augment* existing attitude by re-instantiating attitude from the same system, or by introducing additional evaluation from another system. Alternatively, an evaluative hashtag may counter-expectantly *disrupt* existing attitude, most often in order to realize some form of sarcasm (Figure 4.3).

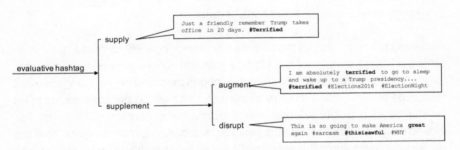

FIGURE 4.3 *Relationship of an evaluative hashtag to the Appraisal in a post.*

For example, a post might open with a description of an event or phenomenon, and then provide the user's emotional response through a hashtag. For example, the following posts construe a reaction to Trump's impending inauguration through hashtags inscribing affect:

```
Trump will become the president in a few days, lets
see what will change … #worried
```

```
11 more days until Trump is President #overjoyed ☺
```

```
Today is the day Donald trump becomes president of the
United States #DonaldTrump #DonaldTrumpInauguration
#happy #great #excited
```

This choice to realize the attitude only in the tag (and not in the body) may be used to construe a range of rhetorical patterns, from emphasizing the attitudinal reaction to creating humour or a sense of drama.

Alternatively, an evaluative hashtag may *supplement* evaluation already present in the post, assisting in radiating the evaluation across the post or, from the perspective of graduation, upscaling the attitude. For example, the hashtags in the following post inscribe negative judgement (capacity) regarding Trump's ability to discharge his role as president. These tags echo similar judgement in the rest of the post (shown underlined):

> It matters because Trump has been chosen to represent the people and most of us know he is <u>incompetent</u>. **#incompetent #unfit**

> If your President can't watch a news report without <u>getting it wrong</u> how can he be trusted in a real crisis? #SwedenIncident #Trump **#Unfit**

> <u>Dumb</u> Donald is so <u>dumb</u>, how <u>dumb</u> is he? #Trump just threatened Toyota - but it looks like he <u>got the facts wrong</u> #MatchGame **#Buffoon #Unfit**

A hashtag may also *disrupt* the attitude presented, typically to invoke humour or sarcasm. Most examples of this kind draw on additional interpersonal resources, for instance, involvement resources (for negotiating solidarity) or engagement resources (for managing the play of voices). This may be because hashtagging an attitude of opposite valence would reduce the coherence of the post. For example, in the following post the hashtag, #justkidding, makes explicit how the reader should interpret the appraisal ('I am joking therefore I mean the reverse of what I am saying'). This in turn invokes solidarity with the ambient reader:

> That Donald Trump tax plan though. Sounds **great**. **#justkidding**

Similarly, negation can be used to explicitly counter the stance presented in the post:

> I get it, Trump has only assumed office a week ago. Give him a break. I get it! #**no**breaksOnClimate **#never #noway** #president**not**GOD

Alternatively, cohesion resources, such as the contrastive 'now' in the post below, can be used to clarify the attitudinal shift:

```
@realDonaldTrump (Mr. Trump,in the beginning I thought
just maybe it could be you that would really do a
great job. Now, #noway #nohumility
```

In addition, use of an expletive can be used to invoke a burst of underspecified affect that inverts the Appraisal:

```
#DACA ... a wonderful program ... full of some bad
hombres! #wtf #Trump
```

Of course, there are many other resources, too numerous to list here, that could be called upon to flip the attitudinal meaning. We will return to this idea of 'evaluative inversion' in Chapter 8.

A topological approach to evaluative metacommentary

As we have seen, evaluative hashtags can span all three systems of attitude: they can express emotion, make moral judgements, and construe aesthetic/value-based assessments. Since hashtags are a 'free text' resource, the possibilities are only limited by the character constraints imposed by the social media channel, inflected by the genre/text type being realized. Most studies have adopted a typological approach to documenting the different classes of hashtags observed. However, the linguistic flexibility of hashtags means that this kind of analysis necessarily generates a 'fuzzy' set. In other words, hashtags can only be partially described[2] through discrete categories and instead require a topological approach:

> A phenomenon that has a topological description ... can never be completely and exhaustively described by a digital or typological code (e.g. the categorical system of phonemes, tonemes, etc. in formal linguistics). It always 'overflows' our attempts to 'capture' it in our category systems. It can be endlessly reclassified according to infinitely many different systems of classification, each of which construes it as having a different set of relevant features (cf. distinctive features in linguistic phonology). (Lemke, 2005, p. 153)

A categorical approach to hashtags encounters the problem, common in linguistics when trying to model agnation (how meanings are related to one and other), that 'a taxonomy is only ever a partial statement of similarity and difference' (Martin & Matthiessen, 1991, p. 346). Taxonomies tend to privilege some criteria, while backgrounding others.

By way of contrast, a topological description of hashtags is useful in illuminating key distinctions in meaning across different dimensions while accounting for such fuzziness. For instance, we might consider tags along a continuum of evaluation (from more to less explicitly evaluative), and along a continuum of stability (from ubiquitous to idiosyncratic). This is a way of understanding their meaning potential across these two dimensions.[3] This approach offers a means of simultaneously distinguishing between evaluative tags with high proliferation that might be considered memes (e.g. *#AlternativeFacts*, the upper right quadrant, Figure 4.4) from tags that are evaluative but relatively unique or uncommon (e.g. *#ICantBelieveTrumpSaidThat,* lower left quadrant, Figure 4.4).

For example, a tag like *#Trump* that incorporates only ideation is less evaluative than a tag such as *#lovetrumpshate* which includes lexicalized attitude. A tag such as *#trump* can imply, but not inscribe, attitude. This tag is extremely frequent in the social stream, having proliferated more

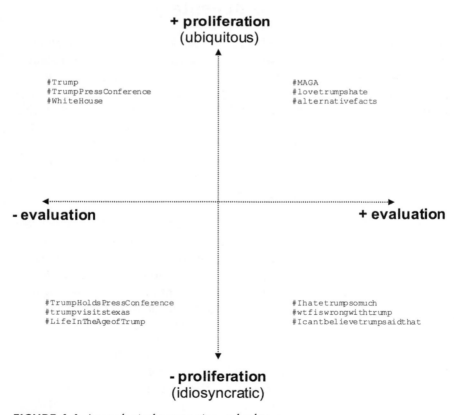

FIGURE 4.4 *A topological perspective on hashtags.*

than, for instance, *#Trumpholdspressconference*: a tag too specific to be widely adopted. While *#lovetrumpshate* might also seem too specific to proliferate, this tag spread 'virally' by virtue of being a slogan used to criticize hateful right wing rhetoric. Similarly, *#AlternativeFacts* proliferated widely, achieving the status of an internet meme. In this meme users contributed their own versions of inaccurate 'facts' as a kind of shared game aimed at ridiculing Trump and his advisers (see Chapter 8). On the other hand, a tag such as *#WTFiswrongwithtrump* remained idiosyncratic, in the sense that it has not been taken up by a large number of users. The interaction of these dimensions is shown in Figure 4.4. Typological approaches to tags will tend to obscure aspects of these dimensions.

5

#SpicerFacts: The Quoted Voice and Intersubjectivity

Introduction

Discourse is inherently multi-voiced, always making connections with other voices (Bakhtin, 1935/1981, p. 89). Hashtags enable a 'polyphony of voices' to compete for discursive visibility in the social stream (Davis, 2013, p. 18). Social media platforms themselves have sought ways of capitalizing on this competition for visibility.[1] As we saw in Chapters 2, 3, and 4, hashtags have afforded a new and expanded form of metadiscourse. The present chapter explores a very interesting dimension of this new meaning potential: how different perspectives and voices are managed, in particular how the quoted voice is construed.

Adding a hashtag to a post amplifies its semiotic 'reach' by making it visible to more potential users/audiences. This also increases the scope of potential intertextual relations (Kristeva, 1984), across multiple contexts. The presence of a hashtag renders a text more 'open' to externalized propositions since it offers the possibility that this audience may engage with the stance construed. For instance, members of the ambient audience may reply, rebroadcast, or rate (via a like/favourite) the post.[2] Intertextual meanings are particularly important in social media environments given the tendency of images, video, and written text to be replicated, modified, and recontextualized at rapid rates and high volume. This has led to the metaphor of 'viral' distribution being used to characterize such proliferation (Hansen, Arvidsson, Nielsen, Colleoni, & Etter, 2011), where 'spreadable media' (Jenkins, Ford, & Green, 2013) is shared across social networks.[3]

This chapter begins by introducing the concept of voice in relation to Bahktin's (1935/1981) ideas about heterolglossia. Bahktin's work on dialogicity influenced the development of the Appraisal framework introduced in the previous chapter. Appraisal was however, largely developed with written texts in mind, and without a means of accounting for multimodal meanings made across semiotic modes. The model for exploring the social media quoted voice proposed in the chapter aims to account for how such multimodal resources are deployed in quotation. For example, it seeks to understand how metadata is involved in attributing stances to voices in social media discourse. Using examples of #SpicerFact posts (responding to Sean Spicer's comments about the size of Trump's inauguration crowd), the chapter details a system network for exploring the quoted social media voice. This network factors in hashtags as a 'metavocalization' resource.

Since social media texts have heteroglossic meaning as their starting point, given that monoglossia is largely impossible in the ambient environment, the chapter concludes by exploring how hashtags support relations between different kinds of perspectives. Social media texts cannot be monoglossic since a post always enters into a relation with the other posts in the social stream. As we will see, rather than simply introducing and evaluating discursive voices, hashtags operate in the service of managing different perspectives. This involves managing relations between the points of view of different potential voices, affording, as we will see, the possibility of interesting permutations of meaning.

Voice

The notion of 'voice' is assumed in most studies of how different stances are introduced into texts. It derives from Bakhtin's (1986, p. 89) ideas about 'heteroglossia', and his central concern that 'all our utterances ... [are] filled with others' words, varying degrees of otherness and varying degrees of "our-own-ness"'.[4] Bakhtin noted 'infinite gradations in the degree of foreignness (or assimilation) of words, their various distances from the speaker' (Bakhtin, 1986, p. 120). Nevertheless, most theories of stance adopt some version of a primary/secondary voice binary. For instance, Sinclair's (1988) distinction between stances that are 'averred' by the author or 'attributed' to a source is similar to Martin and White's (2005) notion of 'authorial' and 'non-authorial' evaluation, and to Hunston's (2000) categorization of sources into 'self' and 'other'. In addition, White (2012, p. 66) has noted that secondary voices are often dialogistically multiple, with the primary voice indicating 'a dialogistic stance on the part of the secondary voice'. For example, 'reporting verbs may have a double functionality of indicating both the "stance" of the primary authorial voice vis-a-vis the attributed material and the "stance" of the secondary, quoted source towards this material' (White, 2012, p. 63).

Hashtags, as a semiotic technology involved in 'new writing' (van Leeuwen, 2008), assist in condensing the play of this otherness/our-own-ness in social media posts. They support 'embedded dialogism' (Han, 2015, p. 64), where multiple voices are abridged and evaluated in the highly condensed manner required by the brief format. Hashtags are also an example of how new media tend to blend established print culture practices for quoting other voices. For instance, conventionalized typographic representations (e.g. 'surface features' (Fairclough, 1992) such as quotation marks) blend with the affordances of new technologies (Puschmann, 2015). Some work has noted that hashtags may invoke a similar tone to quotation marks for signalling ironic or self-conscious distance (Scheible, 2015), or for providing emphasis (Heyd, 2014).

Hashtags are unavoidably polyvocal in the sense that they imply the presence of other voices in the social stream who may use the same tag. Hashtags have been argued to 'encapsulate a variety of "voices", whether the user is responding to the "voice" represented in the content ... or to a collection of unnamed "voices"' (Evans, 2016). However, identifying which voices are implied can be difficult since the original context of social media texts can so easily be lost. In addition, social media users themselves may be uncertain of who might interact with the material that they post. This indeterminacy has been termed 'context collapse': the impossibly of a user being able to exhaustively assess, and attune to, the various parameters of a given context because the social media audience is largely unknown (Wesch, 2009). For instance, a vlogger[5] recording a YouTube video is in the difficult position that they must set a tone for their video, and conform to various norms (that might differ across communities), without necessarily being able to specify the scope of their audience:

> The problem is not lack of context. It is context collapse: an infinite number of contexts collapsing upon one another into that single moment of recording. The images, actions, and words captured by the lens at any moment can be transported to anywhere on the planet and preserved (the performer must assume) for all time. The little glass lens [of the webcam] becomes the gateway to a black hole sucking all of time and space – virtually all possible contexts – in on itself. (Wesch, 2009, p. 23)

Often social media texts quote other texts without using any punctuation resources such as quotation marks, instead relying on the ambient audience's ability to resolve important cultural moments from, either their observations of what has been happening in the social stream, or from knowledge of the relevant contextual meaning. For example, the posts below span a wide range of apparent fields of meaning (e.g. science, comedy, protest, and sport) but the hashtags give clues to the voices in play; it is this meaning potential that will be explored in this chapter.

Consider, for example, the following posts which do not contain traditional 'surface features' indicating that they incorporate a quotation:

This was the largest cell count to ever flow through a cytometer, period! **#AlternativeFACS**

I've been watching **#snl** since it came on. This was one of the best skits ever. Period. *[GIF featuring a moment in a Saturday Night Live sketch where the actor playing Spicer lifts up the podium to attack the audience with it]*

This was the largest March ever to be witnessed on a Scottish Street, period. **#MuslimBan #Edinburgh #Spicerism** *[embedded image of a protest crowd]*

This was the funniest @nbcsnl skit ever. Period. @seanspicer @PressSec **#SpicerLies** *[embedded image of Sean Spicer speaking at press briefing]*

This was the largest ever #Liverpool win against Swansea – period **#SpicerFacts**

These posts all, however, reference the underlined section (below) from a statement made by US press secretary Sean Spicer during his first White House press briefing about the size of Donald Trump's inauguration:

We do know a few things so let's go through the facts. We know that from the platform where the President was sworn in to 4th Street holds about 250,000 people. From 4th Street to the media tent is about another 220,000. And from the media tent to the Washington Monument another 250,000 people. All of this space was full when the President took the Oath of Office. We know that 420,000 people used the D.C. Metro public transit yesterday which actually compares to 317,000 that used it for President Obama's last inaugural. **This was the largest audience to ever witness an inauguration. Period.** Both in person and around the globe. Even the New York Times printed a photog- a photograph showing the- the- a- a misrepresentation of the crowd in the original Tweet in their paper which showed the full extent of the support, depth in crowd and intensity that existed. These attempts to lessen the enthusiasm of the inauguration are shameful and wrong …

Quotation of Spicer's utterance was widespread, with users producing their own amusing iterations using his hyperbolic phrasing as a kind of template.

For example, the following examples insert a different value into by using a hashtag to invoke an additional set of perspectives on the discursive situation:

> Watch it @seanspicer, this is propaganda! "This was the largest audience to ever witness an inauguration, period" **#WeWontBeFooled** by you!

> Sean Spicer: "No one has numbers" …"this was the largest audience ever to witness an inauguration ever. Period." **#waronfacts**

> "This was the largest audience to ever witness an inauguration, period, both in person and around the globe." @realDonaldTrump **#FAKENEWS**

> If "no one had numbers," then how so sure "this was the largest audience to ever witness an inauguration, period"? **#DoubleSpeak #SoItBegins** *[embedded tweet by Politico: White House doubles down on Trump crowd claims, media complaints http://politi.co/2jMZLKH [embedded photo of Sean Spicer speaking at press conference]*

> "This was the largest audience to ever witness an inauguration period." "Inauguration period". Is that the **#WomensMarch?**

> "This was the largest audience ever to witness an inauguration, period" OK, so Spicer was having trouble with his periods.**#inaug2017**

The direct quotation marks in the above tweets signal more explicitly to the audience that some kind of 'in-joke' (spawning from a statement that someone has made) is at stake. This chapter explores how hashtags support these different kinds of quotation practices (both implicit and explicit). It also considers the functions that they play in supporting how discursive voices are managed in social media texts.

Attribution and engagement

One way in which the source of a stance is managed in discourse is through direct and indirect quotation. While it might be tempting to view understanding quotation as relatively simple, to be interpreted only by resolving who is the source of propositions or proposals in a text, attribution in fact involves a complex discourse semantic patterning. How well we can describe this patterning indicates how adequately our models of discourse cope with the intersubjective nature of communication. As a resource, attribution can function both to positively assess a source as valuable or to distance the authorial voice from the source. It can also function as part of meanings that 'open up' or 'close down' the dialogic space available to different textual viewpoints (Martin & White, 2005).

Linguistic studies of attribution patterns in social media discourse are still in their infancy. Work has tended to focus on the role of features such as the @ symbol (e.g. @realDonaldTrump) in relation to forms of address (Honeycutt & Herring, 2009) rather than on the sourcing of stances. Puschmann (2015) has explored re-tweeting as a form of quotation, suggesting that quotation has expanded its role in new media communication to emphasize 'phatic and sociocommunicative aspects in addition to argumentative and informational needs' (Puschmann, 2015, p. 36).

Beyond resolving a particular ideational source, attribution can be modelled as part of a broader region of interpersonal meaning that Appraisal terms 'engagement'. Engagement is a region of discourse semantics 'by which the speaker/writer negotiates relationships of alignment/disalignment vis-à-vis the various value positions referenced by the text and hence vis-à-vis the socially-constituted communities of shared attitude and belief associated with those positions' (Martin & White, 2005, p. 95). Engagement systematizes the kinds of meanings that can be made in a text in relation to managing textual voices. The complete engagement system is beyond the scope of this book. However a relevant domain of meaning is shown in Figure 5.1: the kinds of meanings that can be made to 'expand' the voices that are incorporated into a text. This network features two systems, 'entertain' and 'attribute'. Entertaining involves foregrounding the subjectivity of the author, while attribution involves presenting some external voice as the source for the proposition. This source may be acknowledged, with the author remaining neutral in terms of presenting a stance about the sourced material, often drawing on mental or material processes such as 'think' or 'say' (top example, Figure 5.1). The

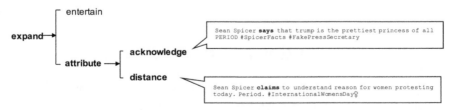

FIGURE 5.1 *Martin and White's (2005) system network describing expansion of the play of voices in a text.*

proposed stance may also be distanced from the authorial perspective via being attributed to an external source that the authorial voice declines to align with (bottom example, Figure 5.1).

Martin and White (2005, p. 111) suggest a range of discursive resources implicated in attribution such as:

1 Projections of speech and thought through direct or indirect reporting with communicative and mental process verbs (e.g. *say, believe, think):*

   e.g. direct reporting – *"Periods are not placed at the end of sentences. Period." **#SeanSpicerSays** #seanspicerfacts*

   e.g. indirect reporting – ***#SeanSpicerSays** Mike Pence has never had a smug look on his face. Period.*

2 Nominalizations of these processes (e.g. *the belief that*):

   e.g. *#spicerfacts #alternativefacts Sean Spicer confirmed **Trump's belief that** millions of votes were cast illegally. Give us the proof, assholes*

3 Adverbial adjuncts (e.g. *according to*):

   e.g. *But **according to** Spicer this is the biggest crowd ever. Period #SpicerFacts [embedded tweet: I'm being told that this REAL pic is VERY upsetting to @PressSec & @POTUS so whatever you do, DO NOT RT this photo.]*

It should be noted that, while the attribute system is concerned with the discourse semantics of attribution, it is 'directed towards analysing dialogistic functionality rather than towards identifying the primary source of the proposition' (Martin & White, 2005, p. 159).

A system network for exploring the quoted voice

The system network shown in Figure 5.2 aims to extend existing monomodal approaches to understanding quotation. This is in order to account for the role of *multimodal* phenomena such as hashtags that play a role, both in both the verbiage and beyond, due to the affordances of metadata. This network is based on White's (1998) work on 'journalistic' voices in which he developed the systems of *extra-vocalization* and *intra-vocalization* as a means

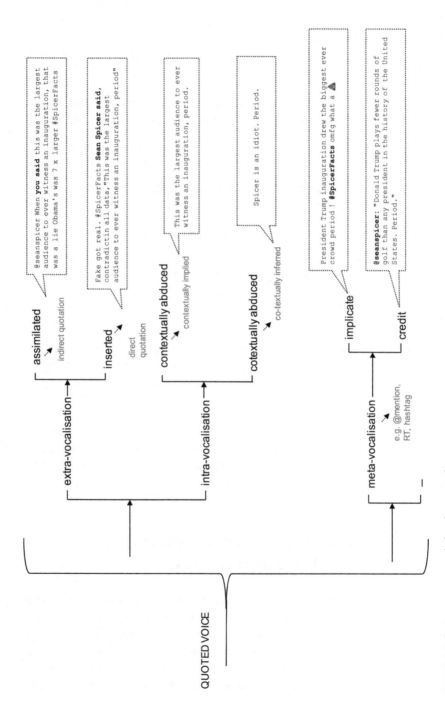

FIGURE 5.2 *System network for the quoted voice.*

for exploring the heteroglossic play of voices in news reporting. Example realizations are shown beneath the diagonal arrows in the network, and example instances, taken from a sample of #SpicerFacts tweets, are shown in speech boxes.

According to White's framework, extra-vocalization visibly incorporates external voices in a text, for example, through explicit quotation. On the other hand, intra-vocalization integrates other voices 'as part of the author's own utterances, rather than as an explicitly external voice or discourse' (White, 1998, p. 127). White (1998, p. 124) identifies two further choices for extra-vocalization: 'insertion', where the external voice is inserted into 'the text without modification or recontextualisation' (e.g. directly reported speech), and 'assimilation', where the external voice is 'merged to some degree with that of the text' (e.g. indirect speech). These ideas are a more elaborated and nuanced modelling of what Fairclough (1992) deals with at the level of structural or typographic features in his notion of 'manifest intertextuality'. This is a form of intertextuality whereby other texts are '"manifestly" marked or cued by features on the surface of the text, such as quotation marks' or seamlessly incorporated into the wording of the text (Fairclough, 1992, p. 104).

I further develop the system of assimilation to distinguish between *contextually abduced* and *co-textually abduced* vocalization in order to account for the particular meaning-potential afforded by Twitter as a communicative channel. Contextually abduced extra-vocalization implicates a source that is unnamed in the cotext through contextual knowledge (e.g. knowledge that a particular phrasing is an internet meme). For instance, the following example relies on knowledge of Sean Spicer's statement to infer the attribution:

```
This was the largest audience to ever witness and
inauguration, period.
```

Another instance of this type of choice is the following:

```
"This was the largest audience to ever witness an
inauguration period." Dictators and despots hand out
obvious, provable lies as facts.
```

```
"This was the largest audience to ever witness an
inauguration - period!" Soz bab, but unlike you and
Trump, the official photos don't lie.
```

```
"This was the largest audience to ever witness an
inauguration, PERIOD, both in person and around the
globe." That's not how periods work.
```

No. Not period. Comma. As in "this was the largest audience to ever witness an inauguration, and then I woke up." *[embedded CNN article titled 'White House press secretary attacks media for accurately reporting inauguration crowds']*

On the other hand, co-textually abduced intra-vocalization is the case where the source may be inferred by being named somewhere in the co-text. The example shown in the network names Spicer, though does not involve Spicer in grammaticalized projection. In this case, the audience may infer a relation between Spicer and the intra-vocalized material. Further examples include:

Ho-ly wow. Just. **Spicer** is losing it. Dude. You're the voice of a racist liar. You own this, enjoy. Period.

Sean Spicer is the best upside-down flag pin wearer ever. Period!

@User Utter nonsense! **Spicer** is the best @**PressSec** America has ever witnessed, period! #**Spicer**Facts

Sean Spicer is the best @**PresSec** ever. Period. #**SeanSpicer**Facts

'Abduction' is used as a concept here to illuminate how sources are implicated rather than inscribed. It is drawn from Bateman and Wildfeuer's (2014, p. 183) suggestion that an 'inherent property of the discourse semantic stratum in any semiotic mode is that it operates abductively'. Abduction is a process of forming a defeasible hypothesis, for example, by drawing on contextual knowledge.

The other optional system, *metavocalization*, considers whether the source is instantiated through metadata such as @mentions, retweets, or hashtags (Figure 5.3). It is the beginning of attempting to systematize how multimodal

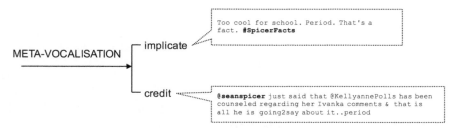

FIGURE 5.3 *System network for metavocalization.*

features (interactive metadata, layout etc.) interact with meanings made in the verbiage or 'body' of a post. Metavocalization, a form of quotation that optionally coordinates with extra- and intra-vocalization, is realized through the use of mode and channel-related features. These include features such as social metadata, and conventions for naming the user account (e.g. @username), or for re-broadcasting material (e.g. retweeting or reblogging).

Metavocalization can be used to simply the origin of a direct quote by implicating a source. It can also assist in contextually abducing the source of an intra-vocalized indirect quote. For instance, in the top example in Figure 5.3, the hashtag *#SpicerFacts* implicates Spicer in the stance presented in the body. The hashtag coordinates with intertextual meanings regarding the phrasal template being mocked (*X is the greatest ever Y. Period*). By way of contrast, the mention, *@seanspicer,* acts as a form of direct reference. It attributes the reported speech directly to Spicer, or to Spicer's account, a distinction which we explore in the next section.

Multimodal attribution: The anchoring function of the social media profile

Before proceeding further, we need to acknowledge that the ways in which a social media text may be multi-voiced are influenced by the multimodal constraints imposed by the social media service. While most approaches to understanding quotation have focused on the written mode, quotation is a multimodal practice (Stec, Huiskes, & Redeker, 2016). In the case of social media texts, quotation in written posts is inflected by the multimodal affordances of the communication technology. This means that we need to consider the structuring of social media services such as Twitter as technologies, and how this structuration interacts with the way that engagement resources are deployed. Some features of social media services allow the user to produce text in relatively 'free-form' ways, as is largely the case with hashtags, while others require adherence to various kinds of template.

While social media platforms are heteroglossic spaces that allow multiple viewpoints to be expressed, this expression is 'anchored' by the communicative resources that a particular service makes available. An important obligatory element of any social media text is the 'authorship' relation established between the social media profile and the posts that appear in the stream linked to that profile (Figure 5.4). Any text thus must integrate two 'fields' of discourse: a personal discourse invoked by the profile, and another secondary discourse. For instance, this secondary discourse might be

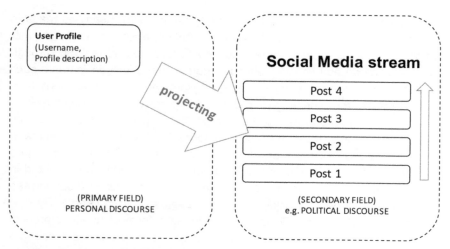

FIGURE 5.4 *The anchoring role of the social media user profile.*

political discourse about the US presidential inauguration that is critical of the incoming administration (see the previous examples of *#Spicerfacts* posts). The primary field of 'personal' discourse combines interpersonal dimensions and the semiotic affordances of the semiotic mode to project the secondary field. In other words, the opinion and sentiment construed about the incoming administration is 'projected by' discourses about the self and the personal. In terms of attribution, this means that the profile affords an intermodal relation indicating that the posts in the unfolding social stream are the projected meaning-making of the profile author. In verbiage 'saying projects locutions and thinking projects ideas' (Martin & Rose, 2008, p. 125); from a multimodal perspective, the user profile affords the possibility of projecting *bonds* that might be shared with the ambient audience.

   This functionality also affords the possibility of metaprocesses of attribution, such as retweeting, which rely on being able to republish another user's post within your own stream of posts. In the following post, User1's tweet has been republished inside another user's feed. The original authorship relation is signalled typographically by *RT @username*:

> **RT @User1:** President #Trump and his team think that
> his inauguration was the biggest ever. Period.

The user profile has special semiotic status in terms of multimodal attribution. For example, in the case of well-known users, establishing the authenticity of the account is valuable. This social capital is visually legitimated through the use of a blue 'tick' verification symbol. This symbol must occur in a particular position in terms of the page layout in order to authenticate the profile. It aims to distinguish a legitimate account from imitation or parody accounts (e.g. @sean_spicier, @SeanSpicerFacts, @spicergoogling).

Visual design choices are also implicated in how address, reference, and attribution are instantiated in the verbiage of social media posts. Twitter requires users to specify a username that uniquely identifies the user account (e.g. @PressSec, Figure 5.5). This is displayed within the profile. The username may be different to the name shown underneath the profile picture. Once this selection is made, other users have the option of addressing, referencing, or targeting (via tagging) the account via the special functionality afforded to the @ symbol (as a marker indicating the string directly following it is a username). We will return to this affordance when considering metavocalization in a later section.

Sean Spicer ✓

@PressSec

@WhiteHouse Press Secretary. Proudly representing @POTUS Trump's Administration. Tweets may be archived: wh.gov/privacy.

◎ Washington, D.C.

🔗 WhiteHouse.gov

📅 Joined January 2017

FIGURE 5.5 *An example of the profile of a 'verified' Twitter account.*

FIGURE 5.6 *Multimodal embedding of another user's post within a tweet.*

There are also various ways, beyond grammaticalized projection within the body of a post, that quotation of another post can occur. For example, another user's post may be quoted as a whole through 'embedding' the quoted post within the primary post, resulting in the structure shown in Figure 5.6. This figure shows projection via the username, as well as embedding via the representation of the secondary post 'inside' the primary post.

Metavocalization within posts

There are a number of key resources involved in social media quotation that draw on the special affordances given to characters such as the @ (for marking a username as introduced above), and the # symbol, for indicating hashtags. Metavocal attribution relies in part on the functionality for special characters defined by the particular social media service. In the case of Twitter, the @ character is the prevailing way of referencing other user accounts, through the concatenation of this character with the account name, e.g. @PressSec (Figure 5.5). The @ symbol is a marker of '*meta*'-vocalization in the sense that it functions at a higher order of abstraction to merely naming a user in a post. Consider the difference in meaning between the following two posts:

> Quoting **Sean Spicer:** "no one had numbers. This was
> the largest audience to ever witness an inauguration,
> period" Bro that is extra stupid

> **@seanspicer** Biggest audience to witness an
> inauguration ever PERIOD. Now thats all the media
> talks about while Trump does anything he wants

The bottom post draws on the particular channel-specific affordances made available by Twitter for coordinating the overlapping exchange structure that characterizes Twitter 'conversations'. These affordances support both addressivity and coherence management (Honeycutt & Herring, 2009). Clicking on an @username will take the user to that microblogger's home timeline. This page features their user profile and a sample of their most recent posts, 'projected' by the profile (as defined in the previous section). In terms of its function within a post, the @, together with the username, can be like a vocative:

> Hey **@seanspicer,** the march against your corrupt boss
> was literally the biggest demonstration ever in the
> history of the world. Period.

It can also function as a form of reference:

> The White House is straight up lying about voter fraud.
> Don't believe a word of what comes out of **@seanspicer's**
> mouth. PERIOD.

Interestingly, hashtags can be used in a similar way, though this is much less common:

> Watched **#SeanSpicer's** briefing yesterday. Conclusion ☞
> He's gone off the DEEP END. Period. Full stop. 👆 *[embedded
> tweet by National Newswatch: White House apologizes to
> British government over spying claims @CNNPolitics]*

The @ symbol can also be used to 'target' a particular user through tagging them in similar manner to appending a hashtag:

> Spicey was very clear today. Period. **@seanspicer**

In terms of establishing the parameters of the quoted voice, @usernames can help to co-textually abduce the source of the quotation.

Hashtagging sources

Individuated voices can be instantiated as hashtags. A hashtag can indicate the potential source of a direct or indirect quote, or it can imply the source. The following are examples, from most to least direct attribution

> 'When I make a mistake, I will own it.' Period!!
> **#Spicer**!! #CNN #SpiceySense😂😂

> **#Spicer** says Trumper doesn't own a bathrobe. Period!
> So … probably roaming around in knee socks and boxers.
> The cheeky girls were the greatest thing to happen in
> popular music ever, period. **#Spicer**

Where these hashtagged personae are not sources, they are often potential targets of evaluation, for example:

> .@User The greatest immediate threat to the US is
> **#Trump,** not **#Kim.** Period.

Layering of sources in social media texts can be quite complicated. For instance, *#spicer* in the below 'implicates' Spicer as the source of the *'statement + period'* structure (that was proliferating as a phrasal template meme at the time of writing):

> The Patriots are winning the #SuperBowl 14-0. PERIOD.
> #spicerfact #spicer #patriots #Falcons *[embedded image
> of Sean Spicer talking at a press conference]*

This is an example of an implicated 'projecting' quoted voice. There is no projecting verbal process (e.g. say, claim, state), or any surface features such as quotation marks. Here, instead, the hashtag helps the audience to abduce Spicer as the source. As the diagram on the right hand side of Figure 5.7 suggests, a number of layers of projection are involved. The microblogger's voice is projected multimodally via the authorship relation instantiated via the social media profile. This comprises projection of both discourse and metadiscourse (realized via the hashtag). Spicer's voice is projected both by the hashtag, *#Spicer,* and by the image (depicting him speaking at a White House press conference).

The above is an example of how a hashtag can be used to 'associate' reported speech with an individual via co-textual abduction. This is supported by implicating metavocalization.

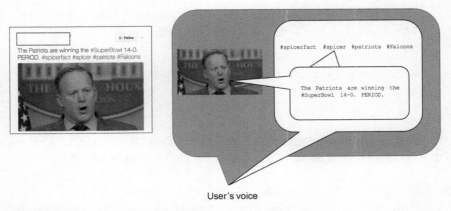

User's voice

FIGURE 5.7 *An example of layered voices in a tweet.*

Verbatim/non-verbatim direct quotation

Since Spicer's original quote is retrievable via transcription of the recorded interview, it is possible to determine whether or not a reiteration of his statement is verbatim or whether it involves modification by the microblogger. Most iterations tended to leave out the circumstance of extent (shown in bold)[6]:

> This was the largest audience to ever witness an inauguration. Period. **Both in person and around the globe.**

Examples reproducing the fuller quotation included:

> @PressSec @nytimes "This was the largest audience to ever witness an inauguration, period, **both in-person and around the globe,"**

> "The largest audience to ever witness an inauguration, period, **both in-person and around the globe,"** LOL – Spicer is a bad liar.

There was debate, at the time that these posts first began to circulate, about whether this circumstance of extent indicated that Spicer had meant the sum total of both offline and online audiences:

> "Both in-person and around the globe" apparently means sum total of those categories, not each individually. Lol. #PressBriefing @PressSec

So Sean Spicer now says 'both in person and around the globe' means the 'total when you add up the in-person and viewing audiences.' Sure.

.@PressSec says he never said it was total largest in-person audience to watch Trump inauguration. Says he combined in-person & around globe

Modified quotations incorporated a range of changes to the original. Options included altering the target of the appraisal, often to humorous effect:

Get used to getting laughed at. All of you! You are a joke. The biggest **joke** ever. Period.#Conway #trump #Spicer

"BIGGEST **#EasterEggRoll** EVER! PERIOD!!!" - #spicey

Ok Listen up, im saying this once. This evening the President hosted the BIGGEST **meeting bewteen the NFL and any POTUS,** period! #SeanSpicer

In addition, the appraisal could be altered in tandem with the modified target:

"Trump tower is the **tallest** building in the world. Period." #SeanSpicerPressReleases #SeanSpicerSays

Trump's people are the **smartest** people ever. Period. #SeanSpicer #MuslimBan *[embedded screen capture of a tweet from a parody account]*

#SeanSpicerSays this is the **most trustworthy** information in the history of investigations. Period.

The polarity of the appraisal could also be adjusted:

#SeanSpicerSays that blood pressure machine is the **worst** machine ever invented in the history of inventions, period.

Shorter Spicer: The AARP is **stupid.** Period. #PressBriefing

Look, I think it's abundantly clear that Nordstrom is a **worthless** brand. Period. #SeanSpicer #SpicerSays #SeanSpicerSays #alternativefacts

Other posts modified the entire proposition, keeping only '*Period.*' as a marker of Spicer's statement. These posts typically proposed ridiculous 'facts':

Donald Trump finished the wall on his second day as President. It is a fact. Period. 🙄#SeanSpicerPressReleases

Earth is a flat disc. Period. " #SeanSpicerSays *[embedded image of Trump making an incredulous expression]*

#ImpeachTrump #ResistTrumpIt is impossible for a woman to become pregnant during a full moon. Period. #SeanSpicerPressReleases #alternativefacts #thisistoomuchfun

This kind of textual play, where users contribute some iteration of a catchphrase (or other well-known utterance), has been labelled as a kind of 'meme'. This term was coined by Richard Dawkins in *The Selish Gene* (2006) to suggest that we think about culture in a similar way to genes (Wiggins & Bowers, 2015). Hashtags associated with this kind of textual play include the examples shown in Table 5.1.

For example, a relevant class of memes are phrasal template memes (see Chapter 9 for more discussion). These are memes where the template is often a phrase taken from a well-known person or fictional character. The template includes 'slots' into which can be inserted different material in order to produce an 'iteration' of the meme (Zappavigna, 2012b). In other words, the '"casing"

TABLE 5.1 Sean Spicer hashtags signalling a play frame

Hashtag	Example
#SeanSpicerPressReleases	#SeanSpicerPressReleases "Whining about crowd sizes will make America great again. Period!"
#spicerfact(s)	"He makes me say these things. Period! no questions." #SpicerFacts #SpiceyFacts @PressSec @POTUS @realDonaldTrump
#SeanSpicerSays	"Trump promised a Muslim ban, and he's delivering on his promise, but it's not a #MuslimBan. Period." #SeanSpicerSays #SpicerFact
#SeanSpicerStatistics	Smoking is actually good for your health. Period. #SeanSpicer #seanspicerfacts #SeanSpicerStatistics
#spiceyfacts	#Spiceyfacts 'That was the largest audience to witness an impeachment, period. Both in person and around the globe.' #TrumpImpeachmentParty

of a phrasal template is a kind of formulaic scaffolding, while items that occur in the slots are customizable' (Zappavigna, 2012b, p. 106). An example of a phrasal template meme is 'I for one welcome our [classifier] overlords'. This template originated from the TV show *The Simpsons*. As is the case with most memes, it can be applied across different contexts for comedic/pithy impact. For instance, the meme was manifest in Spicer-related in tweets such as:

```
I for one welcome the era of alternative truths,
championed by the baby-handed zoophile @seanspicer.
I, for one, welcome our Orange Overlord. His
inauguration audience was 10 BILLION+. Biggest in all
of the Multiverse. Huge.

I for one welcome our orange skinned, pussy grabbing
new Galactic Overlord. #Inauguration
```

Modification of Spicer's statement about the inauguration size incorporated three main types of phrasal template (or sub-templates):

[modified target] + biggest + Period. + [Spicer-related hashtag]
[modified target] + [modified appraisal] + Period. + [Spicer-related hashtag]
[ridiculous/hyperbolic statement] + Period. + [Spicer-related hashtag]

Aside from source-marking hashtags such as *#spicer*, other hashtags could be used to indicate the 'play frame' signalling that the post is humorous (Table 5.1) (Bateson, 1955; 1987).

The type of memetic play identified above tended to invoke negative judgement of Spicer and the Trump administration through ridicule and mockery. It is an example of how the quoted voice functions to do more than source particular information (in the sense of resolved attribution). The quoted voice can also function as part of processes of 'ambient affiliation', whereby the microblogger is aligning with other users who have presented the same stance within the social stream (Zappavigna, 2011, 2014c, 2014d). We will return to this idea in Chapter 7 as we explore affiliation, in Chapter 8 when we explore the *#AlternativeFacts* tag (which is used in similar ways to *#SpicerFacts*), and in Chapter 9 when we explore the concept of a meme in more detail.

'my voice as your voices'

Narrative studies of point of view typically distinguish between the voice 'who tells' us the story and the persona through whose eyes we 'see' the unfolding narrative. These are perspectives that may shift as the narrative unfolds. However, in social media texts because of the nature of the medium, an expanded repertoire of relations between perspectives is possible. This can involve, as we saw in Figure 5.7, a complex pallet for layering voices. Work on print media has taken for granted the idea that there is a stable text that can be analysed. It has thus focused on how other voices are incorporated into that stable text. However, social media texts have as their starting point heteroglossia. Monoglossing is largely impossible by virtue of the constraints of most social media platforms. The examples introduced above have shown how even something as simple as indirect and direct quotation multiplies its heteroglossic meaning potential when supported by the affordances of metavocalization.

While attribution research has suggested that quotation highlights the distinction between the authorial voice and other voices ('my voice' and your 'voice') social media seems to disrupt this binary. It affords a 'my voice/voices' relation.[7] This is in part because of the anchoring function of the social media profile, with the profile and @username enabling metavocalization of the social media user's voice via multimodal projection and embedding. In other words, all posts are, at one level of abstraction, the projected voice of the user, even as they incorporate other voices at the level of individual posts.

Thus an individual user can adopt a stance that has been uttered by someone else and present it as their own. This is often done for the purposes of mockery. An example, the following post which is lampooning the idea that there were more Patriots visiting the White House than in previous years:

The biggest crowd of #Patriots ever. Period. #TRUMP
#First100Daysu

Simply rallying around negative assessment of a quoted stance is clearly possible. However, what is achieved through the quoted voice (as exemplified above) is more nuanced, and perhaps more rhetorically powerful, than directly indicating that the quoted statement is incorrect or unwarranted. Instead, the position is mocked through humourously 'performing' the stance as if it were the user's own. The posts analysed in this chapter suggest that, beyond resolving the source of a particular voice, it is important to consider the perspective of affiliation (i.e. the social bonds at stake), since a source is always envisaged in relation to a potential reader or audience. It is also for this reason that we need to consider intersubjectivity: the possible relations that are established between perspectives, a concept to which we now turn.

Intersubjectivity: Relations between perspectives

Hashtags are not only involved in construing voices with stances, they are involved in construing relations between subjectivities. Interpreting the significance of Foucault's reframing of authorship as a discourse rather than an individuated persona, Fairclough (1992) has also noted the importance for linguistics of coming to terms with the issue of subjectivity. Subjectivity has tended to be marginalized in language studies. These often do not move 'beyond theories of "expression" and "expressive meaning"' and issues of identity such as 'social provenance, gender, class, attitudes, beliefs and so forth' (Fairclough, 1992, p. 45). However, how we theorize subjectivity impacts upon the basic concepts that are assumed in theories of attribution, in particular the textual distinctions between authorial and 'other' voices introduced at the beginning of this chapter.

Gillespie and Cornish (2010, p. 19) (building on Stryker (1956)) offer a framework for approaching intersubjectivity as 'the variety of relations between perspectives' that are possible, where those 'perspectives can belong to individuals, groups, or traditions and discourses'. This approach specifies three levels of relationships involved in intersubjectivity. Each of these incorporates a relation between the self (S) and the other (O) in relation to a phenomenon (X):

1) Direct perspective: the self's perspective on something (S → X) e.g. *I think this was the largest audience to witness an inauguration ever.*

2) Metaperspective: the other's perspective on the self's perspective on something (S → O → X) e.g. *He said that this was the largest audience to witness an inauguration ever.*

3) Meta-metaperspective: the self's perspective on the other's perspective on the self's perspective on something (S → O → S → X) e.g. *I think he said this was the largest audience to witness an inauguration ever.*

These forms of intersubjectivity can be construed explicitly or implicitly in language, as well as in other modes such as images (see, for example, Zappavigna (in press-c); Zhao and Zappavigna (2015, in press) on how multiple perspectives are construed in selfies). When a person makes a statement such as "I think this was the largest audience to witness an inauguration ever", they communicate explicitly a *direct perspective* – a self's (*I*) perspective on a phenomenon (*inauguration audience size*).

Similarly, when a statement such as "He said that this was the largest audience to witness an inauguration ever" is uttered, a metaperspective is being communicated – another's perspective (*his*) on a self's perspective on 'inauguration audience size'.

The major resource implicated in the layering of intersubjectivity in language is 'projection'. This is a logico-semantic relation that implicates resources concerned with, not simply the direct representation of (material) experience, but the representation of a (linguistic) representation of experience. In terms of a distinction between meaning and wording at the content plane of language, projection can involve both levels. For example, an idea can be projected:

```
Spicer thinks you can tell crowd size by level of
cheering audio …
```

In addition, a wording may be projected:

```
Sean Spicer said that the use of magnetometers for
security effected size of the Inaugural crowd. Secret
Service says magnetometers not used.
```

According to Halliday and Matthiessen (2004, p. 443), projection involves three dimensions: level (idea versus locution, as noted above), mode (hypotactic reporting versus paratactic quoting), and speech function (projected proposition versus projected proposal). Examples are shown in Figure 5.8. Projection is a recursive system since, theoretically, language can project infinitely, for instance:

I think that he thinks that I think that he thinks that I think …

Returning to the notion of the layering of perspectives, hashtags add an additional dimension of complexity. They introduce an additional set of potential layers of projection by virtue of the kind of abstraction that they afford.

For example, Table 5.1 applies Gillepsie and Cornish's (2010) framework to some example tweets. Instead of the notation S to denote a self, we adopt the more social semiotic notation, P, to indicate a textual persona (who might be the author, or another participant such as an interlocutor in a dialogue). The layering involved in the projection shown is relatively straightforward in the first three examples (rows 1–3 of Table 5.2). However, when we introduce a hashtag into a text (something Gillepsie and Cornish's model doesn't account for as it is largely based on traditional dialogue) matters rapidly become quite complex (rows 4–6 of Table 5.2).

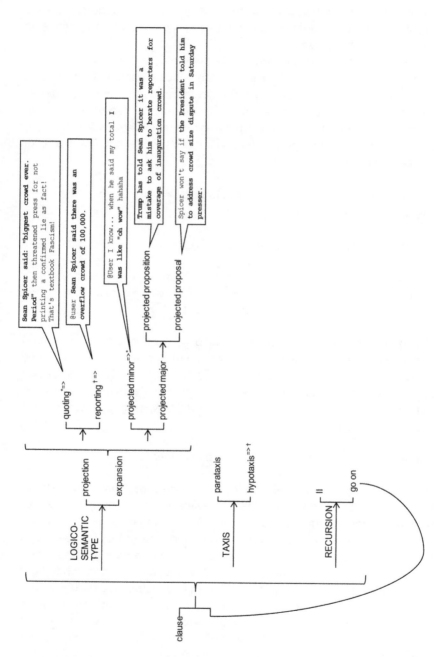

FIGURE 5.8 *The system of projection, adapted from Halliday and Matthiessen (2004, p. 445).*

TABLE 5.2 Layering of perspectives

Level		Example
Direct perspective (P1→X)	1	This was the biggest inauguration crowd ever. Period.
Metaperspective (P2→P1→X)	2	Spicer said "This was the biggest inauguration crowd ever. Period."
Meta-metaperspective (P3→P2→P1→X)	3	The media reported that Spicer said that "This was the biggest inauguration crowd ever. Period."
Inter-perspective	4	This was the biggest inauguration crowd ever. Period. **#Spicerfacts**
	5	Trump: My prison cell is gonna be the biggest ever. The greatest. Period. **#Trumprussia**
	6	The passing of the #AHCA is the biggest ever legislative victory in presidential history. Period. #SeanSpicerFacts Also. WINNING!

Establishing whose perspective is construed in rows 4–6 (Table 5.2) is not straightforward. The hashtag in row 4 implicates Spicer as the source of the intra-vocalized stance:

`This was the biggest inauguration crowd ever. Period.`
`#Spicerfacts`

The tag also suggests this is just one amongst other potential stances ('spicer facts'). The relation might be summarized as:

User's perspective (P1) on (implicated) Spicer's perspective (O) on statement (X)

However, the hashtag functions not only to construe an individualized perspective (P1) on the stance. It is also involved in intertextual perspectives. These accumulate with concurrent deployment of the tag by other users across different semantic fields, for instance:

> #IKnewWeWereDoomed when This was the largest audience to ever witness an Inauguration. Period **#SpicerFacts** *[embedded image of Sean Spicer speaking at press briefing]*
>
> Too cool for school. Period. That's a fact. **#SpicerFacts**
>
> This was actually a march celebrating the introduction of @realDonaldTrump 's new Loyalty Day. PERIOD! **#SpicerFacts** *[embedded tweet about the #climatemarch in Washington DC]*
>
> This was the most lauded draft pick in Bears' history. Period. **#SpicerFacts**
>
> This was the biggest team WH visit turn out PERIOD! **#SpicerFacts** #sizematters

Viewed across aggregated instances, the hashtag can be interpreted as affording an ambient perspective. It incorporates multiple individualized perspectives as it accumulates meaning (hence the circular representation in Table 5.2). In other words, it is simultaneously the perspective of the user and the perspective of the shared social media stream. It is also this intersubjective relation that fuels the humour realized in these posts: they are only really funny if other people are playing with the same phrasal template.

Example 5 in Table 5.2 is an example of how intersubjectivity can function to support a form of ridicule that involves turning the words of someone (or their associates) against them (see also Chapter 8):

> Trump: My prison cell is gonna be the biggest ever. The greatest. Period. **#Trumprussia**

In this example, Spicer's statement is recast as the voice of Trump. The original ideational target, the 'crowd' (affording positive attitude) has been replaced with the 'prison cell' (affording negative attitude). The quote itself is a kind of inserted extra-vocalization. The colon acts as a surface feature indicating the proceeding material is a quotation. The exaggerated punctuation is also suggestive of transcribed speech. The hashtag adds contextual information, implying that there is a relationship between Trump and Russia, and that is the reason for the extra-vocalized statement regarding his future prison cell. The relations between perspectives is again complex, involving the user, the extra-vocalized perspective sourced as Trump, and the ambient perspective of the hashtag.

Example 6 makes matters even more complex through the addition of an image of Spicer speaking at a White House press conference (similar to the image of Spicer in Figure 5.7):

> The passing of the #AHCA is the biggest ever
> legislative victory in presidential history. Period.
> #SeanSpicerFacts. Also. WINNING!

This example incorporates all the dimensions covered in the previous two examples, and adds two more dimensions: an image and a further instance of contextually abduced intra-vocalization. The intermodal relation established by embedding the image of Spicer in the post coordinates with the implied attribution. This coordination functions to suggest that it is Spicer's perspective that is presented. However, the phrase *WINNING!* also invokes the voice of the American actor, Charlie Sheen, who used 'winning' as a catchphrase at the time that he lost his role on a popular US TV sitcom. The slang meaning of this phrase is described in urban dictionary as:

> Charlie Sheen Winning (also known as CSW for short) Is a disorder in which one feels that no matter what they do, they are always 'winning' at life. CSW is quite similar to insanity except with CSW, you KNOW you're being crazy. You just don't give a fuck. (Urban Dictionary, 2011)

Winning is an interesting textual reference because it is not simply a catchy phrase, but the re-appropriation of a perspective on events. As the definition above suggests, it evokes a persona with a high degree of hubris who is out of touch with reality (in a similar vein to *#SpicerFacts*). This, in turn, intersects with the widely lampooned claim that Trump made during his presidential campaign that the American people would become sick of winning if he was elected president:

> because we're going to turn it around and we're going to start winning again. We're going to win so much. We're going to win at every level. We're going to win economically. We're going to win with the economy. We're going to win with military. We're going to win with healthcare and for our veterans. We're going to win with every single facet. We're going to win so much you may even get tired of **winning** and you'll say, 'Please, please, it's too much **winning**. We can't take it anymore. Mr President it's too much' and I'll say 'No, it isn't. We have to keep **winning**. We have to win more!

We're going to win more. We're going to win so much'

What is at stake (in a tweet packing up intertextual references of this kind) is not only the amusing ridicule engendered, but the intersection of multiple perspectives. It is the frisson of these perspectives coming together that makes the post so funny. This interperspective can also be used to comment on another perspective. This may be achieved by embedding another perspective (that embeds an additional perspective), for example:

```
Trump is so tired of winning that he's losing money
on purpose! PERIOD! #alternativefacts #SpicerFacts
#Trump #MAGA [embedded tweet: Trump's DC hotel told
government it lost almost $1.2 million in first two
months of operation [embedded Bloomberg article
titled 'Trump lost $1.2 million at hotel he should
see, Democrats Say]
```

When we factor in retweeting and liking/favouriting, another layer of perspective is incorporated. What we are analysing in these posts appears a kind of *cacophony* of voices and stances, as different perspectives, and relations between perspectives, accumulate in the unfolding social stream. In order to explore this more fully we introduce the concept of 'coupling' in the next chapter. That is, how a voice construes a *value* as a social bond around which personae may commune.

6

#YouAreFakeNews: Construing Values

Introduction

In the previous chapter, I focused on evaluative language in hashtagged metacommentary. However, attitudes are not offered to the ambient audience without reference to experience (Martin, 2010). Adopting a discursive stance by proposing a value to a social stream involves making an evaluation 'about something' (Martin, 2004, p. 337). For example, consider the interaction between Donald Trump and a CNN reporter during one of Trump's belligerent press conferences. Trump makes repeated claims that the mainstream media is 'fake news', and refuses to take a question from the reporter, Jim Acosta:

Acosta: Mr President elect, can you give us a question?

Trump: Don´t be =rude.=

Acosta: You're =attacking us = Can you give us a question?

Trump: Don´t be rude.

Acosta: =Can you give us a question?=

Trump: =No, I´m not going to give you a qu-.= I´m not going to give you a question.

Acosta: =Can you- can you- state= categorically-

Trump: =You're fake news [pointing at CNN reporter].

Acosta: =Sir-

Trump: Go ahead. [pointing at another reporter]

Acosta: Can you- can you- state categorically that nobody. No, Mr President elect, =that's not appropriate=

Trump: =Go ahead.=

This interaction involves a number of competing judgements that the interactants make including:

negative propriety (*rude*)

t-negative propriety (*attacking*)[1]

negative propriety (*rude*)

t-negative veracity (*fake news*[2])

negative propriety (*not appropriate*)

However, what is significant in this exchange, from the perspective of understanding how these participants are negotiating values, is not only the unfolding prosody of negative judgement, but the targets of that judgement:

Target = Acosta; Evaluation = negative propriety (*rude*)

Target = Trump; Evaluation = negative propriety (*attacking*)

Target = Acosta; Evaluation = negative propriety (*rude*)

Target = Acosta (and by implication his news organization); Evaluation = negative t-veracity (*fake news*)

Target = Trump's behaviour/verbiage; Evaluation = negative propriety (*not appropriate*)

As the interaction unfolds, there is a repeated coupling of media-related targets with negative judgement (propriety and veracity) by Trump. This motif is repeated in his discourse across a range of contexts – for example the following extracts sampled around the time of writing. These were sampled respectively from a rally, a conference, an interview, and tweet:

I also want to speak to you without the filter of the **fake** news. The **dishonest** media which has published one **false** story after another with no sources, even though they **pretend** they have them, they **make them up** in many cases, they just **don't want to report the truth** and they've been calling us wrong now for two years. (Speech at a rally in Florida 18/2/17)

And I want you all to know we are fighting the **fake** news. It's **fake**. **Phony**. **Fake**. [*audience applause*] A few days ago I called the **fake** news **the enemy of the people**, and they are. They are **the enemy of the p**eople. (Speech to Conservative Political Action Conference on 24/2/17)

Well, let me tell you about Twitter. I think that maybe I wouldn't be here if it wasn't for Twitter, because I get such a **fake** press, such a **dishonest** press. (Interview with Fox news 15/3/2017

'BuzzFeed Runs **Unverifiable** Trump-Russia Claims' #**Fake**News (tweet, 10/1/17)

Fake news may be defined as 'news stories that have no factual basis but are presented as facts', and excluding, for instance, satirical news sites (Allcott & Gentzkow, 2017, p. 5). Interestingly, in terms of the context of the above examples, 'fake news' is a term that Trump has appropriated from discourse which would have otherwise harmed him politically. The term was prominent in the 2016 US presidential election. This was initially due to incidents such as 'pizzagate', a debunked conspiracy theory supposedly linking a paedophile ring to members of the Democratic Party. The bogus claim was that food-related code words had been found in e-mails leaked by Wikileaks (Douglas, Ang, & Deravi, 2017 in press). This conspiracy theory resulted in millions of posts tagged #pizzagate:

#SaveOurChildren #StopChildAbuse **#PizzaGate** God please protect the innocence!!

NPR going all in on their assessment that **#pizzagate** is "fake news." How long would the MSM have referred to the Lewinsky story as fake news

Just because U don't want to believe it, doesn't mean is not true. **#pizzagate** #wikileaks #PodestaTheMolester #Bidenpedo #NWO #uk #60Minutes

@User Always the Criminal Clintons are Connected! This is a sick ring of degenerates abusing children! #PizzaGate.

PIZZAGATE SMOKING GUN! LITTLE RED FOX CONNECTION TO CLINTONS! **#PIZZAGATE** ... *[link to YouTube video]*

Disturbingly, these posts included the following tweet by the son, and chief of staff, to then national security adviser, Michael Flynn:

Until #Pizzagate proven to be false, it'll remain a story. The left seems to forget #PodestaEmails and the many 'coincidences' tied to it

The term 'fake news' was originally associated with fictitious conspiracy theories of this kind, as well as fictitious stories propagating on Facebook.

Nevertheless, Trump managed to re-appropriate and redirect the power of this original association for his own advantage. He shifted the target of the coupling from the content of the news story to the newsmakers themselves.

Trump's repetition of the news media as the ideational target of his negatively charged axiology is clearly interesting in terms of what it tells us about the kinds of potential 'bonds' Trump is inviting his audience to share. It may be viewed as a kind of invitation to engage in what amounted to a coupling war over credibility. The tag, *#fakenews,* proliferated on social media, generating a huge number of posts adopting Trump's orientation towards the media and praising his administration, for example:

Remember when the fear mongering **#FakeNews** said Trump's election would crash all the markets? We are now seeing record highs! #AmericaFirst

The ShitScream Media is DESPERATE and DYING. Every week further and further down the **#fakenews** rat hole. Bye bye dummies. Lol #MAGA

If the Mainstream MEDIA wasn't so openly UNTRUTHFUL, BIAS & the bearer of **#fakenews** @realDonaldTrump WOULDN'T need to use Twitter #WakeUpMSM *[embedded image of Donald Trump with the inscription 'Donald J. Trump 45th President of the United States of America' and the American flag as a background]*

CNN can't get viewers anymore because they are known as #FakeNews They have to get her on so people will tune in. *[embedded tweet: What is the news value of constantly interviewing Kellyanne Conway, other than to create ephemeral, distracting controversies for cable TV?]*

@CNN @cnnbrk keep up the fake job. Ur lies n **#fakenews** is just creating more future votes for #Trump @realDonaldTrump n @GOP *[embedded tweet: You guys better share this so hard haha! #VeryFakeNews @CNN is TRIGGERED!]*

The tag also featured in posts that condemned or mocked Trump, though this remains a much less common use of the tag:

Trump continuously lies outright on @FoxNews & DO THEY EVER CALL HIM ON IT..for viewer sake? Unethical. Unwatchable. **#fakenews** #cnntownhall

Remember when @POTUS told @FoxNews that Cruz's dad
killed JFK? **#FakeNews** *[embedded tweet: Remember when
CNN interviewed their own camera man pretending to be
a protester lol* 🌀 *#CNNLeaks #FakeNewsMedia #TheFive]*

#Obama released tiny dinosaurs in my sock drawer. Bad
(or sick) guy!³ @POTUS44 @realdonaldtrump **#fakenews**
#wiretap #soSad #alternativeFacts

All these posts have taken up Trump's coupling as a *value* to be negotiated. Hashtags, as we will see throughout this book, offer a way of increasing the scope and visibility of this negotiation by increasing the searchability of the post. Their use increases the potential prominence of the value in the social network. This chapter demonstrates how to analyse the structure and function of this kind of coupling. It provides an analytical tool needed in the next chapter in order to make sense of the role couplings play in forging social bonds.

Coupling

At the most abstract level, *coupling* refers to the combination of meanings across a range of semiotic dimensions 'as pairs, triplets, quadruplets or any number of coordinated choices' (Martin, 2008b, p. 39). It concerns a 'relation of "with": variable *x* comes with variable *y*' (Zhao, 2011, p. 144). This co-selection can occur across ranks, metafunctions, strata, or modalities, and will have some coordinated discursive function. Martin (2000, p. 164) first introduced the notion of coupling to explain humour 'as involving discordant couplings – either between appraisal selections and what is being appraised, or among the appraisal variables themselves' (p. 164). For example, we can note a coupling between features across simultaneous appraisal systems (attitude and force) in the hashtag, #reallystupid, below:

Stupid enough to believe all the fake news and conspiracy
theories that helped get him elected in the first place.
#ReallyStupid *[embedded tweet: I just … if Americans are
really this stupid, we deserve what's coming. Because
how stupid do you have to be to believe this shit?]*

Here 'really' is an instance of graduation raising force, and 'stupid' is an instance of negative judgement of capacity. These two systemic features, from different discursive systems, coordinate to construe the meaning produced in the tag (criticizing the capacity of Americans) (Figure 6.1).

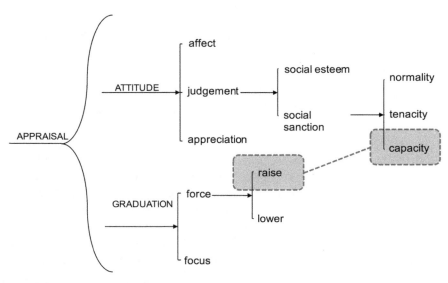

FIGURE 6.1 *Coupling of features across Appraisal systems, based on Martin (2008b).*

Some early work in SFL considered the coordination of systemic features from the perspective of probability, that is, the probability that particular linguistic features will be co-realized. The aim was to generate corpus-based systemic profiles at different levels of generalization (e.g. within particular registers) (Christie & Derewianka, 2008; Halliday, 1991; Matthiessen, 2006; Nesbitt & Plum, 1988). Research adopting this perspective would, for example, be predominately interested in the frequency of the features 'raise' and 'capacity' (Figure 6.1) in a particular text or set of texts. However, since the meanings modelled by a system network are largely meanings that are made within a particular dimension, 'an indefinitely large set of possible combinations is left open' (Martin, 2010, p. 19). It is, as Almutairi (2014, p. 7) has pointed out, it is technically possible to consider relative frequencies, and conditional probabilities, for systemic co-choices in order to achieve 'a synoptic view on local probabilities of system co-choices in a text or group of texts'. However this capacity is limited in terms of the number of features that can be considered, and in terms of the lack of dynamism of the representation:

When more systems are included in the network, the intersections between all features become very hard, if not impossible, to represent. Second, it does not provide a dynamic view on the couplings. In other words, it does not show how 'transitional probabilities' of couplings change over text time, or how features interact with each other logogenetically to couple and decouple as we move from one phase (or moment) of the text to another. (Almutairi, 2014, p. 7)

The synoptic perspective afforded by frequency information about features also tends to efface how they pattern across a text. Probability can only get us so far in terms of modelling meanings that are combinatorial. It does not capture, for instance, the case where particular features never occur together at particular points in the unfolding (with potential implications for the meaning being made) (Zappavigna, Dwyer, & Martin, 2008).

Exploring combinations of meaning quantitatively depends on the insights afforded by measures such as correlation that indicate the strength of association between features. A challenge for this arena of analysis is how to present aggregated views of complex patterns in ways that do not obscure the unfolding of meanings in a text or collection of texts (Caldwell & Zappavigna, 2011; Zappavigna, Cléirigh, Dwyer, & Martin, 2010b; Zappavigna et al., 2008). This is a challenge which will require the help of software applications in order to capture paradigmatic and syntagmatic patterns not necessarily apparent to the manual analyst (Almutairi, 2013).

Coupling along the cline of instantiation

The concept of coupling aims to account for the permutations and combinations that occur when different kinds of meanings combine in unfolding discourse. How this meaning is patterned can be modelled in SFL with reference to the cline of instantiation – the relationship between language as a system and language as text (Figure 6.2). Instantiation focuses on the way the meaning potential of language, as system, is activated in a particular text. It considers which features, from the 'reservoir' of meaning potential constituting a linguistic or semiotic system, are instanced in a text. Texts are primed by (and in turn prime) the situational context.[4] SFL appropriates two broad types of context from Malinowski: *the context of culture* and *the context of situation*. An 'instance', depending upon the level of generalization from which it is viewed/interpreted, will display different kinds of consistency across register, genre, or other ways of aggregating discourse (e.g. by identity, community) (for this theoretical orientation, see Martin (2010), and for studies using this approach, see Bednarek and Martin (2010)).

Theoretically speaking, coupling can be approached from the perspective of any point along the cline of instantiation (as increasingly generalized increments towards the system end of the cline). For instance, consider the perspective of looking at the meanings made in a single tweet containing the hashtag *#fakenews*. Compare this with a corpus-based perspective that factors in the meanings made in a large corpus of texts containing the tag collected at a particular point in time (e.g. just after the exchange between the CNN report and Trump sampled at the beginning of this chapter).

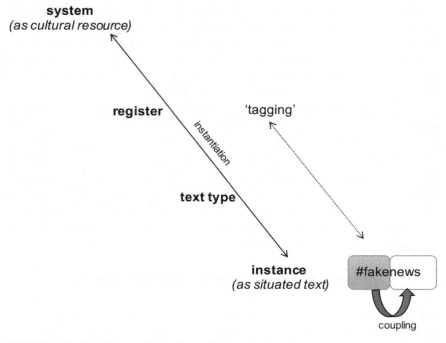

FIGURE 6.2 *Coupling and the cline of instantiation.*

As noted earlier, Halliday viewed the system-text relationship as probabilistic, where 'frequency in text' is 'the instantiation of probability' (Halliday, 1991, p. 31). However, probability (in the simple sense of frequencies of features) does not readily account for temporal sequencing. Thus additional perspectives are needed to account for logogenesis, that is, 'the creation of meaning in the course of the unfolding of text' (Halliday & Matthiessen, 2004, p. 530). Zhao (2011, p. 144) attempts to factor in such temporality by considering coupling as the 'relation formed between two semiotic elements at one given point in time within the logogenetic timeframe' (Zhao, 2011, p. 144). This temporal perspective might be applied to different kinds of timeframes, for instance, historical time, in the sense of describing the meanings made in particular eras:

> The theoretical hypothesis here is that although there exists potentially an indefinable amount of coupling possibilities between semiotic variables ([inter-]metafunctional, [inter-]stratal, intersemiotic, etc.), a given culture at a particular historic period will produce a set of stable coupling patterns that can be theoretical described. This is compatible with Bakhtin's (1981) notion of speech genres as stable patterns of utterance ... (Zhao, 2011, p. 145)

As we will see in the various case studies considered in this book, much smaller time scales attuned (for instance) to the very fast news cycle currently influencing political discourse might feature distinctive coupling patterns.

Zhao's work defines three types of time-based relations, or logogenetic patterns, relevant to how meanings are made in a text: *sequencing* (where the value of a feature is made in relation to its position in the text, e.g. in terms of what comes before or after it in the co-text), *coupling* (what occurs 'with' a feature, that is, the relations of two features at a particular point in the logogenetic unfolding), and *non-linear coupling*, where linear couplings are clustered and reconfigured. We will return to this framework in Chapter 9, which considers intermodal image-text couplings in relation to the *#TinyTrump* meme (images where Trump is presented in miniature, while other visual participants are at normal scale).

Another perspective on coupling that seeks to account for its dynamism is Tann's (2010, 2013) work on iconography. Tann has considered how icons can be interpreted as repeated couplings of linguistic features. This coupling forms syndromes which coalesce over time within a given culture, becoming 'signs around which communities rally' (Tann, 2013, p. 32) (Figure 6.3). For instance, propaganda and political slogans are examples where this type of process is actively encouraged through various rhetorical strategies. For example, the Trump campaign slogan 'Make America great again' is essentially an ideation-attitude coupling of America with underspecified positive appreciation. This ultimately became a fully charged 'bonding icon' (Stenglin, 2008 a & b). As an icon, this campaign slogan came to stand for a particular political identity. Because of the underspecification of both the ideation and the attitude, the coupling was ripe for iconization since it could be co-opted for many kinds of uses across different contexts. It could be charged in relation to different ideational targets (e.g. *great* in the sense of improving the economy, or *great* in the sense of reducing crime). 'Great' is an example of a broad class of meanings that are very general in terms of the appreciation that they instantiate (e.g. good, bad, ok). Dreyfus and Tilakaratna (forthcoming) proposes the category of 'general appreciation' to account for these meanings.

For example, consider the following concordance lines for #MAGA, a hashtag used to reference Trump's campaign slogan. These were sampled on the day (11/1/17) that Trump's exchange with Jim Acosta (which opened this chapter) occurred:

```
So glad @realDonaldTrump stood up to #fakenews ….
it's way passed time they are held accountable #MAGA
[embedded link to Fox news broadcast of extract of
Trump-Acosta exchange]
```

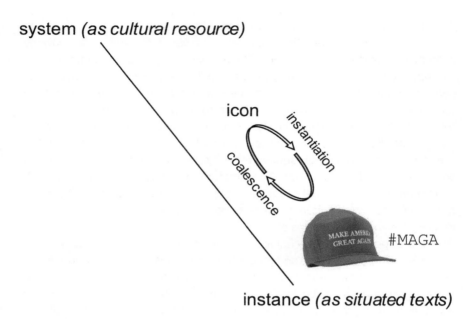

FIGURE 6.3 *An example of the coalescence and instantiation of an icon, based on Tann (2013, p. 33).*

Mr. Trump thanks for calling stupid reporters fake news. **#MAGA** *[embedded link to Fox news broadcast of extract of Trump-Acosta exchange]*

I like to shout a question at Jim @Acosta. Why did you and @CNN rig the presidential debates? ala Donna Brazile **#MAGA**

OUCH! Trump b*tch-slaps @CNN reporter Jim Acosta for #FakeNews & calls @BuzzFeed a 'failing pile of garbage'. 😂 #TrumpPressConference **#MAGA**

#GullibleAmerica needs to understand #fakenews urnalists like @jaketapper & @Acosta make 6 to 7 figures a year to lie @CNN **#MAGA**

Why does @CNN think Trump owes them answers when they are going to spin the response anyway. What a joke. #TrumpPressConference **#MAGA**

@Acosta You got smacked in the mouth and we LOVED IT!!!! **#MAGA**

The repeated use of this tag is a concentrated example of this coalescing process in action. The use of #*fakenews* together with #*MAGA* in the first tweet is an example of the coordination of particular charged couplings. This viewed synoptically might characterize a particular identity or community.

It should be noted that the use of the same tag to mock Trump was also present in the stream of public tweets occurring at the same time. This might be interpreted as forces working to disrupt this 'coalescing' (to use Tann's term) or to undo the hyper-charging of the coupling as a bonding icon. These posts appear to redeploy the power of the icon in the service of a different (i.e. anti-Trump) rhetoric, for example:

@realDonaldTrump is a complete conman. #TrumpPressConference **#maga** *[embedded image of Trump wearing a red 'Make America Great Again' hat in Russian inscription]*

Trump had his paid staff go against the media at his press conf http://politi.co/2jF5gvq @cspanwj #NotMyPresident **#MAGA** #TheResistance #tcot *[link to politico article title "Trump pits his staff against the media"]*

NEWSFLASH: Idiot on the idiotbox doing a press conference. #notmypresident #selectednotelected #fucktrump **#MAGA** #douchebag #trash #IDGAF

"Mr. Trump, can we ask you one more question? M-m-muh RUSSIA! REEEEE!" #goldenshowers **#MAGA**

These posts include hashtags such as #notmypresident and #theResistance which are bonding icons for difference communities. Interestingly, a post containing #MAGA or #theResistance may remain ambiguous, since we cannot necessarily infer who is mocking whom. Necessary contextualization is often lost in the ambient environment. It can only be retrieved by inspecting the user's stream, or by retrieving the original interaction, in the case of posts with replies.

A Google image search for 'MAGA hat parody' reveals many iterations of this iconized phrase, acting in the service of different forms of mockery (Figure 6.4). We will return to the function of quotation in relation to ridicule in Chapter 8. These hats modify the phrasal template 'Make America [X] Again'. The original phrasing features the underspecified appreciate 'great'. The modified iterations are able to substitute, not only attitude (e.g. *Make America **Smart** Again*), but also ideation[5] for attitude (e.g. *Make America **Read** Again*). These examples rely on the intertextual reference to the original as a means of recoupling the political stance, for example, by reversing the valence from positive to negative (e.g. *psycho*). We will explore recoupling in more detail later in the chapter.

FIGURE 6.4 *Examples of hats modifying the phrasal template 'Make America [X] Again'.*

Tabling an ideation-attitude coupling

The form of coupling that has received the most attention to date in social semiotic research is ideation-attitude coupling. This is a coupling across interpersonal and experiential metafunctions, between attitude and an ideational target. This type of coupling has been the principal focus of research because of the key role it plays in terms of how values are *tabled*[6] in discourse. Understanding this coupling will assist, as we will see in the next chapter, in understanding social alignments (how people share, reject, or laugh off particular bonds). To date, ideation-attitude coupling has been studied in relation to casual conversation (Knight, 2008, 2010a, 2010b, 2013), academic discourse (Hao & Humphrey, 2009; Hood, 2010), business writing (Szenes, 2016), and Youth Justice Conferencing (Martin, Zappavigna, Dwyer, & Cleirigh, 2013; Zappavigna et al., 2008).

Knight's work (2008, 2010a, 2010b, 2013) on ideation-attitude couplings is the basis of affiliation theory. It is foundational for the understanding of ambient affiliation adopted in this book (and introduced in Chapter 7). The original data which Knight used was casual conversation involving young female university students discussing food that they enjoy in the holidays. For example, one of the interlocutors in this conversations states:

This was an **awesome** <u>pie party</u> guys

This may be interpreted as proposing the following coupling to her group of friends:

[ideation: pie party/attitude: positive appreciation]

The above notation for indicating a coupling, based on Martin, Zappavigna, Dwyer, and Cléirigh (2013), will be used throughout this book. It may be generalized as:

[ideation: <<>>/ attitude: <<>>]

The square brackets are intended to suggest that the ideational and attitudinal meaning is fused together so that it can be negotiated by interlocutors as a whole. For instance, consider the post below:

@realDonaldTrump So the leaks are **real,** but the news is **fake**? Like how your words are **real,** but what you say is **fake.** Is that what you mean?

This contains a number of ideation-attitude couplings:

[ideation: leaks/attitude: +*t*-veracity]; [ideation: news/attitude: −*t*-veracity]; [ideation: words/attitude: +*t*-veracity]; [ideation: what you say/attitude: −*t*-veracity]

The post was a response to these two tweets by Trump:

1. James Clapper and others stated that there is no evidence Potus **colluded** with Russia. This story is **FAKE NEWS** and everyone knows it!

2. The **real** story that Congress, the FBI and all others should be looking into is the **leaking** of Classified information. Must find **leaker** now!

These posts contain the following couplings

1. [ideation: Potus/attitude: -propriety]; [ideation: story/attitude: −*t*-veracity]

2. [ideation: story/attitude: +*t*-veracity]; [ideation: leaking/attitude: -propriety]; [ideation: leaker/attitude: -propriety]

Clearly credibility is at risk in these couplings, even as Trump attempts to close down any negotiation via the nominalization 'fake news'.

Ideation and attitude may be instantiated within a single hashtag, or across the tag and co-text in varying combinations (e.g. ideation in tag/ evaluation in co-text or vice versa). We will leave aside for now the significance of when ideation or evaluation is tagged or untagged, barring mentioning that it seems to be related to which couplings are likely to be more bondable (in the sense of generating more instances of posts aligning with the coupling) or searchable. *#fakenews* obviously conforms to both being highly bondable and highly searchable since the term has been so prevalent in popular discourse. Indeed, both Trump and Conway respectively have used the tag:

'BuzzFeed   Runs   Unverifiable   Trump-Russia   Claims'
#FakeNews *[embedded link to a lifezette article with same title]*

#fakenews. Rush to judgment. *[embedded tweet by The Hill: Daily Beast falsely identifies Quebec mosque shooters as fictitious white supremacists http://hill.cm/FokfaD1]*

These posts offer a number of couplings to the ambient audience regarding the status that these political figures believe should be given to news media, as shown in Table 6.1.

Hood (2010, p. 144) favours a yin-yang symbol to represent the combining of ideational and attitudinal meanings (Figure 6.5). The yin-yang representation is intended to convey the idea of semiotic complementarity and that 'meaning has to do with the relations among signs'[7] (Martin, 2013, p. 3). It was originally used by Martin (2013, p. 2) to 'highlight the intextricable and interpenetrating bonding of signifié and significant that constitutes … [Saussure's] conception of the sign'.

TABLE 6.1 Couplings in Trump's tweet about his ties with Russia (inscribed attitude in bold; ideation underlined)

Tweet	Coupling
'BuzzFeed Runs **Unverifiable** <u>Trump-Russia Claims</u>[A]' **#Fake**<u>News</u> [B]	[A] [ideation: Trump-Russia claims/attitude: -*t*-veracity]
	[B] [ideation: News/attitude: -*t*-veracity]
#fake<u>news</u>[A]. **Rush to judgment** [B].	[A] [ideation: news /attitude: - valuation]
[embedded tweet by The Hill: Daily Beast **falsely**[C] identifies Quebec mosque shooters as **fictitious**[D] white supremacists http://hill.cm/ FokfaD1]	[B] [ideation: Daily Beast (inferred)/ attitude: - judgement (afforded)]
	[C] [ideation: Daily Beast/ attitude: - veracity]
	[D] [ideation: white supremacists/ attitude: -veracity]

Szenes (2016) adopts this form of representation because it 'lends itself to the visualisation of layers of couplings'. For instance, it might enable us to represent *'I care about #freespeech'* as a coupling nested inside another coupling (Figure 6.6). One limitation of this form of representation is, however, that it does not scale across analysis of many instances in a long text. In addition, since it is an image rather than notational convention, it cannot be applied as a form of in-text annotation.

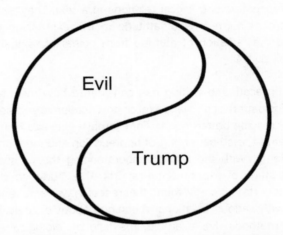

FIGURE 6.5 *A yin-yang diagram used to represent ideation-attitude coupling.*

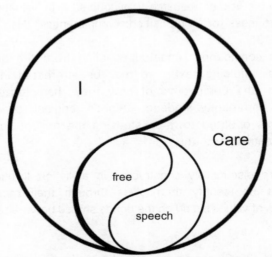

FIGURE 6.6 *A yin-yang diagram used to represent a recoupling.*

Syndromes of meaning

As Hood's (2010) work on academic discourse has made apparent, there is much more going on in a text than a single coupling can reveal. For example, her study of academic research articles has revealed various ways in which prosodies of attitude can spread across phases of discourse, including 'radiating', not just from an attitude, but from a coupling:

> These means include the coupling of attitude and ideation enabling a value to propagate along lexical relations in a text. They also include the development of harmonies of attitude in the expression of consistent values, and the radiation of attitude from points of textual prominence. (Hood, 2010, p. 169)

Similar work on academic writing has considered how identifying ideation-attitude coupling patterns can make explicit how academic genres function, and thus how they may be better taught. For example, Hao and Humphrey (2009) have investigated the co-patterning of appreciation and ideation in published research warrants, with the aim of understanding the persuasive rhetoric typical of this stage of experimental reports. This study, which focused on experimental reports in biology, found that research warrants tended to couple appreciation with various ideational meanings about biological phenomena and research methods. For example, the field of 'biological phenomenon' was coupled with 'valuation: prominence' or 'valuation: benefit'; the field of 'methodology' was coupled with 'valuation: effectiveness' or 'composition: efficiency'; and the field of 'research' was coupled with 'valuation: necessity', 'valuation: worthiness' or 'composition: completeness' (Hao & Humphrey, 2009, pp. 190–191).

As well as considering repeated coupling from the perspective of logogesis (the unfolding text), we may be interested in approaching couplings from the perspective of how they characterize a particular personae or community. Indeed Knight's original conceptualization of coupling was oriented towards studying the role of coupling in the discursive formation of identity:

> Identities are discursively constructed in affiliation through couplings, and interactants identify themselves through their memberships to communities of values based on the bonds shared between them. (Knight, 2010a, p. 212)

Zappavigna et al. (2008), analogizing with the medical concept of a cluster of associated symptoms, have used the term 'syndrome' to refer to repeated patterns of coupling in a text or corpus. In the next chapter will return to how this idea might be used in characterizing different identities.

Recoupling

In addition to considering how couplings unfold across a text through forms of radiating prosody, we might consider how a particular coupling is transformed in a text. For instance, an initial coupling might be 'recoupled' locally, for example, within a clause. Szenes's (2016) work on business discourse has shown how recoupling can be grammaticalized at this level. For example, the following is an extract taken from an undergraduate business report in her dataset:

> The vibrant Brazilian agricultural industry represents a considerable opportunity (Szenes, 2016, pp. 220–221)

Here the initial coupling [ideation: Brazilian agricultural industry/attitude: + reaction] is recoupled as [ideation: initial coupling/evaluation: +valuation]. The first coupling occurs within the nominal group structure. The Epithet vibrant transfers positive attitudinal value to the Target, *Brazilian agricultural industry,* realized by a Classifier^Classifier^Thing structure (Szenes, 2016, p. 219). Hood's (2010) yin-yang representation strategy introduced earlier is particularly useful in visually representing this recoupling (Figure 6.7).

A similar recoupling can be seen in posts that incorporate competing hashtags (though grammaticalization is optional). For example, posts incorporating an opposition between *#fakenews* and *#realnews* are typically directed at Trump himself:

> @realDonaldTrump you're in trouble now you can't blame Obama nor Hillary any longer. Put your hands up Donnie. **#realnews** not **#fakenews**

> @realDonaldTrump What everyone knows is that you are an incorrigible liar. When you label something **#FakeNews,** it's probably **#RealNews.**

> It's not **#fakenews** when it actually happened @realDonaldTrump! It's called **#realnews** #MICHAELFLYNN is a criminal. Stop defending him #resist

> @POTUS: it's not 1933 Germany. People speaking out against you aren't **#FakeNews.** You're the worst POTUS history, that's **#RealNews.** #Resist

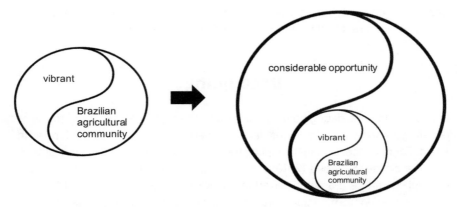

FIGURE 6.7 *An example of recoupling, based on (Szenes, 2016, p. 222).*

Posts can also attempt to solidify an original coupling by introducing a recoupling featuring a similar ideation-attitude combination. An example is posts incorporating the tags *#fakenews* and *#crookedmedia*:

> realDonaldTrump **#fakenews** is right😒 **#CrookedMedia**
>
> @Reuters @ReutersTV **#fakenews** #reutershacks **#crookedmedia**
>
> **#CrookedMedia** focus on Donald Trump and Russia is any attempt to obscure their **#FakeNews** problem and normalize anonymous criminal leaks.
>
> FULL DISCLOSURE is the most effective tool to against **#CrookedMedia #FakeNews**. It's important to report that which the MSM wants to ignore.
>
> @user The #MSM keeps validating my decision to #VoteTrump The more the **#CrookedMedia** reports **#FakeNews** the more I want to #MAGA

This kind of recoupling might feature similar ideation or similar evaluation to the original coupling.

This chapter has focused on how couplings are instantiated in texts from the perspective of how a coupling may be *tabled* in discourse as a value that may be potentially shared or rejected. Even the small volume of 'fake news' posts used to illustrate couplings has likely left the reader keenly aware of the polarization of political discourse currently seen on social media. In the aftermath of the Brexit decision and the 2017 US presidential election, commentators have begun worrying about whether we are entering a 'post truth' era in which facts and experts are devalued in favour of emotional reactions to events. Media commentary has suggested that the public have become more tolerant of politicians who lie or ignore expert knowledge (e.g. scientific consensus about climate change) due to an emergent 'post-truth' ethos:

'Don't bother me with facts' is no longer a punchline. It has become a political stance. It's worth remembering that it has not always been this way: the exposure of former US president Richard Nixon's lies was greeted with outrage. (Higgins, 2016)

Terms such as 'media bubbles', 'silos', and 'echo chambers' (Berghel, 2017) have been used to describe how particular social media communities tend to exclude outside viewpoints which are seen as incommensurable. For example, a study of self-identified supporters of Hillary Clinton and Donald Trump displayed particular patterns of conventional (used by the official accounts of the two politicians) and fringe (user-generated) hashtags on Twitter (Bouma, de Groot, Adriaanse, Polak, & Zorz, 2017). The study found that users supporting each of these candidates tended to link to the same media even where they used different hashtags (conventional v fringe), suggesting that they existed in discrete 'bubbles' (Table 6.2).

TABLE 6.2 Clinton v Trump supporter hashtags identified by Bouma et al. (2017)

Clinton-supporter hashtags		Trump-supporter hashtags	
#Conventional	#Fringe	#Conventional	#Fringe
#NeverTrump	#ImWithHer	#DrainTheSwamp	#LockHerUp
#DumpTrump	#VoteBlue	#TrumpPence16	#MAGA3x
#StopTrump	#StrongerTogether	#MAGA	#HillaryForPrison
#DonTheCon	#HillaryClinton	#VoteTrump	#CrookedHillary
#RememberWhenTrump	#HillYes	#AmericaFirst	#TrumpsArmy
#NotMyPresident	#Hillary2016	#Trump2016	#PodestaEmails
	#ClintonKaine	#MakeAmericaGreatAgain	
	#Dems	#NeverHillary	

Adopting the perspective on coupling presented in this chapter, we might see these communities as 'coupling chambers', where an initial coupling in a phrase such as 'fake news' is reinstantiated many times over. It remains to be seen whether, 'post-truth' is the optimal term for accounting for the coupling patterns prevalent in the #Trump/#Brexit era. We might question whether attitude is taking prominence over ideation, or whether ideation is being used as a prop for sharing attitude.

This chapter has suggested the role that hashtags play in establishing and propagating couplings in social media discourse. The focus has been on how ideation-attitude couplings fuse attitudinal and ideational meaning in order to form a value that can be reacted to in various ways by interlocutors or audiences. In order to explore how this reaction is construed we considered how an initial coupling might be recoupled by being reiterated, substituted, or inverted. The examples offered in this chapter have been largely mono-modal. However, intermodal coupling is clearly an important dimension of meaning-making, which we will return to in Chapter 9. The key thing now to consider is how coupling acts in the service of affiliation, that is, how a coupling can be used to share a 'bond'. It is to this issue that we turn in the next chapter.

7

Ambient Affiliation: Sharing Social Bonds by Negotiating and Communing around Couplings

Introduction

Although language is a rich resource as far as community building is concerned, including naming practices, slang, and many kinds of semantic variation (Martin, 2010),[1] the language used in social media, particularly microblogging, is under significant interpersonal pressure due to brevity imposed by the semiotic technology. Resources such as hashtags have accordingly developed as a means of condensing language used in the service of affiliation, that is, in the service of sharing social bonds. An ongoing theme in social media research is the idea that hashtags are instrumental in forming communities,[2] acting both as 'virtual sites for constructing communities' (Lin, Margolin, Keegan, Baronchelli, & Lazer, 2013, p. 370) and as markers or 'symbol[s] of community membership' (Yang, Sun, Zhang, & Mei, 2012, p. 2). The concept of a 'public'[3] has also been used to characterize the way hashtags coordinate public discussion about issues and events, forming 'hashtag publics' (Bruns & Burgess, 2011b, 2012a; Bruns & Moe, 2014; Bruns et al., 2016; Rambukanna, 2015; Rambukkana, 2015b; Sauter & Bruns, 2015), and 'ad hoc issue publics' (Bruns & Burgess, 2011a, 2011b, 2015; Montemurro & Kamerer, 2016; Sauter & Bruns, 2014).[4] Activist tags such as *#BringBackOurGirls* and *#BlackLivesMatter* have been seen as 'framing devices that allow crowds to be rendered into publics; networked publics that want to tell their story collaboratively and on their own terms' (Papacharissi, 2016, p. 308).

Most studies of hashtag communities focus on an ideational core around which the hashtagged discussion is thought to centre. Alternatively they use field variables to define the community boundaries in which affiliation occurs (e.g. nursing community (Moorley & Chinn, 2014), cancer support communities (Myrick, Holton, Himelboim, & Love, 2015) etc.). In contrast, the social semiotic approach adopted in this book defines affiliation and community in terms of the values that are shared. Drawing on the concept of ideation-attitude coupling introduced in the previous chapter, it offers a way of understanding affiliation in terms of the values that are at stake, rather than simply the field of experience (i.e. just the target of appraisal). We have seen in Chapter 2 how hashtags, as metadata, can render attitude-ideation couplings more prominent in the social stream; in this chapter we will consider how a hashtag makes a coupling more 'bondable'.

Ideation-attitude couplings do not typically 'hang in the air' without response, at least in dialogic discourse. Instead they are negotiated by interlocutors or communed around in the ambient social media stream, forming social bonds. This chapter explores how interlocutors and ambient users/audiences affirm, co-opt, re-construe, laugh off, or reject couplings as different kinds of social bonds are shared or contested. The chapter begins by providing an overview of social semiotic work on dialogic affiliation, with reference to Knight's (2008, 2010a, 2010b, 2013) model of affiliation developed for explaining conversational humour. We then move from dialogic affiliation to consider ambient affiliation in social media, where the 'affiliation is ambient in the sense that the users may not have interacted directly and likely do not know each other, and may not interact again' (Zappavigna, 2011, p. 801). Direct exchanges between users cannot be assumed as the only basis of bonding in social media given that any particular post will not necessarily receive a reply. Oulasvirta, Lehtonen, Kurvinen, and Raento (2010, p. 244) refer to this asymmetry as a kind of 'dilution of conversational obligations'. In light of this, the discursive systems of *convoking, finessing*, and *promoting* (a coupling) are introduced to explain how couplings can be communed around in social media discourse, in addition to being interactively negotiated.

Knight's model of dialogic affiliation

From the point of view of functional linguistics and social semiotics, the key thing to look at in order to explore how values are negotiated in discourse is interpersonal meaning. Interpersonal meaning, according to this perspective, centres on how relationships are enacted (Halliday, 1978). Knight's model of affiliation was developed to explore the interpersonal dimension of conversation in order to understand how social bonds are realized interactively in dialogic communication. This work focused on how interpersonal meanings function in conversational humour between friends chatting about their everyday experiences. The approach was informed by Poynton's (1984, 1991) description of how social solidarity is realized in spoken texts, and Stenglin and Martin's studies of how language functions to align personae into communities (e.g. see Stenglin (2008 a and b), Martin (2004), Martin (2010), Martin and Stenglin (2007)).

Knight's approach also drew on Martin and White's (2005) appraisal framework to explore the community-building significance of evaluative language in terms of how evaluation and experience are fused as couplings, and how these couplings are negotiated in dialogic discourse. The previous chapter presented a snippet of discourse from Knight's dataset: a young woman tabling the following ideation-attitude coupling to her friends:

[ideation: pie/attitude: + appreciation]

More of this exchange is shown in the extract in Table 7.1. This extract gives an indication of the kind of unfolding prosodies of attitude that are often produced in casual conversation and which were identified repeatedly in Knight's larger dataset. In this particular example we see interlocutors rallying around mutual appreciation of pie parties. Knight interprets the unfolding as 'three conversational participants [who] commune around a bond realised by a coupling of intensified positive appreciation for a pie party that they regularly participate in together' (Knight, 2010a, p. 219). They later laugh off an implicated 'gluttony bond' incommensurate with another bond that they share: 'beautiful thinness' (Table 7.1).

According to Knight's model, there are three affiliation strategies that can be deployed in proposing and reacting to a bond: *communing, laughing,* and

TABLE 7.1 Positive evaluation of a pie party in a casual conversation, adapted from (Knight, 2010a, p. 219)

Speaker	Talk	Coupling	Bond (*deferred* or shared)
A	Party's over. For me;		**Fun pie party**
B	No more pie party ==		
C	== This was an **awesome** pie party guys	[ideation: pie party/attitude: + appreciation]	
B	I **love** pie parties	[ideation: pie party/attitude: + t-appreciation /]	
C	I **can't wait** to have another one	[ideation: pie party/ evaluation: + t-appreciation]	

¹The *t-* notation here is used to indicate that the affect (*love*) is a 'token' of appreciation i.e. it is a good pie party.

condemning. Communing affiliation is 'where participants come together to share a bond' as in epideictic or rallying discourses (Knight, 2010a, p. 217). For example, the extract in Table 7.1 involves interlocutors communing around what Knight terms a 'fun pie party' bond by rallying around the [ideation: pie/evaluation: + *t*-appreciation] coupling.

Laughing affiliation, on the other hand, involves tension which is discharged by deferring a bond that is not shareable at a particular moment. For instance, the pie party conversation extract in Table 7.2 shows how a 'happy fatness' bond, instantiated as the coupling [ideation: eating/attitude: +appreciation], is laughed off by the women so that they might share a 'beautiful thinness' bond, commensurate with other body conscious values that they share. The happy fatness bond generates a 'wrinkle' that interrupts the bonding process, creating social tension because it 'a *potential* bond that cannot be shared by the conversational participants and which contrasts in a laughable way with an *implicated* bond that they share together' (Knight, 2010a, p. 208).

The final affiliation strategy identified by Knight is condemning affiliation which also involves a form of social tension. However, rather than being

TABLE 7.2 Positive evaluation of a pie party in a casual conversation, (part 2) adapted from (Knight, 2010a, p. 219)

Speaker	Talk	Coupling	Bond (*deferred* or shared)
A	== Yeah I saw like my family and friends … I **ate well** ((laughs))	[ideation: eating/attitude: +appreciation]	*Happy fatness* **Beautiful thinness**
B	We all **ate well**.	[ideation: eating/attitude: +appreciation]	
all	((all laugh))		
B	Dude we all ((laughing)) ate ***good*** pie!	[ideation: pie/attitude: +appreciation]	
all	((continuous laughing))		
B	Yes I agree. ((continuous laughing)) **On a diet** now.	[ideation: self/attitude: -judgement[i]]	
all	(all laugh))		

[i] Knight analyses this as invoked attitude where negative judgement is flagged by counterexpectancy (Knight, 2010a, p. 305).

TABLE 7.3 An example of condemning, adapted from (Knight, 2010a, p. 233)

Speaker	Talk	Coupling	Bond (*rejected* or shared)
A	It was the way she would act sometimes would be very...kinda **negative**.	[ideation: she/attitude: -appreciation]	*destructive criticism*
	[pause- 2 secs] And we'd-we'd try like to **keep a positive environment**	[ideation: keeping positive/attitude: +appreciation]	**motivating encouragement**
	...(at the tech), you can motivating be but it's not very motivating to have	[ideation: motivation/ attitude: +appreciation]	
	someone **yelling at you** for stuff, and	[ideation: yelling/ attitude:-*t*-appreciation]	*destructive criticism*
B	Mm hm		

laughed off, the tension is instead resolved by rejecting the unshareable bond in order to commune around some other bond that the interactants are able to share. For instance a 'destructive criticism' bond is rejected in favour of a 'motivating encouragement' bond (Table 7.3).

Identity as 'coupling disposition'

Knight's work has also informed social semiotic research into identity, the 'flipside' of affiliation in the sense that any act of communing is also an act of construing the self (as a textual persona). For example, we may think about identities as being characterized by particular 'coupling dispositions' (Zappavigna, 2014c). This disposition is the tendency to construe particular patterns of values. For instance Zappavigna (2014b) explored this idea in relation to Twitter discourse about coffee, an everyday bonding icon. This study found two general tendencies in coupling patterns in this discourse, suggestive of two broad identities enacted in relation to coffee. The first coupling disposition was that of the 'coffee connoisseur' concerned with assessing the quality of coffee from the aesthetic perspective of 'taste'. The coupling pattern typifying this identity was [ideation: coffee/attitude: positive reaction], for example:

> @User thanks very much, I'm looking forward to tasting all the **amazing** coffees we have coming in through the Synesso, and Aurelia.
>
> The sun is shining. I am off to Donington Market to stock up on **rare** and **exotic** coffee blends.
>
> Ditto! RT @User: Just had an Allagash Black. **Fantastic! Notes of roasted coffee, chocolate, and fruity Belgian yeast. (Zappavigna, 2014b, p. 153)**

Agnate identities identified were wine and chocolate connoisseurs, and the more generalized 'foodie', or more ideologically charged 'food snob'. The other dominant coupling pattern manifest in this dataset was a 'coffee addict' persona 'bound to consuming coffee in order to survive the day' (Zappavigna, 2014b, p. 153). This persona construed repeated couplings such as [ideation: microblogger/attitude: desire], for instance, using the hashtag *#ineedcoffee*:

> I hate waking up at 6am everyday. Ughh #**needcoffee**
>
> I'm so out of it this morning. #**needcoffee** or #moresleep
>
> I want to fast forward to 3:30, to where I'm laying in bed, taking a nap. #**needcoffee**
>
> Getting out of bed can be so difficult some days...its one of those days #**needcoffee**
>
> I feel like a zombie. #**ineedcoffee**
>
> Well that was a "fun" morning commute..gggrrrr **#INeedCoffee (Zappavigna, 2014b, p. 154)**

Returning to Trump discourse, a very different context, we can see how appreciation in combination with a bonding icon can be used to align people. For example, Trump's proposed US-Mexico border wall was a bonding icon for his followers (see #BuildThatWall in glossary), around which the 'Trump supporter' identity coalesced. A common coupling was [ideation: wall/attitude: +reaction]:

Oh yes we're building that **beautiful** <u>wall</u>! #BuildThatWall
#MAGA 💙 [GIF of the cast of the TV show Friends clapping]

Excited for our **#Beautiful**<u>Wall</u>! Keep it ugly on the
#Mexico side until they pay for it! #TRUMP #MAGA #WinAgain
#AmericaFirst #Illegal #Crime

BUILD THAT HUGE, Massive, Tall **BEAUTIFUL** <u>WALL</u> Mr.
President @realDonaldTrump... We are with you!!!! #MAGA

Yes my friend:"A BIG **BEAUTIFUL** <u>WALL</u>" 🇺🇸It's long
over-due and it will get built~! It won't happen over
night but it will happen~!#MAGA 🇺🇸😎

Build the big, **beautiful** <u>wall</u> then catapult the
traitors over it. #MAGA

Our country will be better off with a **beautiful** <u>wall</u>!
#MAGA

These examples echo Trump's use of the phrase 'big, beautiful wall' in many of
his campaign speeches. Here users are rallying around aesthetic appreciation
of a wall, and avoiding the racist implications of this act. This is an example of
how appreciation can act in the service of propaganda in order to rally people
around a particular issue.

Examples of dialogic affiliation in tweets

Dialogic affiliation, while not obligatory (and indeed most tweets do not
receive a reply (Liu, Kliman-Silver, & Mislove, 2014)), is possible in social
media discourse. For example, consider the following post by Trump regarding
Alec Baldwin's portrayal of the president on *Saturday Night Live,* an American
sketch comedy TV show:

Just tried watching Saturday Night Live - unwatchable!
Totally biased, not funny and the Baldwin impersonation
just can't get any worse. Sad

This post tabled a number of couplings including a repeated [ideation: SNL/
attitude: -reaction] coupling (Table 7.4). It also featured Trump's characteristic
criticism of people who have challenged him – 'sad' – which he often appends
to the end of a post (see discussion of the '*[evaluatively loaded observation]
Sad!*' phrasal template in Chapter 9). The tabling of the coupling in this post

TABLE 7.4 Couplings tabled in Trump's tweet about SNL

Tweet (inscribed attitude in bold)	Coupling	Bond
Just tried watching Saturday Night Live - **unwatchable**[A]! Totally **biased** [B], not **funny**[C] and the Baldwin impersonation just can't get any **worse**[D]. **Sad**[E]	[A] [ideation: SNL/attitude: -reaction] [B] [ideation: SNL/attitude: -reaction] [C] [ideation: SNL/attitude: -reaction] [D] [ideation: Baldwin impersonation/ attitude: -reaction] [E] [ideation: SNL/attitude: -t-attitude]	'sad SNL'

proposes a 'sad SNL'[5] bond to the ambient audience. Sad is coded in Table 12 as general attitude since the phrasal template is inherently ambiguous: it could be Baldwin's performance, SNL, or the entire situation that is the ideational target of the appraisal. Given Trump's online persona, it is likely that negative judgement is an appropriate coding, especially given his tendency to refer to people and institutions as 'losers' in a similar manner at the end of his tweets:

There are no buyers for the worthless @NYDailyNews but little Mort Zuckerman is frantically looking. It is bleeding red ink - a total **loser!**

I have watched sloppy Graydon Carter fail and close Spy Magazine and now am watching him fail at @ VanityFair Magazine. He is a total **loser!**

Have a good chance to win Texas on Tuesday. Cruz is a nasty guy, not one Senate endorsement and, despite talk, gets nothing done. **Loser**!

Trump's assessment of SNL was contested by other users in a cascade of hundreds of replies to Trump's posts (examples in Table 7.5). Theses replies re-construed Trump's [ideation: SNL/attitude: -reaction] via recoupling, with Trump, rather than SNL, the new target of the negative attitude. These competing couplings tended to be realized as [ideation: Trump (or Trump's behaviour)/-t-propriety], with the attitude realized as token of judgement of Trump's propriety. These posts reject the 'sad SNL' bond offered by Trump and instead share a 'sad Trump' bond. The rejection of Trump's bond is a form of condemning affiliation, and users instead rally around an anti-Trump bond that they do share.

The key idea of dialogic affiliation is that social alignments are negotiated through couplings since we 'don't after all simply affiliate with feelings; we affiliate with feelings about people, places and things, and the activities they participate in, however abstract or concrete' (Martin, 2008a, p. 58).

TABLE 7.5 Examples of condemnation of Trump's 'sad SNL' bond

	Tweet (inscribed attitude in bold)	Coupling	Bond (*rejected* or shared)
1	the fact that you tweet about a comedy sketch instead of going to security briefings is **sad**. Do your homework.	A [ideation: The fact of Trump's behaviour/ attitude: –*t*-propriety]	*'sad SNL'* **'sad Trump'**
2	@realDonaldTrump And yet you watch it Every. Single. Week. THAT's the definition of **sad** ^A.	A [ideation: Trump watching SNL/attitude: –*t*-propriety]	*'sad SNL'* **'sad Trump'**
3	@realDonaldTrump what's more **sad** A is your inability to laugh at yourself. Real presidential^B. Worry about more important things! #noyoure**sad**^c	A [ideation: Trump's inability to laugh at himself/attitude: : –*t*-propriety] ^B [ideation: you (elided)/ attitude: –*t*- propriety] ^c [ideation: you/–*t*-propriety]	*'sad SNL'* **'sad Trump'**

For instance, we do not merely align with (or de-align from) the negative appreciation expressed in Trump's tweet about Saturday Night Live. We also align (or de-align) with the coupling of this appreciation with Saturday Night Live, and hence with how this coupling coordinates with other values that we hold. Social alignments are forged as we negotiate these couplings in discourse since the bonds that they realize 'make up the value sets of our communities and culture' (Knight, 2010b, p. 43). The 114,458 likes and 27,691 retweets (which Trump's post had received at the time of writing) are also an example of how the social media channel itself offers condensed/ speedy ways to signal an acceptance of a tabled coupling, or to at least present it as worth sharing (since users may retweet material with which they do not necessarily agree).

A system network for exploring affiliation

Figure 7.1, developed with J.R. Martin, is a system network for exploring both dialogic and ambient affiliation. The fundamental choice is between tabling a coupling or ignoring an interlocutor entirely. Each of the subsequent choices in the network is about how a speaker/respondent tables, augments, or replies to a coupling. The choices shown in grey relate to how a particular coupling in enhanced in order to be more bondable, and will be explored in more detail in the section 'Convoking, promoting, and finessing' below.

Once an initial coupling has been tabled in discourse (first choice shown in Figure 7.1), a respondent may either ignore the coupling entirely, or proceed to react to it by managing the coupling in various ways. The first choice is between *supporting* or *rejecting* the coupling. Supporting can be realized by reaffirming the coupling, for example:

```
User1: The border wall will be beautiful!
[ideation: border wall/attitude: +reaction]

User2: @User1 I know! The border wall will be so
beautiful!
[ideation: border wall/attitude: + reaction]
```

Alternatively, the coupling may be rejected, for instance, by *dismissing* it and not offering an opposing coupling:

```
User1: The border wall will be beautiful!
[ideation: border wall/attitude: +reaction]

User2: @User1 Whatever!
```

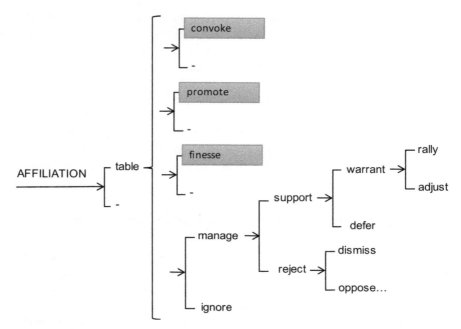

FIGURE 7.1 *A system network for exploring affiliation.*

Alternatively, a coupling may be supported by either *deferring* or *warranting*. The border wall (introduced earlier) is an instance of warranting by rallying around [ideation: border wall/attitude: +reaction]. The alternative to rallying is *adjusting* by modifying the attitude, either within or across systems, for example:

> **User1:** The border wall will be beautiful!
> [ideation: border wall/attitude: +reaction]
>
> **User2:** @User1 I know! The border wall will be the best thing that has ever happened!
> [ideation: border wall/attitude: +valuation]

On the other hand, if the coupling is *deferred* (because it cannot be rallied around by the interactants due to some opposing bond that they share) they may laugh it off, in the sense introduced by Knight (2010a,b) at the beginning of this chapter:

> **User1:** The border wall will be beautiful!
> [ideation: border wall/attitude: +reaction]
>
> **User2:** @User1 haha!:P
> Laughs off [ideation: border wall/attitude: +reaction]
>
> **User1::P**
> Laughs off [ideation: border wall/attitude: +reaction]
>
> **User2:** Gosh, I hate Trump!
> [ideation: Trump/attitude: -happiness]

In Knight's terms, the coupling [ideation: border wall/attitude: +reaction] is laughed off. Instead interlocutors align around another bond that they share: dislike of Trump [ideation: Trump/attitude: -happiness].

Where a coupling is rejected, the choice is between *dismissing* (as in the example shown earlier) and *opposing*. An example of opposing is the following where, rather than the coupling being cast aside, an alternative recoupling is tabled:

> **User1:** The border wall will be beautiful!
> [ideation: border wall/attitude: +reaction]
>
> **User2:** @User1 No way! The wall will be a moral outrage.
> [ideation: border wall/attitude: -propriety]

Tabling a coupling, particularly on social media platforms, where posts do not necessarily receive dialogic replies, also involves orienting the ambient interlocutor/reader/audience to the coupling. This may be acheived by calling together or 'mustering' a particular community (*convoking*), increasing the prominence of the coupling (*promoting*), and entering the coupling into heteroglossic relations with other potential couplings (*finessing*). These are resources of *communing*, rather than dialogic negotiation. They are not necessarily specific to online communication, and might be found in, for example, broadcast communication. Thus they should not be interpreted as mutually exclusive choices, but as simultaneous choices, which may be inflected by the communicative possibilities and constraints of a particular mode of communication. For example, promoting resources can be used at the same time as rallying resources. Convoking, promoting, and finessing (shown in grey in Figure 7.1) are the focus of this chapter, since they are most closely associated with hashtag use, and are explained in more detail in the sections which follow.

Convoking, promoting, and finessing

Tabling a coupling via a social media platform means construing a value in the absence of paralanguage, and often, repartee. While Knight's model accounts for the dialogic dimension of affiliation, when there is a direct interaction between interlocutors, here we aim to better account for the 'ambient' or 'broadcast' dimension of affiliation. This is important for understanding social media communication because users do not necessarily interact directly. They nevertheless participate in shared practices of aligning or de-aligning with particular stances and perspectives. Ambient affiliation involves *communing* around, rather than necessarily directly *negotiating,* particular couplings in a clearly defined conversational exchange.

Hashtags are a resource amongst others (e.g. emoticons/emoji) involved in augmenting written language in light of the absence of paralanguage and clearly defined dialogue. However, it should be noted that, in making this claim, I am not suggesting that online discourse is an impoverished form of either spoken or written discourse. In light of the absence of paralanguage, it is interesting to explore how hashtags are used to maximize the potential interpersonal impact of ideation-attitude couplings, and the kinds of resources that are drawn upon in order to forge communion of feeling around a coupling. Three systems of meaning are relevant to this communion:

- *convoking* – mustering community around a coupling, for instance, via naming or classifying, e.g. *#TrumpTrain*

- *finessing* – heteroglossically positioning a coupling in relation to other potential couplings, e.g. via engagement resources such as negation, for instance, via negation, e.g. *#NotMyPresident*

- *promoting* – interpersonally emphasizing a coupling, for instance, via graduation or typographic emphasis, e.g. *#EVIL*

These systems of meaning are concerned with 'alignment to the coupling' (Han, 2015, p. 30). Briefly, the *convoking* system involves proposing a coupling to a particular community by calling together a group to bond around the coupling. *Finessing*, on the other hand, modulates the coupling in relation to other potential stances that may be present in the social stream. Finally, *promoting* interpersonally foregrounds the coupling. Each of these systems is explained below in terms of how they may be realized via a hashtag. It should be noted that, while the hashtag is an important resource for construing this meaning potential, communing is not necessarily limited to this type of semiotic resource.

Convoking a community around a coupling with a hashtag

The system of convocation considers how a post 'calls together' a community to bond around a coupling. This is perhaps the most general function of hashtags from the perspective of affiliation. It is most likely in play to a certain extent in all tagging, since using a tag presupposes that there are other like-minded people in the social network who may also use the same tag. Convoking is a 'mustering' function of garnering the attention of a particular community, and is important in social media environments where the ambient audience is largely unknown where the individual user is posting to a social stream that may contain millions of unrelated posts. In other words, the user needs some way of bringing together potential personae who will bond with the coupling that is tabled.

For example, the *#MAGA* (*Make America Great Again*) hashtag was used for convocation, acting as a marker of a generalized Trump-supporter identity, along with other resources such as the 'Pepe the frog' emoticon, co-opted as a symbol of the 'alt-right' (alternative right) movement in US politics. For instance, *#MAGA* was used to convoke personae around the coupling [ideation: media/attitude: -propriety]:

```
I trust #Russia more than I trust the corrupt
Democratic Party and the corrupt media! 🐸☕ Stop
trying to start WWIII #Snowflakes ❄! #MAGA
```

> The liberal **media** is all hypocrisy. **#maga** 🐸☕
>
> We the People will not let the corrupt **media** influence elections any longer. Period. **#MAGA** 🐸 *[embedded tweet: News outlets should step up and instill confidence in America's election system. Watch @Users essay here]*
>
> It is becoming increasingly rare when the corrupt **media** asks serious questions of both parties rather than pushing the lefts agenda **#MAGA** 🐸
>
> @realDonaldTrump boycott Saturday night live. They and the **media** are your enemies. **#maga** #PresidentTrump #SNL ✝🚩🐸

From the perspective of affiliation, a post needs to be visible for any potential audience to align with the coupling that it tables, and hashtags afford this possibility. In the above post, *#MAGA* both calls together Trump supporters and means that more users, beyond an individual's network of followers, will be convoked by the tag.

Calling together a 'college of potential bonders' using a hashtag is the interpersonal corollary of classifying a post with a tag. For example, the hashtag *#Trump* in the following, viewed through the lens of ideational meaning alone, indicates that this post is about Trump; viewed through the lens of affiliation, the tag functions to link the post with other posts tabling similar couplings, in this case [ideation: media/attitude: -propriety]:

> The corrupt **Fake**[6] news **media** has not said anything positive about our President. **#Trump** 4 the people!

In this way it also links the post to other posts proposing similar anti-media bonds. This point is more apparent if we look at a collection of posts containing the same tag. An example of a tag with a very clear (likely prefabricated) convoking function, in relation to the above coupling, is *#TrumpTrain*:

> But CNN is **faaaaakeee** newsss! **Sad! Biased! Corrupt!** #maga #trumptrain #buildthewall #corruptmedia #fakenews😎😎😎🚩🚩🚩🚩😎😎😂😂😂
>
> **Corrupt** media folks that **sold out** to Clinton **lost** all **credibility** as journalists. They became **commentators.** #MAGA TrumpNation #TrumpTrain
>
> Time for the **#TrumpTrain** to take on the **corrupt** news media.Start with out of context clip editing and cut and paste vidclip antics #FakeNews

```
#Trump has proven - after overcoming GOP hopefuls, a
crooked media, and the corrupt Clinton machine - that
the #TrumpTrain has no brakes! [image of Trump leaning
on a boardroom desk]
```

```
Wow, you guys will believe whatever you hear from the
corrupt media. #MAGA #TrumpTrain #Libtards
```

In these examples *#TrumpTrain* convokes potential bonders who share the [ideation: media/attitude: -propriety] coupling.

As we saw in Chapter 2, by clicking on a hashtag such as *#TrumpTrain* (appearing as a link when viewed natively inside the Twitter service), the user is presented with the most recent posts using that tag in the unfolding social stream. This gives them access to the unfolding feed of couplings related to that tag, and to posts containing related tags (e.g. *#MAGA*). In addition to a convoking function, there are tags which have a clear exclusion function, aimed at creating an out-group. For instance, in the final *#TrumpTrain* example above, *#Libtards* (liberal retards) performs the function of out-grouping anti-Trump personae. Table 7.6 gives examples of these kinds of tags that out-group pro-Trump or anti-Trump personae.

Convoking can, of course, occur directly as part of dialogic exchanges and incorporate interlocutors in the form of named users. For example, some posts draw on the @mention convention, where the @ character is used to refer to another user account in a manner similar to a vocative in a face-to-face conversation. For instance, this resource is used in the following exchange in which users are arguing about Trump's proposed border wall. This exchange occurred as a reaction to the following tweet by the news organization CNN:

```
Trump's debt is spread across 150 companies, according
to a Wall Street Journal analysis [link to a CNN
article titled 'Trump's debt spread across 150
companies, Wall Street Journal says']
```

An extract from the thread of posts replying to the CNN's tweet included the following exchange:

```
User 1: stupid voters that voted 4 him without showing
his taxes screwed the whole country! #TreasonousTrump
```

```
User 2: @User1 @CNN we will depart you Mexican #MAGA
```

```
User 1: @User2 @CNN what? You're not even making sense.
Can you read and write, gather a thought and write it down?
```

User 2: **@User1** **@CNN** looks like you need to go! #BuildTheWall #MAGA

User 1: **@User2** **@CNN** oh, and you get to pay for that wall on your 7.50 an hour!

User 2: **@User1** **@CNN** Mexicos paying for it and guess what you're going back #buildthewall #MAGA

User 1: **@User2** **@CNN** listen to your Fuher. He just said the USA will be paying for it. Catch up, the adults are talking.

User 2: **@User1** **@CNN** the CNN is 100% false and you are going back America isn't for losers it's only for winners like Trump #MAGA

User 1: **@User2** *[image of white text with black background]* "Hello, Trussian Troll Please stuff your propaganda up Putin's ass. Others will now block you without engaging to reduce your impact.

User 2: **@User1** **@CNN** cry more Trump is president Russia is our Ally and you will be departed #MAGA

In each of these posts, the @ symbol, appended to the username, is employed to direct the particular couplings at the relevant interlocutor (including CNN as the author of the original post). In addition, the hashtags *#TreasonousTrump*, *#buildthewall*, and *#MAGA* function to call upon anti-Trump or pro-Trump alignment (as we saw earlier), and to invoke the value positions that these communities hold. In this way, social media texts can incorporate elements of both dialogic affiliation and ambient affiliation, in terms of how the text identifies and convokes the bonders to align with the couplings that are tabled.

We will now consider how, once the text has convoked an appropriate audience, the couplings that are tabled enter into relationship with further potential stances that may be held by other members of the ambient audience.

Finessing a coupling with a hashtag

Finessing manages how couplings are presented to potential bonders, and in this sense, is related to the discursive system of engagement, as described by Martin and White's (2005) Appraisal framework. Engagement is the region of meaning associated with managing relationships to voices, stances, and other texts, and is concerned with 'meaning making processes by which the speaker/writer negotiates relationships of alignment/dis-alignment vis-à-vis the various value positions referenced by the text and hence vis-à-vis the

TABLE 7.6 Examples of hashtags with an out-grouping function

	Hashtag	Example
Out-grouping pro-Trump personae	#LiberalSnowflakes; #Snowflakes	#Day100 and @POTUS has done excellent for #WeThePeople! Keep going sir - after today, the #liberalsnowflakes will need a new excuse!
	#Libtards	Man, those #libtards R triggered. Just walked past some protesters demanding Trump's tax returns..again. They're running on empty! Losers.
Out-grouping anti-Trump personae	#deplorables	They want you to accept the fact Russia got Trump elected and move on so he can continue using the US as his personal cash cow #deplorables
	#drumpfsupporters	#drumpfsupporters cry #MAGA but @realDonaldTrump picks are all bad for American jobs and great for outsourcing. What say you bigoted sheep?

socially-constituted communities of shared attitude and belief associated with those positions' (Martin & White, 2005: 95). However, while engagement accounts for the patterning of attitude, finessing deals with how ideation-evaluation couplings are modulated. For example, consider the following posts tabling couplings of negative propriety (*evil*) with Trump, his administration, or an act of his administration:

```
Trump's EO undoing Obama's protection for Women on
#EqualPayDay is so gross. 45 is pure effing evil.
#NotMyPresident #GoToJail

He who accepts evil without protesting against it is
really cooperating with it." - Martin Luther King, Jr
Trump is #NotMyPresident
```

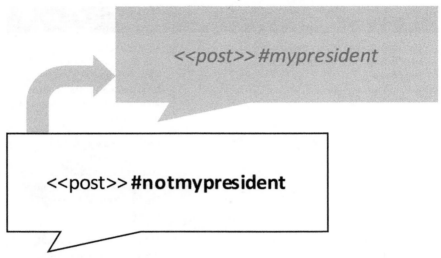

voice of putative ambient other

<<post>> #mypresident

<<post>> **#notmypresident**

FIGURE 7.2 *Invoking an opposing coupling through engagement together with a hashtag.*

Rex Tillerson is Exxon. Exxon/Trump/Russia all the same **evil** conglomerate. **#NotMyPresident** #TrumpTreason #Resist *[embedded tweet by CNN White House statement congratulating ExxonMobil investment pulls lines from oil giant's statement without citation [URL]]*

Donald Trump is evil. He is a villain & deserves to be impeached. We just need the GOP to get some frickin' courage. #resist **#NotMyPresident**

Trump you are **evil** and - SICK! All you have done in your one-hundred days is start war and taken away health care we NEED! **#notmypresident** 😡😡

Trump is **evil**. He is horrible. The whole family needs to vanish. #notmypresident

In these examples, the hashtag *#NotMyPresident* employs heteroglossic contraction (*Not*) to critique Trump, with the ideation affording judgement (i.e. not being the president is bad). The construction invokes the stance of a putative ambient other that holds an opposing view (shown in grey in Figure 7.2, based on Han's (2015) diagramming of a similar pattern in *#feminism* tweets). The

FIGURE 7.3 *Discharging and recharging couplings.*

coupling in the hashtag invokes this potentially opposing voice. This finesses the [ideation: Trump/attitude: -propriety] couplings in the posts, casting them against a background of potentially opposing perspectives.

In Han's (2015) terms, this type of hashtag contributes to an interpersonal pattern 'discharging' positive judgement of Trump, and opening space for a 'recharging' of Trump with negative evaluation (*evil*). In this way, negation can function to 'invoke or activate the positive' (White, 2003, p. 271). This type of discharging/recharging pattern has also been noted by Zappavigna (forthcoming) in posts about depression that recouple [ideation: depression/attitude: -capacity] as [ideation: depressed person/attitude: +capacity] (Figure 7.3). Zappavigna's example is different, in terms of structural realization, to *#NotMyPresident* since the coupling occurs across an entire post, rather than within a single tag. However, the rhetorical strategy is quite similar in terms of the role that finessing via negation is playing in supporting the tabling of the particular coupling (in reaction to other real or potential couplings in the social stream).

Promoting a coupling with a hashtag

In addition to the convoking and finessing functions already identified above, hashtags can function to interpersonally promote a coupling in a tweet, performing a similar function to upscaling or intensifying attitude via the system of graduation. Graduation is a resource 'whereby feelings are amplified and categories blurred' (Martin & White, 2005, p. 35) (for further explanation of the graduation system see Chapter 9). Here, however, it is not just an attitude that is interpersonally foregrounded but an entire coupling around which the potential audience may commune. For instance, this is most obvious where the coupling itself occurs in the hashtag, for instance, *#TrumpisEvil* [ideation: Trump/attitude: -propriety]:

Trump and the GOP are going to destroy our country
and maybe the world. #AntiChrist **#TrumpIsEvil**
#TrumpResistance [GIF of a nuclear bomb explosion]

The only cure for a coup is another coup. #FireTrump
#GOPMustGoDown #TrumpHasDementia **#TrumpIsEvil**
#GOPHatesAmerica #GOPIsEvil

The press doesn't "bash" trump. They report on him.
All that bad stuff is "real" trump. #pussygrabber
#resist **#trumpisevil**

The mob is linked to Trump. There is so much
corruption and infiltration. #trumprussia **#trumpisevil**
#TrumpTaxes #Resistance

@PressSec if Assad is worse than Hitler then how does
Trumpjustify refusing to accept refugees. **#trumpisevil**
#spicerisstupid

Yo fat man! Release your taxes or we will keep
marching and shouting. You will not sell us to Russia.
#TaxMarch **#TrumpIsEvil** #RESISTANCE

Other resources such as typographic emphasis via all CAPS (e.g. #EVIL) can
be used to foreground a coupling:

and #TrumpCriminal just can't wait 2 start more wars
There's one word for #Trump & the @GOP & that word is
#EVIL #impeachTrump #VoteThemOut

First protected DREAMer is deported under Trump. **#EVIL**
#TrumpIsGoingToHell *[embedded article by USATODAY
titled' First protected DREAMer is deported under
Trump]* via @USATODAY

In the face of #atrocity #Trump shows no ability to
lead. MORALLY vacuous. Corrupt. I actually think the
word is **#EVIL**

To a certain extent, any hashtag usage highlights the values expressed in a
tweet because of the multimodal affordances of the tag that we explored in
Chapter 2 which render the tweet more findable and hence more bondable
as a form of searchable talk. Employing a hashtag meme (see Chapter 9) is
another way of promoting the coupling in a tweet, and there are probably

many other resources that can render a coupling more likely to be communed around in the ambient environment.

This chapter has explained affiliation from the perspective of negotiating couplings in dialogic discourse, and the perspective of communing around couplings in ambient discourse. Knight's (2010a,b) three general affiliation strategies were described in relation to dialogic affiliation: rallying, laughing, and condemning, each assuming a different reaction to a tabled coupling. A system network was then proposed to account for not only dialogic but also ambient affiliation. The network models how tabled couplings are managed by being rallied around, adjusted, deferred, dismissed, or opposed, and by being convoked, finessed, and promoted. The next chapter draws on the model developed here to explore how hashtags can act as resources for construing ridicule.

8

#AlternativeFacts:
Censuring and Mocking the
Quoted Voice

Introduction

As we saw in Chapter 5, social media discourse is inherently heteroglossic (Bakhtin, 1986). Voices, stances, and intersubjectivities (relations between perspectives) from many different arenas compete for discursive space, attention, and control. Public comment on political issues is a fertile domain in which different social bonds are shared and rejected. Taunting politicians is an interesting part of this social practice. The views of politicians and public figures are regularly mocked on social media, particularly when they have made a careless or embarrassing comment, or a verbal gaffe likely to be offensive to a sector of the public. This mockery largely relies on directly or indirectly quoting short snippets of secondary quoted material. In the case of political issues that have generated a lot of public interest, these quoted snippets can proliferate rapidly through an online social network, resulting in mass re-articulation and re-contextualization across 'collapsing' contexts (Wesch, 2009).

Displaying one's wit is a form of social currency on Twitter, particularly in political discourse (Zappavigna, 2012b). While outright condemning of politicians and particular political views is widespread, humorous ridicule via derisive imitation is also extremely common. It has also become commonplace to mock political gaffes by using a taunting hashtag that imitates the unusual or memorable phrasing. These hashtags often achieve the status of internet memes that become part of public consciousness, a concept we will explore in the next chapter. For example, commentators termed the 2012 US presidential election the 'meme election' due to the prominent role that hashtag memes based on political gaffes appeared to play.[1] This tendency was echoed in the highly polarized political discourse seen during the 2016 US presidential election, which again generated many hashtag memes that both sides of the political spectrum used to mock and insult each other.

This chapter explores two associated affiliation strategies: *censure* and *ridicule* of the quoted political voice using a hashtag. It draws on the model of affiliation developed in the previous chapter to explore hashtags in the service of these strategies. The chapter focuses on *#AlternativeFacts*, used to signal mockery of US presidential adviser Kellyanne Conway, and White House press secretary Sean Spicer. As we will see, *#AlternativeFacts* appears to function as a manifestation of Bateson's (1955, 1987) notion of a play-frame, a form of metacommunication which indicates playful rather than serious meaning. This is a concept that has been used by humour theorists interested in understanding how interactants know when another party is being jocular (cf. Coates (2007) and Knight (2013) in relation to conversational humour).

Ridicule and bonding

Rhetorical strategies that are typically associated with ridicule, such as irony, mockery, and sarcasm, are notoriously difficult to analyse, since the meanings at stake often rely on implicating rather than explicating interpersonal meanings. These resources also tend to draw on the semiotic dexterity of language: they simultaneously construe incongruous or contradictory meanings without losing, and most often fuelling, communicative power. Teasing, insulting, taunting, and other forms of jocular mockery have been the subject of much attention in linguistics (Haugh, 2010). This has been informed by work on the bonding role of joking more generally (Boxer & Cortés-Conde, 1997; Norrick, 2003). It has been suggested that biting forms of joking, such as sarcasm and mockery, 'can express both aggression and solidarity – aggression in the message, attacking others for their foibles and errors, and solidarity in the metamessage, including others in a playful relationship with increased involvement' (Norrick, 1994, p. 423). Martin (2000, p. 164) has suggested that sarcasm might be thought of as involving 'discordant couplings – either between appraisal selections and what is being appraised, or among the appraisal variables themselves' (cf. Swain (2003)).

Many studies have posited a relation between hashtags and the communication of 'non-verbal cues like irony' (Lin et al., 2013). Detecting sarcasm in social media texts, particularly in tweets, is an entire area of computational inquiry, due to the problems that sarcasm and irony create for automatic sentiment analysis (Khattri, Joshi, Bhattacharyya, & Carman, 2015).[2] Some computational studies have used tweets marked *#sarcasm* as training data to improve sarcasm identification (Davidov, Tsur, & Rappoport, 2010; González-Ibánez, Muresan, & Wacholder, 2011; Riloff et al., 2013). For instance, Kunneman et al. (2015) collected a large corpus of tweets featuring the hashtags *#sarcasm*, *#not*, *#irony*, and *#cynicism*. This study found that posts containing these kinds of tags tended to include fewer additional communicative features for signalling sarcasm such as exclamations and intensifiers. In these posts, hashtags appeared to function as a 'digital extralinguistic equivalent' to paralinguistic expressions for conveying sarcasm seen in face-to-face interaction (Kunneman et al., 2015). Thus hashtags appear a promising resource for understanding humour, of the kind we will explore in this chapter in relation to *#AlternativeFacts*.

As I flagged in Chapter 1, we know from research into gossip that criticizing someone can be a highly aligning activity (Bosson et al., 2006; Dunbar, 2004; Eggins & Slade, 1997/2005), and is closely related to the establishment of in-group/out-group boundaries (Gagnon & Bourhis, 1996; Jaworski & Coupland, 2005; Tajfel, 1970; Wert & Salovey, 2004). When the negative assessment is humorous or witty, this appears to augment affiliation. In the case where the humour involves a bond that the participants cannot share, it creates what Knight (2010b, p. 46) refers to as a semiotic 'wrinkle' that allows meanings that are too controversial to be laughed off. When the humour involves a bond that is targeted in direct opposition to something ('laughing at' rather than 'laughing off'), it assists the interactants in their rallying around negative attitude.

'Alternative facts'

This chapter explores how affiliation is enacted in public censure and mockery of the discourse of Kellyanne Conway, an adviser to US president Donald Trump. The focus is on social media response to her use of phrase 'alternative facts' in an interview with Chuck Todd during a broadcast of *Meet the Press* on 22 January 2017. The interview featured the exchange below, in which Conway defended false claims made by the White House press secretary, Sean Spicer, regarding the size of the crowd that attended Donald Trump's presidential inauguration. Spicer, as we saw in Chapter 5, had claimed that it 'was the largest audience to ever witness an inauguration. Period.'. This statement was itself widely lampooned, resulting in the #SeanSpicerSays meme (amongst others). In her exchange with Todd, Conway attempted to avoid answering the question of why Spicer chose to make these claims in his very first White House press conference:

Chuck Todd: = You did not answer =

Kellyanne Conway: = Yes I did. =

Chuck Todd: the question of why the president asked the White House press secretary to come out in front of the podium for the first time and utter a falsehood. Why did he do that? It undermines the credibility of the entire White House press office

Kellyanne Conway: = No it doesn't. Don't be so- =

Chuck Todd: = on day one.=

Kellyanne Conway: Don't be so overly dramatic about it, Chuck. What it - You're saying it's a falsehood. And they're giving Sean Spicer, our press secretary, gave **alternative facts** to that. But the point = remains that there's–

Chuck Todd: = Wait a minute, alternative facts? = **Alternative facts**. Four of the five facts he uttered, = the one thing he got right was =

Kellyanne Conway: = hey, Chuck, why- Hey Chuck- =

Chuck Todd: Zeke Miller. Four of the five facts he uttered were just not true. Look, **alternative facts** are not facts. They're falsehoods.

The phrasing 'alternative facts to that' in Conway's exchange above is a nominal group (Figure 8.1). Within this nominal group 'alternative' functions as a classifier of 'facts'. 'Alternative' is not always attitudinally loaded, in the sense that it may merely mean, for instance, one choice in relation to another choice. However, when used as a classifier for 'fact' it takes on an attitudinal meaning. Conway's phrase is an attempt to assert legitimacy. It involves an unusual coupling that disrupts the typical fact–not-fact binary by implying that there are either different types of facts, or that facts are gradable. This prompts the challenge by the interviewer ('Wait a minute, alternative facts?'). As a disturbance in the kind of coupling pattern that might be expected from a political adviser, the statement was open to ridicule. As Zhao (2011, p. 145) has noted, '[s]ince a given culture is inclined towards a stable set of coupling patterns, the disruption of these patterns can often create comical, satiric, artistic or other effects'.

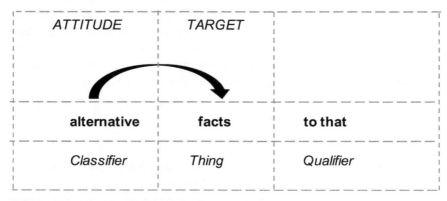

FIGURE 8.1 *Nominal group and Appraisal analysis of 'alternative facts to that'.*

Given the prosody of positive evaluation that Conway targets at Spicer, Trump, and the Trump administration in her television interviews, it can be argued that 'alternative' invokes positive appreciation of the type 'valuation' (i.e. answering the question, 'is this worthwhile?'). This in turn can be seen as a token of positive veracity, a choice in the judgement system. This dual meaning is coded as *t*-veracity throughout this chapter (see the *t*- notation introduced in the previous chapter). The choice of Classifier asserts that Spicer's propositions are a valid alternative to 'that' (the propositions about crowd size made by the media and experts).

The phrase 'alternative facts' was swiftly parodied across social media, adding to an outpouring of criticism regarding what has been characterized as a 'post-truth' climate in which facts and experts are not respected (see, for example, discourse about *#brexit* (Zappavigna, in press-b)). Conway's statement was also the focus of many news reports with titles such as:

"Kellyanne Conway says Donald Trump's team has **'alternative facts.'** Which pretty much says it all." [Aaron Blake, 22/1/17, Washington Post]

"White House Pushes **Alternative Facts**. Here Are the Real Ones". [Nicholas Fandos, 22/1/17, The New York Times]

"Trump aides defend inflated inauguration figures as **'alternative facts'**" [Brian Bennett, 22/1/17, Los Angeles Times]

"Even rightwing sites call out Trump administration over **'alternative facts'**". [Adam Gabbatt, 23/1/17, The Guardian]

"**'Alternative Facts'**: The Needless Lies of the Trump Administration". [Graham, David, 22/1/17, The Atlantic]

A Wikipedia page for the phrase arose (https://en.wikipedia.org/wiki/Alternative_facts). There was a purportedly related spike in sales of George Orwell's dystopian novel *Nineteen Eighty Four*. Alternative facts were likened to Orwell's notion of 'newspeak', described in his novel as a form of language designed to 'narrow the range of thought' (Orwell, 1949/1987, p. 124). It was also referred to as a form of 'disinformation' (from the Russian term дезинформация (*dezinformatsiya*) for state-sanctioned false information). This is discourse aimed at fuelling confusion and mistrust, and associated with propaganda (see also *#PropagandaBarbie* in the glossary).

#AlternativeFacts

Unsurprisingly, Conway's phrase spawned the hashtag *#AlternativeFacts*, alongside *#SpicerFacts* and *#SeanSpicerSays,* in reference to the position she was defending. The tag was typically appended to a ridiculous proposition, for example:

Slaves were immigrants. **#alternativefacts**

Hey kids! If you get in trouble or caught doing something bad, just scream #fakenews or **#alternativefacts** and it goes away! Thx Merica!

FIGURE 8.2 *An example of a widely shared image appearing with the #alternativefacts tag.*

This is a red chair.**#alternativefacts** @KellyannePolls
@realDonaldTrump *[embedded image of a blue chair]*

Black is white **#alternativefacts** #TrumpRally #cartoon
*[image of a cartoon featuring Trump pointing at a
black square]*

These posts rely on contextually abduced intra-vocalization (see Chapter 5) since there is no projection, and we have to abduce, using contextual knowledge, that Conway is the source of the phrase in the hashtag.

Images involving visual jokes featuring discordant visual couplings were also tagged *#Alternativefacts*, for instance Figure 8.2 was a widely shared example. This image features the cover of a 'Little Golden Book', a popular children's book series that began in 1940 that has kept the same distinctive appearance throughout its popularity during the twentieth century. The remixed cover includes retro images that are incorrectly labelled, e.g. the picture of the dog is labelled 'cat'.

Affiliation through censure and ridicule

If we read *#AlternativeFacts* posts as replies to Conway's gaffe, we can interpret them as managing the initial coupling by *opposing* it. We need to augment the affiliation network introduced in the previous chapter to include a choice between *censure* and *ridicule* in the oppose system (Figure 8.3).

Figure 8.3 indicates that the distinction between censure and ridicule is essentially a choice between criticizing a stance or imitating it, though imitation is likely not the only means of realizing ridicule. Censure involves critiquing a position, for example, explicitly recasting 'alternative facts' as 'lies':

We need to stop normalizing fake news, conspiracy theories,
#alternativefacts and call them what they are **lies**

@MELANIAJTRUMP @WashTimes last month Trump told Jill
stein there were no fraudulent votes **#alternativefacts**
are **lies.**

The war on National Parks is a conservative war
against Nature. Stop using **#alternativefacts**. They are
lies. Say so. https://t.co/W3DWIpIVsL

Not **#alternativefacts** not #falsehoods ... **LIES.** They are
LIES. Just call them what they are. https://t.co/Mvp4vPBRWX

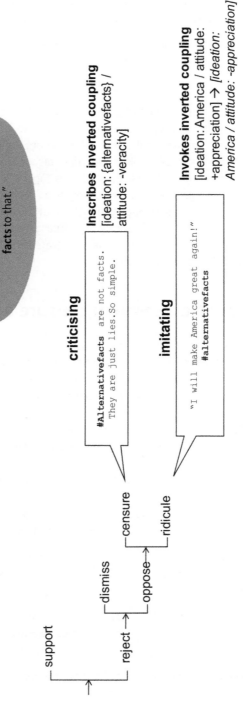

FIGURE 8.3 *Censure and ridicule as dimensions of affiliation.*

Compare these examples to imitation where the user performs an opposing position (that Trump will make America great again) as if it were their own for the purposes of mockery:

```
Trump is making America great again quicker than you
can blink! #alternativefacts 👀
```

```
RT @User: So far, @realDonaldTrump is really making
#America great again! #alternativefacts #ResistTrump
```

```
Making America great again! Say Thank you! 2 @
realDonaldTrump's #alternativefacts
```

```
#alternativefacts #altfacts @realDonaldTrump Donald
Trump will make America Great Again.
```

These tweets are sarcastic in the sense that they reverse the meaning construed in the body of the post: we are to interpret them as stating that Trump will not make America great again. Recall how in Chapter 5 we noted the potential that social media channels offer for presenting other voices as the voice of the primary user (a 'my voice/voices' intersubjectivity) for various rhetorical ends. This is an example of this relation employed in the service of mockery.

Returning to the system network for exploring affiliation, censure involves tabling an opposing coupling that directly negatively reappraises the initial coupling. This can be achieved by inscribing an inverted coupling in which the polarity of the attitude is reversed. For example, in the following example the coupling [ideation: facts/attitude: +veracity] is recoupled as [ideation: (alternativefacts)[3]/attitude: -veracity]:

```
#alternativefacts are lies
```

```
[ideation: facts/attitude: +veracity] → [ideation:
(alternativefacts)/attitude: -veracity]
```

The reader is reminded that veracity (a choice in the judgement system) is invoked via valuation (a choice in the appreciation system) in all the examples considered in this chapter and for the sake of simplicity I will refer to +veracity without attending the invocation hereon. The recoupling is more easily represented using the yin-yang diagrams introduced in Chapter 6 (Figure 8.4).

In contrast to censure, ridicule *invokes* an inverted coupling by repeating (imitating) the initial coupling articulated by the quoted voice, for example:

```
'I will make America great again' #alternativefacts
```

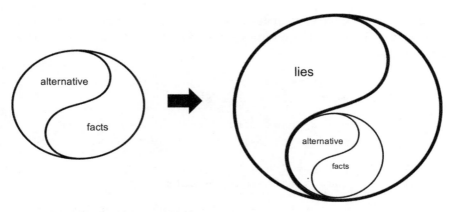

FIGURE 8.4 *Alternative facts are lies.*

This is an example of imitation used for mockery, that is, performing a stance which is the reverse of the intended meaning for the purposes of satirical humour. The post involves two couplings: [ideation: America/attitude: +appreciation (general[4])] and [ideation: fact/attitude: +veracity]. Both of these couplings are inverted as [ideation: America/attitude: -appreciation] and [ideation: fact/attitude: -veracity], a process that I refer to as double inversion (Figure 8.5).

In double inversion the hashtag functions as a play frame to indicate the humorously inverted meaning. The inversion is 'double' in the sense that the

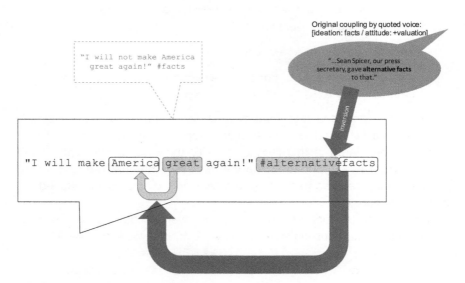

FIGURE 8.5 *An example of double inversion used for ridicule.*

hashtag inverts Conway's original coupling which, in turn, as metadiscourse, inverts the coupling in the body of the post (as shown in Figure 8.5). Other examples of the same pattern are shown below:

> donald trump is going to make america great again
> **#alternativefacts**

> Make America Great Again - President Trump
> **#AlternativeFacts** #FakeNews #ConfuseTheIdiots

> Donald Trump will make America great again
> **#alternativefacts**

> Make America Great Again! #nastyhombre
> **#alternativefacts** @User [URL]

> Once we get rid of environmental regulations, America will be great again! **#alternativefacts** *[image of lead in tap water]*

Having outlined the distinction to be made between censuring and ridiculing, the sections which follow consider in more detail the types of meanings that can be made, and the types of bonds that are shared via these two affiliation strategies.

Bonding by censuring

Censure is a more direct opposition strategy than ridicule and involves explicitly opposing a coupling. In terms of *#AlternativeFacts*, censure was most often achieved by recoupling (as defined in Chapter 6). The following are examples of the pattern, summarized earlier in Figure 8.4, which recasts 'alternative facts' explicitly as 'lies':

> We need to stop normalizing fake news, conspiracy theories, #alternativefacts and call them what they are **lies**

> @MELANIAJTRUMP @WashTimes last month Trump told Jill stein there were no fraudulent votes #alternativefacts are **lies.**

> The war on National Parks is a conservative war against Nature. Stop using #alternativefacts. They are **lies.** Say so. https://t.co/W3DWIpIVsL

Not #alternativefacts not #falsehoods ... **LIES.** They
are **LIES.** Just call them what they are. https://t.co/
Mvp4vPBRWX

@POTUS @KellyannePolls stop with #alternativefacts
call things as they are, **lies** #tellthetruth #stoplying
#dishonestdonald

'Lie after lie after lie'. You are my go to source
for #FakeNews (lies) & #AlternativeFacts (also **lies**)!
#FakePOTUS

In these examples, Conway's [ideation: facts/attitude: +veracity] is recoupled
as [ideation: alternativefacts (original coupling)/attitude: -veracity]. The region of
attitudinal meaning at stake is negative judgement of social sanction in terms
of veracity (where a person or behaviour is appraised). Another strategy for
making this attitudinal meaning prominent was to realize the negative veracity
as a hashtag in its own right (in tandem with the #alternativefacts tag):

@User1 @User2 @User3 @User4 @User5 @User6 @User7 Wow -
knew she **#lied** but come on #alternativefacts

If #SeanSpicer has a shred of integrity He should
#TellThe**Truth** & #SpicerResign #AlternativeFacts
#Trump**Lies** #Delusional **#Liar** #Propaganda

@POTUS @KellyannePolls stop with #alternativefacts
call things as they are, lies #tellthe**truth** #stop**lying**
#**dishonest**donald

Grammaticalized recoupling was also possible inside the hashtag. For example,
tags such as *#alternativefactsarelies* and *#alternativefactsarefalsehoods*
echoed the opposing coupling that the interviewer Chuck Todd himself made
in the original interview ('alternative facts are falsehoods'), for example:

Why do you continue to have a proven liar kellyanne on
CNN? U are ruining ur own reputation by having her on
#ALTERNATIVEFACTSARELIES

Look up narcissistic. There you'll find a
picture of our president, @realDonaldTrump.
#alternativefactsareLIES #ridiculousfalseclaim

@thedailybeast @KellyannePolls you seriously can't fix
the stupid that is you 😏 **#alternativefactsarelies**
#Trumprussia #SpecialProsecutor

> Reporters Just Demanded The Media Stop Interviewing Paid
> **Liar** Kellyanne Conway – [URL] #AlternativeFactsAre**Lies**

Censure thus seems to rely heavily upon opposing via 'substitution', whereby one coupling is replaced by another, though further research is needed to determine whether other coupling patterns are possible.

In terms of the bonds being shared and rejected, the examples presented in this section reject a 'falsity' bond and share a 'truthfulness' bond. This is manifest in discourse as the coupling [ideation: news/attitude: +veracity] being replaced with [ideation: news/attitude: -veracity] (Table 8.1). Other hashtags (that co-occurred with *#AlternativeFacts*) supporting this kind of bonding with included *#fakenews*, *#falsenews*, *#RealFacts*, *#ActualFacts*, *#TrueFacts*, *#disinformation*, *#misinformation*, *#lies*, *#nottrue*, *#falsehoods*, *#upsidedown*, *#posttruth*, and *#bullshit*:

> Spicer and Conway are some **#posttruth** havin,
> **#alternativefacts** believin, **#bullshit** peddlers.
> They're called **#lies** and #misinformation.

> The correct terms are #disinformation and #propaganda
> … not **#fakenews** and #alternativefacts. We don't need
> new labels for old strategies.

> #alternativefacts aren't #facts they're **#falsehoods**

> Nothing is going Nicely @realdonaldtrump, **#FalseNews**,
> #AlternativeFacts, just simply **#NotTrue**! @cnn

> Trump's **#UpsideDown** world of #alternativefacts, or
> what I call lies #Resist

> @User I feel like some in the current administration
> would spout this as **#realfacts** and not #alternativefacts

> @Salon More #alternativefacts from @KellyannePolls.
> According to **#Actualfacts**, only 60% of Americans
> dislike Trump.

> These are NOT #alternativefacts these are **#truefacts**
> @realDonaldTrump *[embedded tweet about the size of
> Obama's inauguration and the women's march]*

TABLE 8.1 Bonds shared or rejected via censure

	Text	Coupling	Bond (rejected or shared)
Original statement	Sean Spicer, our press secretary, gave **alternative**[a] facts to that	[a] [ideation: news/ attitude: +veracity]	**'truthfulness'**
Reaction 1	@User so sorry, we only deal in REAL news[a], not #alternativefacts[a] & #fakenews[a]	[a] [ideation: news/ attitude: +veracity] [b] [ideation: facts/ attitude: -veracity] [c] [ideation: news/ attitude: -veracity]	'falsity' **'truthfulness'**
Reaction 2	@POTUS @ KellyannePolls stop with #**alternative**facts [a] call things as they are, **lies** [b] #tellthetruth [c] #stop**lying** [d] #**dishones**tdonald [e]	[a] [ideation: she lie/ attitude: -veracity] [b] [ideation: facts/ attitude: -veracity] [c] [ideation: tell/ attitude: +veracity] [d] [ideation: Trump/ attitude: -veracity] [e] [ideation: Trump/ attitude: -veracity]	'falsity' **'truthfulness'**
Reaction 3	Reporters Just Demanded The Media Stop Interviewing Paid **Liar** [a] Kellyanne Conway – [URL] #Alternative Facts**AreLies** [b]	[a] [ideation: Kellyanne Conway/ attitude: -veracity] [b] [ideation: alternativefacts/ attitude: -veracity]	'falsity' **'truthfulness'**

Bonding by ridiculing

The examples of censure considered in the previous section are very obvious instances where a bond incommensurate with a particular user's values is rejected. A similar kind of rejection can be achieved less directly via humorous ridicule in the form of mockery via imitation. This section considers examples where *#AlternativeFacts* is used to reject a 'falsity' bond by imitating Conway's original coupling in her interview with Todd and 'flipping' the meaning from this original context. Consider, for example, the following posts:

This isn't a beer; it's an alternative kale smoothie. #AlternativeFacts

The pizza, cake, wings, and sweet potato fries I ate yesterday are alternative healthy #alternativefacts

The food groups: Coffee, cake, waffles, and ice-cream. #alternativefacts

Table 8.2 provides a coupling analysis of these posts, showing how the 'falsity' bond is rejected and a 'truthfulness' bond is shared. This 'truthfulness' bond is proposed as an opposing bond to that offered by Conway in her original 'alternative facts' comment. These examples

TABLE 8.2 Bonds shared or rejected via ridicule

	Text	Coupling	Bond (rejected or shared)
Original statement	Sean Spicer, our press secretary, gave **alternative** [a] facts to that.	[a] [ideation: facts/ attitude: +t-veracity]	**'truthfulness'**
Reaction 1	This isn't a **beer** [a]; it's an **alternative kale smoothie** [b]. **#Alternative**Facts [c]	[a] [ideation: it (beer)/ attitude: ∀-quality (afforded by ideation *beer*)]] [b] [ideation: it/attitude: ∀+quality (afforded by ideation *Kale smoothie*)]] [c][ideation: facts/ attitude: -t-veracity]	'falsity' **'truthfulness'**
Reaction 2	The pizza, cake, wings, and sweet potato fries I ate yesterday are **alternative healthy** [a] #**alternative**facts [b]	[a] [ideation: pizza, cake, wings and sweet potato fries/ attitude: ∀+quality] [b][ideation: facts/ attitude: -t-veracity]	'falsity' **'truthfulness'**
Reaction 3	Candy is totally **good for you** [a]. #**alternative** facts [b]	[a] [ideation: candy/ attitude: ∀ +quality] [b][ideation: fact/ attitude: -t-veracity]	'falsity' **'truthfulness'**

include references to food and display a moralizing discourse (invoked via appreciation) that is characteristic of modern discourse about food, and which groups foods into 'good' or 'bad/naughty' categories. The humour in part relies on how this is a summoning of a configuration of values from another context (i.e. outside politics). Indeed incongruity has been commonly noted to have an important function in humour, and 'there have been several widely known explanations that have attributed humour to an incongruous conflict between two scenarios, scripts, schemas, frames, or whatever one chooses to call the ways humans have of categorizing chunks of experience' (Chafe, 2007, p. 147).

The incongruity is, however, not only at the level of the field of experience but also at the level of irreconcilable bonds realized as incommensurate couplings. Conway's 'truthfulness' bond, in the examples shown in Table 8.2, is opposed by her coupling being inverted via the hashtag. As I noted in the section 'Affiliation through censure and ridicule', this is a double inversion. For example, the coupling [ideation: candy/ attitude: ∀+social sanction (invoked via appreciation))]] is inverted (indicated by the ∀ symbol) and we interpret the meaning as 'Candy is totally not good for you'. Similarly, Conway's use of 'alternative' to mean 'legitimate' is inverted and we interpret the tag as meaning 'false facts'. In this way, the tag is an enactment of humorous inversion at the same time as signalling the play frame that tells us the post is humorous. As one user quipped:

`'We hold these #alternativefacts to be self-evident' just doesn't have quite the same ring …`

Fake news bond complex

This chapter has shown how hashtags, by referencing or quoting snippets of discourse, can be used as a resource to censure or ridicule a political voice. To put it in folk terms, a hashtag can be employed to 'use someone's own words against them'. On one level, what is at stake is moral control. #AlternativeFacts involves competing discourses about what is fake and what is real; what is true and what is false; what is authentic and what is contrived; and what is, by implication, fundamentally virtuous or immoral. On another level, what is at stake is a 'bond complex' involving a configuration of related 'truthfulness' bonds (realized as texts incorporating tags such as *#AlternativeFacts, #PostTruth, #FakeNews*, and *#AlternativeFactsAreLies*) (Figure 8.6). By the term 'bond complex' I mean clusters of 'shared values at ever higher levels of abstraction' (Martin, Zappavigna, Dwyer, & Cleirigh, 2013, p. 490). These clusters can be said to characterize particular personae, groups, communities, and, ultimately, cultures.

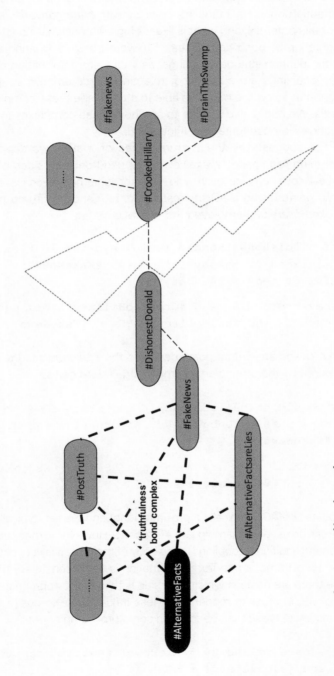

FIGURE 8.6 *Configurations of bond complexes.*

The 'falsity'/'truthfulness' opposition is just one small pair of bonds amongst many other potential bonds. Hashtags that co-occur with *#AlternativeFacts* give us a glimpse of this potential, and what is likely a high-dimensional, constantly shifting configuration of bond complexes. If it were possible to annotate a large dataset for ideation-attitude couplings, as well as for information about whether those couplings are supporting, rejecting, or deferring a coupling proposed by another voice, we might be able to start to see these complexes of related bonds. We might also be able to see how these complexes in turn cluster into higher-order configurations (Figure 8.6).

As Figure 8.6 suggests by the two instances of *#fakenews* depicted, and by the lightning rod shape, *#FakeNews* was used on both sides of the polarized political spectrum, as each side vied for legitimacy. For instance, both anti-Trump posts (using a *#DishonestDonald* tag) and pro-Trump posts (using a *#CrookedHillary* tag) employed the *#FakeNews* tag:

```
Filthy rich #dishonestDonald Trump enjoying in Florida
wasting millions of taxpayers' money. #FakeNews
Channel Fox is okay with that.

All you have to do is read #CrookedHillary's Wikipedia
page & you know the whole site is BS 🙄 #FakeNews
```

Similarly, both pro- and anti-Trump posts deployed the *#fakenews* tag to cast the media favoured by the other side as propaganda (*state news*):

```
Fox News should be called what it is: State News. Your
source for—> Unfair. Unbalanced. Alternative Facts.
#Resist #fakenews

@CNN is comical, they are more than "State News" they
are paid to run #Fakenews #MAGA
```

In the above posts, *#MAGA* (typically a pro-Trump tag) and *#resist* (typically an anti-Trump tag) can be used to disambiguate *#fakenews*. However, in many posts, without considering additional couplings in the body of the post, it is very difficult to tell whether a pro-Trump or anti-Trump orientation is being construed. This is in part because there are posts in which each side is trying to re-appropriate the other side's slogans in order to render them less influential or to co-opt their influence. For instance, *#resist* can be found in some pro-Trump tweets:

```
More of garbage piling by #FakeNews! #Resist frenzied
#Lefties and #globalists! #MAGA
```

It is also because, at their most extreme ends, political discourse of both the right and the left can look quite similar in terms of coupling patterns.

Analysing affiliation in ambient environments is no small task. Analysing humour is also notoriously difficult. This chapter has deliberately chosen some of the less complicated instances of each as a place to begin. As we saw in Chapter 5, the relations between perspectives that are made possible in social media are very complex, inflecting the strategies personae use to commune – Bahktin's dream perhaps!

9

#TinyTrump: Intermodal Coupling and Visual Hashtag Memes

Tagging images

Up until this point we have predominately been concerned with tagging in relation to the written verbiage of social media posts. However, since social media texts are multimodal, image tagging, amongst other forms of multimedia tagging, is also highly relevant. While research into social media communication has tended to focus on language, visual meaning-making is crucial given the multimodal nature of social media environments, and the tendency of users to embedded images, animations, and video into their texts (Adami & Jewitt, 2016). Hashtags enter into relationship with these forms of media, as well as verbiage. Just as written social media texts involve internal and external relations, of the kind we have surveyed across the previous chapters, 'the social media image directs our attention from the inside toward the outside: toward its potential positioning in relation to other images with the same tags across spatial and temporal boundaries' (Hochman, 2014, p. 5).

Research into hashtags as an image tagging resource is still in its infancy. Some work has considered how these tags function in particular domains, for instance, Instagram images[1] about birth and death tagged *#ultrasound/#funeral* (Gibbs et al., 2015; Highfield & Leaver, 2016; Meese, Gibbs, & Kohn, 2015), and images dealing with the representation of the self, tagged *#selfie* (Wendt, 2014). There has been an interest in how tags are used to manage the temporality of the social stream, in terms of the relation between taking an image and posting it online (Veszelszki, 2016). Tags such as *#latergram*, *#latepost*, and *#tbt* (Throw Back Thursday), that explicitly indicate that the time of posting and the time of image production are divergent, have emerged as a result of the social value assigned to posting in 'real-time' (Highfield & Leaver, 2016). Some computational work has considered the descriptive power of Instagram hashtags to indicate the content of an image, with a view to using this information as part of training datasets for automatic image annotation (Giannoulakis & Tsapatsoulis). Within different disciplinary areas, there has also been interest in the insights that can be gained from studying images collected via particular hashtags, for example, tags such as *#zikavirus* (Fung et al., 2017), *#pharmacist* (Hindman, Bukowitz, Reed, & Mattingly Ii, 2017), *#selfharm* (Moreno, Ton, Selkie, & Evans, 2016) in the medical domain, and tags such as *#sharingcph* (Guerrero, Møller, Olafsson, & Snizek, 2016) in urban planning.

Matley (in press), in one of the first linguistic studies of image tagging, has explored how hashtags can function as a metacomment involved in image-text relations, in particular text-image incongruity. This study focused on the hashtags *#fitness, #brag,* and *#humblebrag,*[2] as used on the image sharing service Instagram. When appended to an image, #humblebrag acted as a face aggravating pragmatic metareference that foregrounds the false modesty construed in the post. Matley notes the self-conscious quality of this type of tagging, where the hashtag, as an apparent irony marker, 'indicates knowingness of and a level of reflexivity on the self-praising speech act' (Matley, in press, p. 19).

This chapter explores a form of image tagging where users add hashtags to a social media image to indicate that is it part of collective practice: generation of internet memes (explained in the following section). Drawing on the concept of coupling from Chapter 6, it explores intermodal couplings between these images, their captions, and tags. We will focus on the 'Tiny Trump' meme, often tagged *#TinyTrump*, a visual meme featuring Trump in miniature. The chapter begins by describing some of the main types of memes: hashtag memes, phrasal template memes, and image macros. It then investigates, using the system of graduation from the Appraisal framework, the discourse about size that is central to the *#TinyTrump* meme and related memes such as *#TinyHands*. The second part of the chapter introduces Zhao's (2011) model for interpreting intermodal coupling in terms of ideational meaning, and extends this to explore some of the interpersonal meanings made in the image-verbiage-tag relations observable in *#TinyTrump* tweets and Instagram posts.

Tiny Trump

The image manipulation applied in the *#TinyTrump* meme involves reducing the size of Donald Trump as a visual participant in relation to the other visual participants in the image. Alternatively, it involves appending Trump's head to the body of a child. Memes that involve image manipulation are sometimes termed 'Photoshop memes' (after the image editing software), and include images that insert visual participants from different texts into an image, or, for instance, alter the face in an image to change the identity of the visual participant. There are two types of images that are typically tagged #TinyTrump: images featuring Trump in miniature (Figure 9.1) and images where Trump appears as a child at normal size (Figure 9.2).

The first instance of miniature Trump photos of this kind was posted to Reddit[3] by user, theLAZYmd, on 16 February 2017 with the accompanying text 'I made Trump 2 ft tall. It makes him look cute next to the secret service' (Figure 9.1). Reddit is a popular source of memes, and, along with the infamous site 4Chan, has been described as manifesting a 'logic of lulz' that celebrates 'the anguish of the laughed at victim' (Milner, 2013a; Phillips, 2015, p. 27). Another popular iteration of the meme deriving from this site was Figure 9.2 posted by user Polymathyx on 17 February with accompanying text 'My new favorite meme'.

Figure 9.2 was followed by many images posted to Reddit, and subsequently to social media services such as Twitter and Instagram, with the hashtag #TinyTrump, mocking Trump by presenting him as a tempestuous child (Figure 9.3). These images relate to a history of discourse mocking Trump's 'small child' temperament and small hands since the 1980s. The visual choice can be traced back to early lampooning of Trump in Spy magazine, a monthly New York satirical magazine. The visual motif of portraying Trump as an infant can be found, for example, on the August 1990 cover. This edition featured an image of a child in a staged tantrum pose, wearing a suit jacket with a

FIGURE 9.1 *A tiny Trump image posted to Reddit by theLAZYmd.*

FIGURE 9.2 *A tiny Trump image posted to Reddit by Polymathyx.*

FIGURE 9.3 *Examples of* **Tiny Trump** *images depicting Trump having a tantrum.*

cut-out of Trump's head superimposed on the infant body. It included the accompanying text, 'WA-A-A-A-H! Little Donald Unhappy at Last' (Figure 9.4). The facial expression in the Trump tantrum image, featuring Trump's open mouth, is very similar to those repeated in 'Tiny Trump' from Reddit, and which appeared online tagged *#TinyTrump*.

Internet memes

Hashtags have been noted as a vehicle aiding in the proliferation of memes through social media (Leavitt, 2013): for instance, memes incorporating hashtags were used to facilitate the 'polyvocal public conversation' that occurred during the Occupy Wall Street Movement[4] (Milner, 2013b, p. 2388). A 'meme' is a folk term employed by internet users to label the 'novel online phenomenon' whereby texts are mimicked, modified, and shared, proliferating through online social networks[5] (Dynel, 2016, p. 662). More broadly, it can be used to refer to a range of faddish or 'catchy' multimodal phenomena such as 'popular tunes, catchphrases, clothing fashions, architectural styles, ways of doing things, icons, jingles' etcetera (Knobel & Lankshear, 2007, p. 199). Types of memes that have been identified include objects (e.g. Trump's MAGA

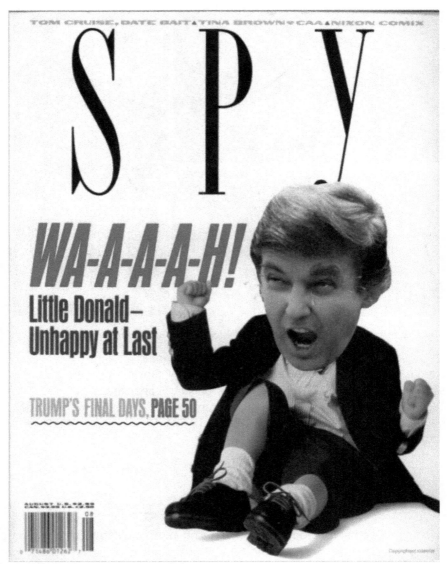

FIGURE 9.4 *Donald Trump on the cover of the August 1990 issue of* Spy *magazine.*

cap), specific characters (e.g. Trump), generic characters (e.g. a politician), actions (e.g. dance movements), and phrases (e.g. *haters gonna hate*) (Segev, Nissenbaum, Stolero, & Shifman, 2015). For example, *#AlternativeFacts*, discussed in the previous chapter, is an example of a phrase meme realized as a hashtag meme.

The term 'meme' was originally coined by Dawkins (1989/2006) to capture the idea that cultural units function in a manner analogous to genes. According to this perspective, memes proliferate through mimicry 'by leaping from brain to brain via a process which, in the broad sense, can be called imitation' (Dawkins, 1989/2006, p. 192). However, if we adopt a social semiotic perspective on communication, we might question whether semiosis can be reduced to imitation, and suggest instead that imitation is but one of the vast repertoire of choices available to humans as they interact and cultures evolve. Some scholars have suggested that the meme is an inferior concept to the sign:

> one does not have to be particularly well versed in semiotics to receive the impression that we have been shown an old hat. The meme, whatever its eventual merits and demerits, is no new thing but the old semiotic idea of sign, in somewhat new clothing, and reintroduced with some bombast. (Kilpinen, 2008, p. 220)

The concept of a meme has also been criticized for minimizing the role of human agency and choice (Shifman, 2012). Research has shown that participation in a meme is influenced by factors such as 'technical limitations (features and affordances), entrenched social behaviors, and inclusion in (or exclusion from) a shared understanding of the meme' (Leavitt, 2013, p. 145).

When applied in internet studies, the concept of a meme has been used to broadly describe 'units of popular culture that are circulated, imitated, and transformed by individual Internet users, creating a shared cultural experience in the process' (Shifman, 2013a, p. 367). Online memes are usually humorous texts, typically requiring knowledge of a particular context to appreciate the witty intertextual references made. They often transform something from this original context and apply it to a new context. This typically involves modifying a source text by substituting items into a template (e.g. a phrasal template). It can also be achieved by forms of repackaging such as mimicry, or by remixing via digital multimedia manipulation (Hill, Monroy-Hernández, & Olson, 2010; Mitchell & Clarke, 2003; Shifman, 2014).

Memes have been thought to 'shape mindsets, forms of behaviour, and actions of social groups' (Shifman, 2013b, p. 18). Perhaps one of the most powerful dimensions by which they do this is via the ability to take something from one context and use it to make a comment on something from a very different context (often to both humorous and insightful effect). For example, a phrase originally produced on a TV show might be used to comment on a political issue. For instance, the overlord meme (introduced in Chapter 5), originating from the animated TV series *The Simpsons*, has an ongoing history of being used to comment on whatever particular issue or event is currently being reported in the media. An example is the following post which criticizes Trump's ties with Russia, mocks his fake tan, and makes reference to the controversy surrounding his nomination of a US Supreme Court justice:

> Well, **I for one, welcome** our tangerine **overlord** and look forward to his appointment of Vladimir Putin to the Supreme Court.

The use of this meme to mock Trump's suspected association with Russian leader Vladimir Putin is also a repeating pattern:

> I for one would like to welcome comrade **Putin** and our luxurious Russian overlords. *[embedded tweet by Politico: Putin on Trump: 'Nobody believed he would win except for us' [link]]*

> @realDonaldTrump I for one welcome our new #ShadowPresident **Vladimir Putin** #InaugurationDay

> I for one would like to welcome our new overlord! Hail **putin**!

> I, for one, welcome my new **Putin** overlord.

> I for one welcome our Russian overlords! **Putin** is great! Bigly so!

This ability to condense cultural references in a humorous and biting way is part of the appeal of memes, as we will see throughout this chapter. The overlord meme can also be invoked through use of a hashtag, *#IForOneWelcome*, though this appears to mostly occur in relation to news stories about robotics, and seems to be less able to move across contexts:

> Siemens has an army of spider robots that work as a team to complete tasks [URL] via #User **#IForOneWelcome**

> This isn't ominous at all … **#Iforonewelcome** *[embedded news article about a Chinese world record in which 1007 robots danced together in unison]*

> I basically can't shut up about my roomba, apparently **#iforonewelcome** @irobot [URL] *[embedded video]*

Knobel and Lankshear (2007, p. 207) suggest that in order to discursively analyse online memes various dimensions need to be considered. These include the referential or ideational system involved in their meaning, the contextual or interpersonal systems involved in the social relations they enact, and the ideology or world views that they convey in terms of the values and beliefs that they construe. In terms of interpersonal meaning, memes are generally 'deployed for social bonding rather than for sharing information' (Zappavigna, 2012b, p. 101). In part this is because of the extent to which they enable humour and displays of wit, but also because of their ability to cut across different contexts in order to use, for example, a phrasal template structure originating from one context to comment on an issue from another context, as we saw above. Knobel and Lankshear (2007, p. 218) also propose taxonomizing memes in terms of their purpose, distinguishing between 'social commentary purposes', 'absurdist humour purposes', 'Otaku or manga fan purposes', and 'hoax purposes'. The *#TinyTrump* meme appears closest to the social commentary type where 'participating as a carrier in passing these kinds of memes on to others marks somebody as being a person of a particular kind who has particular desirable characteristics and worldviews within groups or social spaces committed to critiques of power and inequity' (Knobel & Lankshear, 2007, p. 219).

There has been some research interest, mostly in computational domains, regarding how memes proliferate and evolve in terms of temporal dynamics, for instance, by using models from mathematical epidemiology (Bauckhage, 2011). Wiggins and Bowers (2015, pp. 12–14) have suggested that internet memes progress from 'spreadable media' (media that virally proliferates without necessarily being modified (see Jenkins et al., 2013)), to 'emergent memes' (altered spreadable media that becomes a separate version), and then to 'meme' (emergent memes that have produced iterations involving some form of modification). Other work has suggested that, unlike simple contagions (like diseases), memes are complex contagions that 'are affected by social reinforcement and homophily', aside from a few viral memes which do appear to 'spread across many communities, like diseases' (Weng, Menczer, & Ahn, 2013, p. 2522).

There has been ongoing research interest into the different possible proliferation and diffusion patterns of different types of memes. For instance, highly topical memes, that are reactions to an event, are likely to be relatively short-lived, whereas other kinds of more general memes might endure over many years. For example, a hashtag meme such as *#Trumps7WordWireTapLeaks* makes a topical reference to a particular political moment (see Glossary) and will likely not endure beyond this context. A tag such as this is unlikely to endure as long as a more general meme such as *#TinyHands,* which mocks a dimension of Trump that is unlikely to change across his presidency.

Hashtag memes

The term 'hashtag meme' may broadly apply to any meme marked by a hashtag. The term has been popularly applied to hashtagged phrases, often in the form of complaints about some aspect of modern experience (e.g. *#IHateItWhen*). These memes may also take the form of any post where users contribute variations on a theme, in what is sometimes described as a 'massively multi-person conversation', where users post their thoughts 'prompted by the hashtag' (Huang et al., 2010, p. 1).[6] As well as personal observations, this might take the form of political comment. For example, a popular hashtag meme criticizing Trump's comments about women was the *#DressLikeAWoman* meme. This tag often co-occurred with *#ActualLivingScientist* as a means of making a comment about women's crucial role in science. These hashtags were typically accompanied by images of women working in their particular discipline. They were often images taken during fieldwork that required clothing which either challenged gender stereotypes, or simply wasn't a dress:

> I am Julie, an **#actuallivingscientist,** anthropologist/ social scientist working to save wildlife in the Americas **#DressLikeAWoman** @TheWCS *[image of a woman doing fieldwork]*

> My journey as #ecologist & #scientist has been long & varied but always interesting! I am an **#actuallivingscientist** and I **#DressLikeAWoman.** *[image of a woman doing fieldwork]*

> Getting ready for a week of dry spraying sample prep for XRD. I'm a scientist and I **#DressLikeAWoman** *[image of a woman in laboratory and image of samples]*

> Trump demands professional appearance at all times. **#dresslikeawoman** *[image of Steve Bannon in scruffy attire]*

> I study how Shetland formed over 3 billion years. I'm an **#actuallivingscientist** and I **#DressLikeAWoman** while I'm doing it. *[embedded image of a woman swinging a sledgehammer at a rock]*

For instance, the last example sampled above was accompanied by the image shown in Figure 9.5. In order to further understand the intermodal relations established between these tags and the images they accompany we need an

 Steph Walker ■ @StephWalker91 · Feb 4
I study how Shetland formed over 3 billion years. I'm an #actuallivingscientist
and I #DressLikeAWoman while I'm doing it.

♡ 138   ↻ 2.2K   ♡ 9.7K   ✉

FIGURE 9.5 *An example of a post using #DressLikeAWoman.*

analytical framework for interpreting the different ideational and interpersonal connections that are possible. This will be offered later in this chapter when we will explore intermodal coupling.

Phrasal template memes

An easily identifiable form of meme is the phrasal template meme which we introduced earlier: the overlord meme (Zappavigna, 2012a). These memes consist of a frame that stays relatively constant, into which users can insert their own (usually humorous) iterations (e.g. *I for one welcome, our [classifier] overlords*). Rintel (2013, p. 256) refers to this potential as the 'templatability' of memes, 'a product of the human capability to separate ideas into two levels – content and structure – and then contextually manipulate that relationship'. Another example is the Russian Reversal meme with the structure *In Soviet Russia [object] [plural verb] you!* (Zappavigna, 2012b, p. 105):

```
Trump, In Soviet Russia, Pussy grabs you!
#Trumps7WordWireTapLeaks
```

The above is an example of the Russian Reversal meme used in the service of a hashtag meme (*#Trumps7WordWireTapLeaks,* introduced earlier). It also involves an intertextual reference to Trump's comments about grabbing women by the genitals (see *#WomensMarch* in the hashtag glossary for the relevant transcript). Complex, overlapping intertextual references are a feature of meme discourse in part because a major rhetorical function of memes is to use phenomena from one domain to comment on issues in another. In addition, incongruity is also part of how humour operates in these memes (see Chapter 8 for more on incongruity in humour and ridicule).

A phrasal template used to mock Trump's tweeting practices involved appending 'sad!' to the end of a post. This meme imitates Trump's tendency to use this phrasing in his tweets when criticizing other people (in his characteristically bombastic manner). The meme applies the following structure:

[evaluatively loaded observation] Sad!

Examples of Trump's tweets conforming to this pattern include:

```
The so-called angry crowds in home districts of some
Republicans are actually, in numerous cases, planned
out by liberal activists. Sad!

FAKE NEWS media knowingly doesn't tell the truth. A
great danger to our country. The failing @nytimes has
become a joke. Likewise @CNN. Sad!

The Great State of Arizona, where I just had a
massive rally (amazing people), has a very weak and
ineffective Senator, Jeff Flake. Sad!

Certain Republicans who have lost to me would rather
save face by fighting me than see the U.S.Supreme Court
get proper appointments. Sad!
```

The media coverage this morning of the very average
Clinton speech and Convention is a joke. @CNN and the
little watched @Morning_Joe = **SAD!**

Examples of users adopting this phrasal template include:

And somehow, trump supporters will find a way to
justify why their King prefers self benefiting from
golfing at his resorts over them. **SAD!**

Republican women must like old white Republican men
telling them what they can and can't do with their own
bodies! **Sad!**

#SallyYates was acting attorney general for 10 days
and she did more for this country than Donald Trump
has done in over 100 days. **Sad!**

There seems to be no limit to the hatred Trump
and White Republican men have for women. **Sad!**
#IAmAPreexistingCondition #FridayFeeling

Reports are that Trump is now leaning toward pulling
the US out of the Paris Climate Agreement, Making
America the Greatest – Loser. **Sad!**

In many instances a hashtag was used, further marking the phrase as
something that is recognizable and shareable:

The failing Pakistan team thinks they defeated us but
if the runs taken away from us by the FAKE umpires
were counted we'd win BIGLY. **#Sad!**

When I see #Scandal trending, I don't know if it's
because of the TV series or because of the TV series
my country has become. **#sad**

Trump isn't throwing out the 1st pitch at Nationals
home opener because he can't. His hands are way too
small to grip a baseball. **#Sad!**

@realDonaldTrump doesn't know how congress works.
It's the art of compromise not bullying. And it is
inclusive not exclusive **#sad**

@SpeakerRyan @HouseGOP @SenateGOP You folks are
truly fools if you believe @realDonaldTrump rotten
manipulative tweets aren't personal. **#Sad**

This is similar to the charging of phrases such as *#Fakenews* and *#AlternativeFacts* (Chapters 6 and 8). The quoted phrasal snippet becomes a bonding icon, and users enjoy a sense of shared ridicule of both the original quoted voice and stances associated with that voice. In the above, users appear to be ridiculing Trump's tendency to criticize or blame people who do not agree with his actions or views.

Image macros

Memes occur within an increasingly visual online culture. Visual witticisms are readily shared as part of an ongoing history of internet jokes construed via 'visual collages assembled from phrases and pictures taken from popular media' (Kuipers, 2002, p. 451). This kind of sharing has been interpreted as a 'form of vernacular rhetoric that may function to build consciousness and interpellate subjects' (Duerringer, 2016, p. 9). Image macros are image-verbiage combinations where a humorous caption is superimposed onto the image. They may be produced by adding the same text to a range of images, or by appending different text to the same or similar images (Davison, 2012, p. 125). The popular term 'image macro' is believed to have derived from the 'Something Awful' forum in which a macro was a shortcut[7] that could be used to summon a default image. The caption text is often rendered in Impact, Arial, or Comic Sans font, with bold white lettering and black outlining (e.g. Figure 9.6), and featuring 'Internet orthographic alterations' (Rintel, 2013, p. 257). While these texts can be hand generated, they are often produced via a captioning tool (e.g. Meme Generator https://memegenerator.net) where the user enters text and the tool defines the position of the words in relation to the image.

Image macros seem to endure longer than other kinds of meme media (such as video) perhaps due to the ease with which iterations can be created via these captioning tools (Wiggins & Bowers, 2015). One of the first and most enduring forms of image macro is the LOLcat (Miltner, 2014). These image macros feature an image of a cat with an amusing caption, and are sometimes referred to as a 'cat macro'. Variations of Lolcat memes have endured for long periods of time due to their wide appeal and ability to be used to comment on topic across many different contexts (Zappavigna, 2012b). For instance, Figure 9.7 shows examples of Lolcat macros tagged *#Trump*.

The intermodal relation between the image and the caption can be quite complex in an image macro, and is related to the concept of 'voice' which we introduced in Chapter 5. In the case of cat macros, the caption text often appears

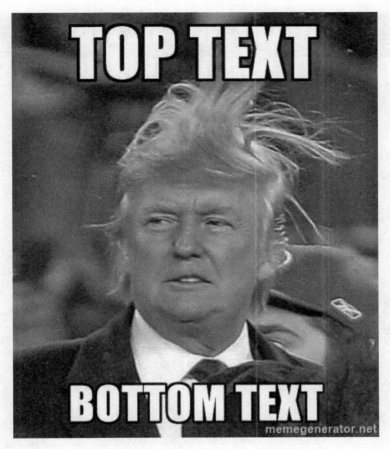

FIGURE 9.6 *An example of the default verbiage position for an image macro generated using a captioning tool.*

FIGURE 9.7 *Examples of cat macros tagged #Trump.*

FIGURE 9.8 *An example of a face substitution #TinyTrump image macro.*

to invoke a projection relation with the cat as the source of the caption (which can be read as quoted text). For instance, verbal projection is suggested in the images in Figure 9.7. The implication is that the cat is the visual participant saying, 'Hey hoomin, you're fired' (mocking Trump's catch phrase on the TV show *The Apprentice*[8]). This effect is also achieved through the use of LOLspeak, a form of language play associated with LOLcats (Gawne & Vaughan, 2011), further suggesting that the quoted voice is the voice of the visual participant (i.e. the cat).

An example of a Tiny Trump image macro is Figure 9.8. This image features Trump's phase superimposed on a child's body in the manner of Figure 9.3 and Figure 9.4. In this example, the caption acts as an evaluative metacomment on Trump as the visual participant. This metacommentary is reinforced via the image manipulation where he appears as a child. The image is an example of how producing 'an image macro and submitting it to a website or posting it to a blog or forum is an act geared toward fashioning semiotic belonging' by allowing users to rally around some shared value or perspective, in this case an anti-Trump stance (Zappavigna, 2012b, p. 103).

Discourse about size

Before proceeding to analyse #TinyTrump memes in more detail, it is necessary to consider the discourse about size that is so central to both the context and realization of this meme. This discourse, which featured both metacommentary about material size and semiotic size (e.g. exaggeration), was unusually prevalent throughout Trump's campaign and into his presidency. His tendency towards hyperbole was widely noted in reporting and commentary, and, as we will see, mocked through a variety of hashtags. While overstatement is a common feature in the talk of politicians, Trump's tendency to use very generalized attitude (e.g. *good, great, best*) makes his repeated exaggeration seem farcical. For example, this tendency is evident in his tweets (examples of upscaling underlined, generalized attitude in bold):

> I started my business with <u>very</u> little and built it into a **great** company, with some of **the best** real estate assets in the World. **Amazing**!

> The polls are now showing that I am **the best** to win the GENERAL ELECTION. States that are <u>never</u> in play for Repubs will be won by me. **Great**!

> I will be **the greatest** job-producing president in American history. #Trump2016 #VoteTrump *[link]*

> My transition team, which is working long hours and doing a **fantastic** job, will be seeing **many great** candidates today. #MAGA

The underlined examples in these tweets show how attitude is a gradable system. The Appraisal framework refers to meanings that are modified in terms of amount, intensity, or preciseness as graduation. The graduation system is aimed at describing how 'feelings are amplified and categories blurred' (Martin & White, 2005, p. 35). Trump's hyperbolic tendencies meant that his discourse was ripe for mockery realized via graduation (Figure 9.9).

The major choice in the graduation system is between force, 'grading according to intensity of amount', and focus, 'grading according to prototypicality and the preciseness by which category boundaries are drawn' (Martin & White, 2005, p. 137). For instance, the hashtag *#yuge* (mocking Trump's pronunciation of 'huge') was used to ridicule his tendency to exaggerate the scale of his achievements via quantification:

> It's a **#yuge** deal! It'll save my #lobbyist companies billions! #TinyTrump

> #trump is a #tiny man w. #tiny hands, #tiny brain, #tiny ideas, #tiny heart. and a **#yuge** ego.#tinytrump

> It seems pretty obvious by now that President Procrustes is not long for @WhiteHouse. #russiagate #tinyTrump likes **#yuge** #bribes. #(sick)

Similarly the hashtag *#bigly* (which we will explore in more detail later) is a reference to Trump's use of the term 'big league', and was used to mock Trump's hyperbole via intensification:

> #TinyTrump losing his shit **#bigly** #LyingDonald the #Temp #TheLooterPresident #amateur #POTUS

> #tinytrump agrees **#bigly**

> This could **#Bigly** annoy #45 ... #Gold #TinyTrump #BLOTUS #LyingTrump

Focus, on the other hand, is a resource for grading the extent to which something conforms to a particular category. For instance, a common device used to criticize Trump via focus was the tag *#FakePresident*, asserting that he is not a legitimate president:

> u are **#Fake**President, kuddos to @nnytimes @CNN for ur reporting KEEP UP THE PRESSURE on #tinytrump

> #DelusionalDonald does not perceive reality!#Crowdsize #TrumpWireTap #alternatefacts **#Fake**president #Trump #tinytrump *[embedded image comparing a flattering and unflattering painting of Trump with the caption 'Donald's delusions' and 'fantasy'/'reality']*

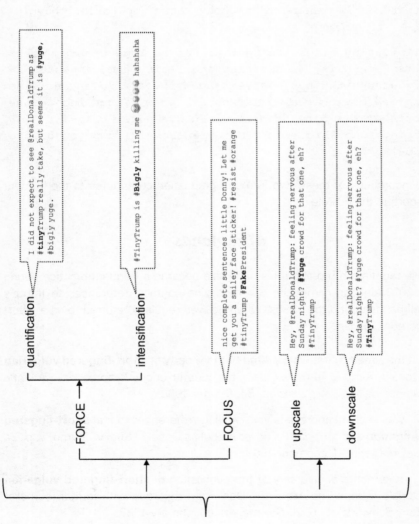

quantification
I did not expect to see @realDonaldTrump as #**tinyTrump** really take, but seems it is #**yuge**, #bigly yuge.

intensification
#TinyTrump is #**Bigly** killing me 😂😂😂 hahahaha

FOCUS
nice complete sentences little Donny! Let me get you a smiley face sticker! #resist #orange #tinyTrump #**Fake**President

upscale
Hey, @realDonaldTrump: feeling nervous after Sunday night? #**Yuge** crowd for that one, eh? #TinyTrump

downscale
Hey, @realDonaldTrump: feeling nervous after Sunday night? #Yuge crowd for that one, eh? #**Tiny**Trump

FORCE

FIGURE 9.9 *A system network for graduation with example hashtags, adapted from (Martin & White, 2005, p. 154).*

```
#FakePresident continues to blow smoke. We need to
all ask #tinyTrump to turn TV off & start reading
reputable newspapers.
```

The other fundamental choice is between upscaling or downscaling the attitudinal meaning. Much of the humour engendered by the Tiny Trump meme, as we will see, is a result of various layers of juxtapositioning of up- and downscaled graduation. For example, the following posts show upscaling in bold and downscaling underlined:

```
-Yuge! The biggest ever. Tremendously bigly! Oh wait,
that was @womensmarch!! Nobody showed up for u, chump!
😂   #tinyTrump

Tiny, tiny hands. So Sad. He has on Yuge problem with
his Teeny Tiny Hands.#tinyhands #tinyTrump #peeotus
#whatsupwithtinyhands [embedded tweet: Did anyone else
notice during the #JointAddress when #Trump had to use
both of his tiny hands to hold his water or …?]
#tinytrump #bigtruck @User @realDonaldTrump you go big
boy!
```

The incongruity of these two forms of graduation contributes to the humour supporting the ridicule.

#TinyHands

While taunting Trump about his hand size became a frequent practice during the 2016 election campaign, *Spy* magazine contains references to Trump's small hands during the 1980s, when he was regularly referred to as a 'short fingered vulgarian'[9]:

... the already ultraswanky 42nd-birthday party of **short-fingered vulgarian** Donald Trump at Trump's Castle, his superluxurious keno parlor in Atlantic City ... p. 142 *Spy* magazine, September 1988

... was I able to appreciate your previous references to that **short-fingered vulgarian** and former SPY cover model as Donald "Stinky" Trump ... p. 24 *Spy* magazine, December 1989

... Two-month anniversary of the publication of **short-fingered vulgarian** Donald Trump's The Art of the Deal (tape recorded with former journalist Tony Schwartz) ... p. 20 *Spy* magazine, February 1988

In the 2016 presidential campaign the phrase 'tiny hands' was used to ridicule Trump across a range of modes and channels. This included protest chants such as 'We don't want your tiny hands anywhere near our underpants' – a reference to a recording of Trump talking about how his celebrity status meant that women would let him 'do anything' to them.[10] It is also a reference to his alignment with conservative views relating to policy about women's health (e.g. anti-abortion agendas). The chant featured in Fiona Apple's protest song, titled 'Tiny Hands', written prior to the Women's March, an international protest aimed at advocating for women's rights held the day after Trump's inauguration.

Unsurprisingly, *#TinyHands* became an ongoing hashtag. For example, the following are instances of the tag used to make fun of the Trump administration's statements about his inauguration crowd size (graduation shown underlined):

Poor Trump, let's just make him feel better. Tell him he had biggest crowds. Tremendous amount of people! **#tiny**hands #lying #impeachhim

Never too much to remember that the orange guy with **#TinyHands** is also the one with tiny inauguration crowd. *[embedded tweet: Noticed you had to use an old Obama inauguration photo for your banner, so we fixed it for you.]*

I just wanted to remind @realDonaldTrump that his tiny inauguration crowd matched the size of his **#tiny**hands

Hey @realDonaldTrump. Your inauguration crowd isn't the only thing of yours that's smaller than Obama's. **#tiny**hands

Trump inaugural crowds are microscopic! Disaster! VERY UNPOPULAR! #Inauguration **#TinyHands** #TinyMind *[Embedded CNN article title 'Comparing Donald Trump and Barak Obama's inaugural crowd sizes']*

Trump himself directly referred to criticism about his hand size, for instance, in this statement during a Republican presidential debate in Detroit with Florida senator Marco Rubio:

And I have to say this- I have to say this. He hit my hands. Nobody has ever hit my hands- I've never heard of this word. Look at those hands. Are they small hands. And he referred to my hands if they're small, something else must be small. I guarantee you there's no problem. I guarantee

Here, Trump is drawing a link between hand size and penis size, an association that is part of popular consciousness, and part of a broader discourse about masculinity. This idea was also made explicit through hashtags in posts containing *#TinyHands* and *#TinyPenis*, for example:

> You have **#tinyhands** which means you have a **#tinypenis**. also, you're a puppet. #notmypres #trump #crazyperson *[embedded tweet by Trump: When will the Democrats give us our Attorney General and rest of Cabinet! They should be ashamed of themselves! No wonder D.C. doesn't work!]*

> No it's not @realDonaldTrump's feminine tiny hands. It's his flaccid tiny brain. **#tinyhands #tinypenis** #Trump @POTUS @GenFlynn

> **#TinyHands #TinyPenis** #TinyBrain #StopPresidentBannon #Impeach #NoBanNoWall #Trump #Resist *[embedded image of a mock PornHub video featuring Trump]*

> Much more intellectually suited for the imbecile #trump #tinybrain **#tinyhands #tinypenis** #bannonspuppet *[embedded tweet by The Hill: Trump screens "Finding Dory" at White House as thousands protest immigration ban outside http://hill.cm/aC1GViJ]*

> HACK TRUMP'S TAX RETURNS!!! #DUMPTRUMP #TRUMP2016 **#TINYHANDS #TINYPENIS** @realDonaldTrump #uniteblue

#bigly

In parallel with discourse about the small size of Trump's hands was mockery of his hyperbole via the hashtag *#bigly*. This tag is a reference to Trump's idiosyncratic use of the phrase 'big league'. This phrasing occurs in many of his speeches and rallies, typically as a modifier of a verbal group. A similar patterning can be found in his tweets (verbal group modified shown underlined):

> .@oreillyfactor please explain to the very dumb and failing @glennbeck that I <u>supported</u> John McCain **big league** in 2008, not Obama!

> .@club4growth asked me for $1 million. I said no. Now falsely advertising that I will raise taxes. I'<u>ll lower</u> **big league** for middle class.

Housing prices will be going up **big league**-a great
time to buy-good luck!

Gas prices are going up **big league** - I told you so -
payback to OPEC!

There was controversy regarding whether Trump was saying 'big league'
or 'bigly' in these instances, in part because it is quite difficult to audibly
disambiguate, and in part because it is unusual to use 'big league' as an
adverb.[11] In addition, since mocking Trump's bombastic language is a highly
aligning activity in anti-Trump communities, it is unsurprising that 'bigly' was
proffered as an example of Trump's linguistic oddity.

The popular belief that Trump was in fact saying 'bigly' spawned the
hashtag *#bigly*, which remains popular at the time of writing. It has been
used, for example, to mock the Republican Party's failure to agree on a bill
for 'repealing and replacing' the Affordable Health Care Act, despite Trump's
grand promises such as the following (that features his characteristic
upscaling of graduation):

I am going to repeal and replace ObamaCare. We will
have MUCH less **expensive** and MUCH **better** healthcare.
With Hillary, costs will triple!

Examples of mockery in this domain using *#bigly* included:

7 years. 52 repeal votes. GOP can't even sell their
own bill to their own party. #TrumpCare; if you're
gonna fail do it terrific and **#Bigly**

Congratulations on the **#bigly** loss @realDonaldTrump
Americans love #OBAMACARE #trumpfail

A plan so great that even lots of the Republicans would
rather have ObamaCare. #Winning **#Bigly** *[embedded tweet
by Trump: After seven horrible years of ObamaCare
(skyrocketing premiums & deductibles, bad healthcare),
this is finally your chance for a great plan!]*

The BLAME game is in full force over here. #SAD **#Bigly**
#KillTheBill #Obamacare #Ryan #ArtOfTheDeal #NotWinning

Mr ART OF THE DEAL FAILED **#BIGLY** and if this is what
he calls winning boy don't lose oh he's a big loser
anyway

Discourse about size also informs the intermodal coupling of *#TinyTrump* with images of miniature Trump to which we now turn.

Intermodal coupling

In order to interpret the meanings being made by tagging an image of Tiny Trump with the hashtag *#TinyTrump*, we need to understand how meanings in verbiage and meanings in images coordinate intermodally. The concept of 'intermodal coupling' has been used to explore how different semiotic modes coordinate as multimodal texts. For instance, how ideation-attitude couplings are negotiated both verbally and nonverbally (via body language) (Martin, Zappavigna, Dwyer, & Cléirigh, 2013), or across gesture and phonology in an interaction (Zappavigna, Cleirigh, Dwyer, & Martin, 2010a), as well as between image and verbiage (Caple, 2008a, 2008b; Painter & Martin, 2011; Zhao, 2011). When approaching intermodal coupling in this way, it is important to recognize that a constituency-based approach, focused on identifying more and more granular units of meaning, may be problematic since 'a multimodal text is not simply made up of smaller texts and images, nor is its meaning an accumulation of separate parts'; instead these texts can be interpreted as 'a meaning making process, in which choice from one semiotic system is constantly coupling with or decoupling from the choice made in another system' (Zhao, 2010, p. 261).

On social media platforms designed specifically for image-sharing such as Instagram, the ideational function of hashtags is foregrounded. This is because image search is more difficult than text search (though image-based search technologies are a developing area). Images will often be tagged with what looks like ideational over-specification, for instance, a close-up image of an eye and eyebrow with make-up tagged:

```
#makeup #instamakeup #cosmetic #cosmetics #mua
#fashion #eyeshadow #lipstick #gloss #mascara
#palettes #eyeliner #lips #tar #concealer #foundation
#powder #eyes #eyebrows #eyelashes #primers #beauty
#beautiful #morphebrushes #anastasiabeverlyhills #abh
#anastasiabrows #hudabeautyrosegoldpalette #hudabeauty
```

This ideational function operates largely in the service of search, enabling, for instance, a user who is interested in a particular make-up product to find examples of its use. However, just as we saw with tags used within written texts, hashtags applied to images can foreground an interpersonal function in the service of forging various kinds of alignments. This is particularly apparent on photo-sharing sites such as Instagram, where the caption to a post may be entirely composed of hashtags. For example, an Instagram image depicting Putin as a ventriloquist and Trump as his doll was tagged:

```
#trumpf #tinytrumps #fucktrump #funnyshit
#politicalart #putin #resist [Image]
```

Some of these tags contribute to the interpersonal meanings relating to ridicule made in the image via presenting a powerful figure with agency (a president) as a powerless figure without agency (a ventriloquist doll). For instance, *#trumpf*, *#tinyTrumps*, *#fucktrump*, and *#resist* are all aimed at imbuing Trump with a negative axiological charge that augments the negative connotations in the image. *#funnyshit* and *#politicalart* appear to be references to the genre and the status of the text as a form of political commentary. *#putin* is the only strictly ideational tag, since, while *#trumpf* does identify a visual participant, the alteration of the name invokes negative appraisal. These tags both supplement the meanings made in the image and frame how the image is to be 'read' by the ambient audience.

Ideational image-verbiage coupling

Zhao's (2011) work on image-verbiage relations in web-based digital learning materials defined a number of types of coupling focused on ideational meaning. These forms of coupling are categorized across organizing principles of *abstraction* (naming, identifying, representing), *generalization* (classifying, exemplifying), and *specification* (circumstantiating) (Table 9.1). This framework for ideational coupling is based on a minimum mapping hypothesis, whereby the mapping between fields (that an individual semiotic resources construes) is constrained. This means that 'if verbiage and image can co-construe one aspect of a social action, e.g. process (what is going on), participant (the participants that engage in the process), etc, they form a verbiage-image coupling' (Zhao, 2011, p. 171). In other words there is a logically resolvable relationship between ideation in an image and ideation in accompanying verbiage, and hence, the intermodal coupling is 'a shared meaning space in the logogenetic unfolding' of the text (Zhao, 2011, p. 171).

Figure 9.10 is an attempt to apply Zhao's framework to internal image-tag relations in an Instagram post. It is necessary to qualify these as 'internal' relations since, as we saw in Chapter 2, tags are involved in both internal and external relations, in terms of meanings made within an individual post or across posts aggregated by a hashtag. This post is from an Instagram account devoted to sharing images of Trump eating food as a means of lampooning his behaviour and ideology. The image of Trump eating a taco was taken from one

TABLE 9.1 Verbiage-image ideational couplings based on Zhao (2011, p. 224)

	Hashtag	Type	Semantic relation	Organizing principle	Example
1	#Trump	Naming	is	abstraction	
2	#potus	Identifying	is		
3	#USA	Representing	stands for		
4	#hat	Classifying - Exemplifying	(co)classifies exemplifies	Generalization	
5	#Maralago	Circumstantiating	specifying circumstances	Specification	

of Trump's tweets, where it accompanied the following text that appears to be invoking the ridiculous claim that Trump's love of tacos means he is not racist:

```
Happy #CincoDeMayo! The best taco bowls are made in
Trump Tower Grill. I love Hispanics! [link to Facebook]¹²
```

There is rarely a one-to-one mapping between a hashtag and an image, given that hashtags are often applied in combination, and also in relation to the rest of the verbiage of the post. Thus teasing out the ideational meanings being made, even if they are internal meanings, is quite complex. As the table in Figure 9.10 suggests, there is somewhat of an over-specification of ideational meanings across abstraction, generalization, and specification in the hashtags. Even though the ambient viewer is likely to recognize the individual in the post, and most likely the context of the image, since it was shared widely during Trump's election campaign, the tags instantiate these ideational meanings. For example, in terms of abstraction, this spanned naming the visual participant (*#trump*), describing the represented activity (*#trumpeating; #trumpeatsstuff*), and identifying the visual participant (*#potus; #president*). Generalization was realized via classifying (*#beef; #food; #tacos*), and specification via circumstantiation (*#trumptower*).

Table 9.1 summarizes Zhao's categorization of the major types of verbiage-image ideational couplings that are possible. Images tagged with Trump-related hashtags are used to illustrate these ideational categories. Applying Zhao's framework to tag-image relations, 'naming' coupling is where the tag assigns a proper name to the visually represented participant, for example, *#Trump* used with an image featuring Donald Trump as a participant (row, 1 Table 9.1). Naming might be used to indicate people, places, or objects, and involves the semantic relation 'is' since it is 'comparable to that between Value and Token in an identifying clause' (2011, p. 191). 'Identifying' coupling, on the other hand, is where the visual participant is verbally identified. However, unlike naming, there is a second layer of relations incorporated, for example, via a possessive deictic in the nominal group (e.g. *Trump's* hat where the deictic (*Trump*) identifies the Thing (*hat*) as a subset of hats (those that belong to Trump)). An example of identifying is the relation between the tag *#potus* (president of the United States) and an image of Trump (row 2, Table 9.1). Both naming and identifying are organized by the principle of abstraction. 'Representing' coupling also involves a form of token-value relation. However, rather than identifying the visual token (or being identified by it), the tag 'stands for' the meaning construed in the language, by 'symbolising, signing or signifying' (Zhao, 2011, p. 209). For instance, the US flag symbolizes the USA in an image tagged *#USA* (row 3, Table 9.1).

Where's the beef? All of it is in his taco bowl.
#helookssoproud #beef #trumpeating #trumpeatsstuff #food
#tacos #trump #potus #trumptower #president #impeachtrump
#impeach #resist

	ideational		interpersonal
abstraction	Generalisation	Specification	
#trump	#beef	#trumptower	#helookssoproud
#trumpeating	#food		#impeachtrump
#trumpeatsstuf f	#tacos		#impeach
#potus			#resist
#president			

FIGURE 9.10 *Ideational and interpersonal image-hashtag couplings in an Instagram post.*

Ideational couplings can also be organized by generalization via classifying-exemplifying coupling. This term was used by Zhao to reflect the bi-directionality of this coupling relation since from 'the perspective of image, the verbiage classifies the visually represented participant as a member of a class, while from the perspective of verbiage; the image exemplifies the characteristics of the members of this class' (Zhao, 2011, p. 214). For example, consider the relationship between the tag *#hat* and the red hat in the image (row 4, Table 9.1). Alternatively the coupling may involve specifying circumstances. For instance, this relation may be construed by visually representing a location, in the case of *#Maralago*, Trump's resort that he frequently visits at great expense to US taxpayers, and which he controversially termed 'the Winter Whitehouse' (row 4, Table 9.1).

Clearly the function of these ideational couplings is very different to the pedagogic function of Zhao's web-based digital leaning materials, and in order to interpret their role in these social media texts, we need to understand how they function in relation to other types of coupling, in particular interpersonal coupling. In addition, as we will see in the next section, intertextual coupling, that is coupling between meanings made in the text and meanings made in other texts, is crucial to explaining the rhetorical function of these resources.

Using intermodal coupling to analyse the #TinyTrump meme

The *#TinyTrump* meme ridicules Trump's relationship with other figures, for instance, with foreign leaders. By rendering Trump in miniature these images place Trump in a subordinate relationship as a visual participant (by virtue of being visually smaller) to the other visual participants. Examples of posts featuring images of this kind include the following, which feature different world leaders depicted together with Tiny Trump:

#tinyTrump *[image of minature Trump shaking hands with Canadian prime minister Justin Trudeau]*

Trump shames Angela Merkel's PDd #tinyTrump *[image of child Trump colouring in with small children while German Chancellor Angela Merkel and other adults look on]*

#trumpmerkel #tinytrump #trumprussia #resist #ImpeachTrump *[image of Tiny Trump sitting next to German Chancellor Angela Merkel during meeting with press]*

Making the internet great again, #TinyTrump ☹☹☹ *[image of miniature Trump sitting on a child's chair next to Canadian prime minister Justin Trudeau]*

This #tinyTrump pic wins the internet!*[image of child Trump meeting Russian leader Vladimir Putin]*

The most frequent image of this kind (featuring Trump and a world leader) was an image of Putin crouching as if interacting with a small child and shaking hands with a reduced-sized Trump (Figure 9.11). This image was originally posted to Reddit with the text, 'Putin meets his biggest tiny fan'. Some iterations of this image include a visual intertextual reference by including Kellyanne Conway kneeling next to Trump, sampled from another image where she is kneeling on a White House lounge as shown in the bottom right image in Figure 9.12 (see also *#CouchGate* in the hashtag glossary). The image was used to ridicule the nature of Trump and his associates' relationship to Russian leader Vladimir Putin. This alleged relationship was an ongoing issue throughout Trump's presidential campaign. It is also the subject of an ongoing FBI inquiry, from which Trump

FIGURE 9.11 *'Putin meets his biggest tiny fan' by user calituna.*

FIGURE 9.12 *Example of #TinyTrump images featuring Putin.*

fired FBI director James Comey, resulting in the selection of special counsel by the US Department of Justice in order to independently investigate the matter.

Tweets with the 'Putin shaking hands with Tiny Trump' image contained a range of hashtags:

#Trump #Putin #Conway

#Putinspuppet #tinyTrump

#tinytrump, of **#Trumpistan**, aims to emulate **#Putin.**

Putin meets his biggest tiny fan *[link to Reddit]* **#TinyTrump #RussianHacking**

An historic photo op for @realDonaldTrump and @ KellyannePolls meeting with **#Putin #tinyTrump**

Times when you're like "f%~k the internet!" Then there are times the internet gifts us with this Thank you internet **#tinyTrump #Putin #potus**

Meeting Putin with @KellyannePolls #TinyTrump By r/ bass-

Putin and his **#TinyTrump**

@realDonaldTrump Oh **#tinyTrump**, always a **#puppet** to **#putin**

```
#Putin meets his biggest (tiny) fan #tinyTrump
#TinyHands #TinyPresident #PresidentsDay

#TinyTrump #PuppetMaster #Putin
```

These tags can be seen to have different ideational and interpersonal functions in terms of their coupling with the image (Table 9.2). Tags that map to specific ideation in the image were treated as ideational, conforming to Zhao's (2011) 'minimum mapping' hypothesis introduced earlier. As Table 9.2 details, there were tags such as *#Trump* with a clearly ideational function (abstraction), similar to topic-marking hashtags explored in Chapter 3. However, the majority of the tags appear to have an interpersonal function, contributing to the visual ridicule achieved by miniaturizing Trump. For instance, the hashtags labelling Trump 'a puppet' are aimed at reducing his status. They are an intertextual reference to Clinton's jibe at Trump (during the third presidential debate) that he was a puppet of Vladimir Putin (see Glossary entry for *#PutinsPuppet*).

While *#TinyTrump, #TinyHands*, and *#TinyPresident* might be treated as ideational, since a miniature sized Trump is evident in the image, these ideational tags afford interpersonal meaning via the graduation 'tiny' (as explained in the section 'Intermodal coupling'). They are used to mock Trump's status as a leader and also his masculinity. It should also be noted that analysing social media images adds another layer of difficulty to the minimum mapping

TABLE 9.2 Ideational and interpersonal hashtags appended to the 'Trump meets Putin' image

Ideational			Interpersonal
Abstraction	**Generalization**	**Specification**	
#Trump	#tinytrumpmeme	#PresidentsDay	#GaslighterGeneral
#Putin			#puppet; #PuppetMaster; #Putinspuppet
#Conway			#RussianHacking
#potus			#Trumpistan
			#TinyTrump; #TinyHands; #TinyPresident
			#resist

hypothesis because some tags may bear relationships to other elements of the post. For instance, *#PresidentsDay* is a reference to the date that this post was made, as well as seeming to have some resolvability in relation to the image (since it contains a president, although the image does not include features that indicate that it is Presidents Day).

An example of tags applied to the 'Tump meets Putin' image (kneeling Kellyanne Conway version) posted to Instagram is the following:

```
#TinyTrump #PutinsBitch #BigDaddyPutin #TinyMind
#TinyHands #Trump #DICKtator #InHisElement #OrangeClown
#TheHateWhisperer #YourPotus #YouVotedForHim #Republicans
#KellyAnneConway #Working #AlternativeFacts #KKKConway
#STFU #WigIsCrooked #Tweets #Twitter #OnHerKnees
```

This caption consisted only of these hashtags. The majority of these tags are interpersonal, supporting the visual ridicule explained earlier (Table 9.3).

TABLE 9.3 Ideational and interpersonal hashtags appended to the 'Trump meets Putin' Instagram post

	Ideational		Interpersonal
Abstraction	**Generalization**	**Specification**	
#Trump	#Republicans	#InHisElement	#WigIsCrooked
#YourPotus	#Working	#OnHerKnees	#PutinsBitch; #BigDaddyPutin
#KellyAnneConway	#Tweets		#DICKtator
	#Twitter		#OrangeClown
			#TheHateWhisperer
			#TinyTrump; #TinyMind; #TinyHands
			#YouVotedForHim
			#AlternativeFacts
			#KKKConway
			#STFU

They serve a similar function to the evaluative metacommentary explained in Chapter 4, and act as a negative comment on Trump. They construe an anti-Trump bond to be shared with the ambient viewer in a similar way to the bonding described in Chapter 7. Here, however, the alignment is not just around the coupling in the verbiage [ideation: Trump/attitude: -judgement (afforded by graduation)]. It is also around this coupling co-realized as the small-sized Trump. The judgement afforded by 'Tiny' in the verbiage is co-construed in the image via this miniaturization.

A major subset of *#TinyTrump* images depicts Trump as Putin's child (Figure 9.12). This inscribes the subordinate position assigned to Trump by the miniaturization of his body. These images draw on contextual meanings about the relationship of children to parents as a way of ridiculing the alleged Trump-Putin relationship. They also cleverly leverage the provenance of existent 'Toddler Trump' memes (sometimes tagged *#ToddlerTrump* or *#ToddlerInChief*) which we introduced earlier in relation to the original image in *Spy* magazine. For instance, a repeated pattern was reference to Putin as Trump's 'daddy':

Here we see @POTUS #DonaldTrump out for a walk with **daddy #Putin** #TinyTrump #TinyHands #TinyPresident *[image of Putin walking Tiny Trump on a leash]*

Daddy Putin took me for a nice walk this morning. #tinyTrump *[image of Putin walking Tiny Trump on a leash]*

☺☺regrann from fucktrumpware – "Don't let go, **Daddy Putin.** Don't let go!" #tinytrump *[image of Putin pushing Tiny Trump on a bike]*

Other posts used 'good boy', a phrase associated with condescending praise, and also often used with dogs, to further mock Trump's subordination:

#Putin pats #TinyTrump Who's my **good Boy**churian Candidate? #PutinGate #Russia #NotMyPresident #ImpeachTrumpNow *[image of Putin sitting at desk patting Trump, who is seated cross-legged on the floor, on the head]*

#tinyTrump #epa #Trumprussia good boy on a walk *[image of Putin walking Tiny Trump on a leash]*

He's such a **good boy** lol @User #TinyTrump *[picture of Putin patting Trump, who is standing the with other children, on the head]*

This phrase was also re-instantiated as the hashtag *#goodboy*, and employed in posts without images to invoke the meanings construed via the image-tag relations already explored, for instance:

#GoodBoy, #молодецтоварищ … Russian ambassador meets @ realDonaldTrump a day after #JamesComey got sacked. Thanks *[link to CNN article titled 'Trump to meet Russian foreign minister amid FBI swirl]*

So nice of #PresidentBannon to let Trump sit in the big boy chair for a photo **#goodboy** #runalong

Trump is now defending Russia **#goodboy** #debatenight

Ideational and interpersonal hashtags used with images that present Trump as a child and Putin as a parent are shown in Table 9.4. Again there is a proliferation of interpersonal tags supporting the general ridicule already introduced. Some of these tags are more explicitly focused on the nature of the relationship (e.g. *#daddyPutin, #PutinsPuppet,* #Goodboy) than in broader TinyTrump memes. Instances of tags that might seem ideational include *#TrumpRussia* and *#Russia*. These have been coded as interpersonal since the images do not appear to depict Russia as a circumstance of location, but rather reference Russia in relation to accusations that Trump held inappropriate ties with the Russian leader. This is in keeping with the principles of Zhao's minimal mapping hypothesis introduced earlier.

The interpersonal functions of tags identified in the visual memes surveyed in this chapter is in accord with the overall function of memes as humorous metacommentary on both the personal and political. The Tiny Trump meme and its interpersonal tags make comments across personal and political domains. The meme uses the personal (e.g. the parent-child relationship) to adopt stances about the political (e.g. Trump's connections with Putin). The tags are multifunctional, at once enacting a textual function (linking a specific instance of a meme to all other potential instances e.g. via *#TinyTrump*), ideational (indicating the topic of the meme e.g. *#Trump* and *#Putin*), and interpersonal (construing evaluative metacommentary e.g. *#PutinsPuppet*). They are, however, an order of magnitude more complex than that tags explored in Chapters 3 and 4, since they incorporate coupling across semiotic modes (image and verbiage) as well as within tags (e.g. ideation + attitude in *#GoodBoy*), and each of these forms of coupling enters into intertextual relationships with other posts containing the same tags.

TABLE 9.4 Examples of hashtags from posts where Trump is presented as Putin's child

	Ideational		Interpersonal
Abstraction	**Generalization**	**Specification**	
#Putin			#TinyTrump; #TinyTrumps; #TinyHands; #TinyPresident
			#TinyTrumpThursday; #tinytrumptuesday
#Trump; #DonaldTrump			#Resistance; #TheResistance
#Conway			#MAGA
#Bannon			#PutinsPuppet
#potus			#inlove
			#daddyPutin
			#fakepotus
			#TrumpTrain
			#BannonPuppet
			#TrumpRussia;
			#putingate
			#sanctions
			#SoCalledPresident;
			#GoodBoy
			#RussianHacking
			#ImpeachTrumpNow

10

Conclusion

Hashtags as searchable talk

This book has explored hashtags using a series of different lenses that illuminate different aspects of their function as a semiotic technology, and of their instantiation as both metadata and metadiscourse. The aim has been to explore their expanded meaning potential as an example of the increasingly interpersonal function, beyond simple classification, that 'searchable talk' is having in social life. Since classification is central to most aspects of existence, it is unsurprising that linguistics, and other disciplines, have refined tools for understanding the ideational dimension of meaning-making. What remains less well understood is the interpersonal, and when to stop approaching what looks on the surface as classification and recognize that something more complicated is going on. The social semiotic approach adopted in this book recognizes that understanding communication means recognizing that both experiential and interpersonal meaning are important:

> …experience is understood in the course of, and by means of, being acted out interpersonally – and, in the same way, interpersonal relations are enacted in the course of, and by means of, being construed ideationally. The grammar flows these two modes of meaning together into a single current, such that everything we say (or write, or listen to, or read) 'means' in both these functions at once. Thus every instance of semiotic practice – every 'act of meaning' – involves both talking about the world and acting on those who are in it. (Halliday, 1996, p. 8)

In arguing that hashtags are a semiotic technology – both metadata and language – we have explored the intersection of their technical *affordances* with their semiotic *functions*. For instance, we have explored how hashtags as metadata support both discovery and navigation. This dual affordance in turn inflects and is inflected by their discursive potential. For instance, their textual potential is manifest in their function as a discourse marker to indicate various kinds of meaning (in the service of garnering attention within the social stream). This textual potential is derived from the ability of hashtags to function as metadiscourse, in the sense that these tags indicate the presence of two orders, or levels, of abstraction in a post.

In Chapter 3 we focused on the ideational and interpersonal dimensions of this potential, drawing on Halliday's (1973) model of linguistic metafunctions. This involved exploring both the cataloguing function of hashtags that mark the topic of a post and their capacity to make interpersonal meanings (both by reflecting back on the body of post and by negotiating a relationship with the ambient reader). This chapter revealed the linguistic flexibility of hashtags, whereby they can take up a full range of experiential and interpersonal linguistic functions at the level of lexicogrammar, as well as enacting metacommentary at the level of discourse semantics. This latter stratum was the focus of Chapter 4, which considered in more detail how hashtags can function as evaluative metacommentary. This chapter drew on Martin and White's (2005) Appraisal framework to interpret how hashtags can be used to construe attitudinal stances, and suggested the utility of topological approaches to interpreting hashtags given their inherent multifunctionality.

The idea of attitudinal stance was also central to Chapter 5 which problematized simple conceptualization of discursive voices projecting stances (that are common in models of evaluation based on traditional written discourse). This chapter, detailed a system network for describing the quoted social media voice It demonstrated that a multimodal perspective is required in order to interpret how voices and stances are managed in social media texts. The system of metavocalization was explained in relation to quotation practices. This chapter also indicated that beyond a simple relation of sources to quoted material, social media texts require theorizing relations between 'perspectives'. This is because social media environments take dialogic meaning as their starting point: a social media text is always projected by some voice, and this voice is always also inherently connected to other voices in the social stream which they can repackage and republish. Thus, I proposed the importance of accounting for 'intersubjectivity', in the sense of how a post manages relations between perspectives, not just relations of sources to stances.

Chapter 6 returned to the concept of evaluative metacommentary, suggesting that more is needed than simply tracing Appraisal patterns in order to understand how values are construed via hashtags. This chapter introduced the notion of attitude-ideation 'coupling' as the central component of a stance involved in construing a value. Couplings were then used in Chapter 7 as the basis of establishing 'bonds': social alignments are formed in social networks. This chapter reviewed Knight's (2008, 2010a, 2010b, 2013) model of dialogic affiliation, and extended this approach to create a model for understanding ambient affiliation. This is affiliation where personae do not necessarily directly interact but instead 'commune' around values. This chapter introduced the following ambient affiliation strategies for such communing:

- *convoking* a coupling by directing it at a potential audience via, for instance, specifying a domain of interest or attitudinal target

- *finessing* a coupling by positioning it in relation to other potential value positions via forms of heteroglossic engagement

- *promoting* a coupling by foregrounding it interpersonally salient via, for example, resources for scaling up or down an attitude

Chapter 8 used the ideas developed in Chapters 6 and 7 to explore the social bonds at stake in posts with a censure or ridicule function. We saw how hashtags can operate in the service of ambient affiliation, acting as 'virtual sites for constructing communities' (Lin et al., 2013, p. 370).

The final chapter of the book returned to the concept of coupling introduced in Chapter 6 in order to explore intermodal coupling. It factored in the image-verbiage-tag relations that are increasingly realized in social media texts. This chapter extended work on ideational image-verbiage relations developed by Zhao (2011) to explore the interpersonal functions of tags used with internet memes, focusing on the *#TinyTrump* meme.

The aim of all of the chapters in this book has been twofold: to introduce linguistic theory and technicality needed for analysing hashtags, and to explore how hashtags have functioned in a real context (ridicule of Trump during his presidential campaign and early presidency). What we have seen across these chapters is that hashtags both enable and are enabled by 'multiplication of meaning' (Lemke, 1998), affording expansion in the meaning potential available to social media users as they create texts. Hashtags have also been revealed to be somewhat of a paradox in terms of the social functions for which they are put to use. On the one hand they can expand the visibility of a social media text, and provide a concise way of intertextually referencing multiple voices and relations between perspectives (intersubjectivity). On the other hand, a hashtag can provide a tool for coordinating discourse within so-called 'bubbles' or 'silos' (see Chapter 6), providing a means for propagating meanings inside 'echo chambers'. In other words, hashtags can act in the service of both homophily and polarization, where homophily is 'the idea that users in a social system tend to bond more with ones who are "similar" to them than ones who are dissimilar' (De Choudhury, Sundaram, John, Seligmann, & Kelliher, 2010, p. 2).

Mockery of Trump has had varying levels of success in terms of influencing the actions of his administration. We should perhaps note with hope the impact that satire and comedy can have in 'speaking truth to power'. However, just how far can hashtagged ridicule take us? We might heed the warning of an Australian commentator:

This was the disastrous year when the centre would not fold, would not concede that only a leftist origami could restore its foundational texts. But. You know. Keep saying that the problem is shit people and their bad taste and their fake news. Hold on to that cup of hope. Hold on to it while the racists drink like ecstatic pigs from the trough of power. (Razer, 2016)

Cast of Characters

Jim Acosta

American journalist. Senior White House correspondent for CNN.

Hillary Clinton

The 67th US secretary of state, former US senator for New York, former First Lady of the United States, and Democratic Party nominee for president of the United States in the 2016 election.

James Comey

Former director of the US Federal Bureau of Investigations (fired in May 2017 by President Donald Trump).

Kellyanne Conway

Counsellor to the US president.

Vladimir Putin

President of Russia.

Sean Spicer

US White House press secretary.

Jake Tapper

American journalist. Chief Washington correspondent for CNN and anchor of *The Lead with Jake Tapper,* CNN International and State of the Union.

Chuck Todd

American journalist. Moderator of NBC's *Meet the Press* and the host of *MTP Daily* on MSNBC.

Donald Trump

The 45th president of the United States.

Hashtag Glossary

#AlternativeFacts; #AltFacts

In an interview with Chuck Todd, during a broadcast of *Meet the Press* on 22 January 2017, Conway attempted to defend false claims that were made by the White House Press Secretary, Sean Spicer, regarding the presidential inauguration crowd size (see also #SpicerFacts). She argued that Spicer's crowd size claim was an 'alternative fact':

Chuck Todd: = You did not answer =

Kellyanne Conway: = Yes I did. =

Chuck Todd: the question of why the president asked the White House press secretary to come out in front of the podium for the first time and utter a falsehood. Why did he do that? It undermines the credibility of the entire White House press office

Kellyanne Conway: = No it doesn't. Don't be so- =

Chuck Todd: = on day one.=

Kellyanne Conway: Don't be so overly dramatic about it, Chuck. What it - You're saying it's a falsehood. And they're giving Sean Spicer, our press secretary, gave alternative facts to that. But the point = remains that there's–

Chuck Todd: = Wait a minute, alternative facts? = Alternative facts. Four of the five facts he uttered, = the one thing he got right was =

Kellyanne Conway: = hey, Chuck, why- Hey Chuck- =

Chuck Todd: Zeke Miller. Four of the five facts he uttered were just not true. Look, alternative facts are not facts. They're falsehoods.

#BowlingGreenMassacre (also, #BowlingGreen; #JeSuisBowlingGreen #NeverForget; #NeverRemember)

The 'Bowling Green Massacre' was a term used by US counsellor to the president, Kellyanne Conway, in an interview with Chris Matthews on MSNBC on 29 January 2017 (as well as a previous interview with *Cosmo* magazine) to refer to an incident that did not occur:

Kellyanne Conway: I bet it'd brand new information to people that President Obama bad a six month ban on the Iraqi refugee program after two Iraqis came here to this country, were radicalized, and they were the master- masterminds behind the Bowling Green massacre. Most people didn't know that because it didn't get covered.

The fictitious nature of Conway's claim meant that this term became a symbol of doublespeak.

#BringBackOurGirls
'Bring Back Our Girls' is a campaign to return 276 female students who were kidnapped by the extremist terrorist organization, 'Boko Haram', from the Government Secondary School in the town of Chibok in Borno State, Nigeria.

#BlackLivesMatter
'Black Lives Matter' is an activist movement campaigning against systemic racism and violence against black people.

#BuildThatWall
A chant often heard at Trump rallies. It is a reference to Trump's claim that he would build a wall along the US-Mexico border in order to prevent 'illegal' immigration.

#DressLikeAWoman
A response to claims made by a White House source that Donald Trump prefers his female staff to 'dress like a woman'.

#FakeNews; #VeryFakeNews
A term initially used to refer to false news reports, particularly those shared via FaceBook during the 2016 US presidential election. The term was appropriated by Donald Trump to refer to traditional news media as a means of discrediting reporting that was critical of his campaign and later his presidency.

#CouchGate
A reference to photos captured by official White House photographers on 28 February 2017 showing Kellyanne Conway kneeling on a White House lounge while taking photographs with her phone of Donald Trump meeting with leaders of historically black colleges. Conway was criticized for his showing of reverence for the oval office and its furniture.

#CrookedHillary
A derogatory label given to Hillary Clinton by Donald Trump when she was the Democratic nominee in the 2016 US presidential election. The tag was intended to suggest that Clinton had engaged in corruption, e.g. Trump claimed that her use of a private e-mail server when she was secretary of state meant that she was hiding unethical activities. Examples of Trump's use of the term include:

#CrookedHillary is nothing more than a Wall Street PUPPET! #BigLeagueTruth #Debate

We must not let **#CrookedHillary** take her CRIMINAL SCHEME into the Oval Office. #DrainTheSwamp

Basically nothing Hillary has said about her secret server has been true. **#CrookedHillary**

#CrookedMedia
A term used by Trump to refer to the mainstream media (see also #FakeNews). The term was adopted by former speech writers and spokesman of President Obama, Jon Favreau, Jon Lovett, and Tommy Vietor, as the name for the pro-Democrat media company which they started in the wake of the Trump presidency.

#LastnightInSweden
A meme mocking Trump's insinuation that there had been a terrorist attack in Sweden. During a rally in Florida on 18 February 2017 Trump used the phrase 'last night in Sweden' to imply an attack had occurred when it had not:

Here's the bottom line. We've got to keep our country safe. You look at what's happening. We've got to keep our country safe. You look at what's happening in Germany, **you look at what's happening last night in Sweden. Sweden, who would believe this. Sweden. They took in large numbers. They're having problems like they never thought possible. You** look at what's happening in Brussels. You look at what's happening all over the world. Take a look at Nice. Take a look at Paris. We've allowed thousands and thousands of people into our country and there was no way to vet those people. There was no documentation. There was no nothing. So we're going to keep our country safe.

#libtard
A portmanteau of *liberal* and *retard* used by Trump supporters as an insult for anti-Trump supporters.

#LittleDonny
A derogatory term intended to mock Trump for being childish. It was used in the title of the satirical children's book series *Little Donny Trump*.

#LockHerUp
'Lock her up' was a rallying cry amongst Trump supporters who wanted to see Hillary Clinton go to prison for her use of a private e-mail server when she was US secretary of state. It was chanted at Trump rallies by supporters, and, controversially, by retired Lt. General Michael Flynn at a Republican National Convention in July 2017 during which he stated:

Michael Flynn: We do not need a reckless President who believes she is above the law.

Crowd: Lock her up.

Michael Flynn: Lock her up. That's right. Yes, that's right. Lock her up. I'm going to tell you what. It's unbelievable. It's unbelievable.

Michael Flynn: yeah I use I use #NeverHillary. That's what I use. I have called on Hillary Clinton. I have called on Hillary Clinton to drop out of the race because she, she put our nation's security at extremely high risk with her careless use of a private email server.

Crowd: [chanting] Lock her up. Lock her up

Michael Flynn: You guys are good.

Crowd: [chanting] Lock her up. Lock her up

Michael Flynn: Damn right. You- you're exactly right

Crowd: [chanting] Lock her up. Lock her up

Michael Flynn: There's nothing wrong with that and you

Crowd: [chanting] Lock her up. Lock her up

Michael Flynn: And know why and you know why- you know why we're saying that? We're saying that because if I, a guy who knows this business, if I did a tenth, a tenth, of what she did I would be in jail today.

Crowd: [Applause]

This was later followed with the tag *#LockHimUp* after Flynn was fired due to lying to Vice President Mike Pence about his communications with the Russian ambassador Sergey Kislyak.

#MAGA; #MakeAmericaGreatAgain
'Make America Great Again' was the slogan used by Donald Trump during the US presidential campaign.

#ManyPeopleAreSaying
References Trump's tendency towards vague attribution, for example, in the following tweet:

> **Many people are saying** that the Iranians killed the scientist who helped the U.S. because of Hillary Clinton's hacked emails.

#MicrowaveCamera; #MicroWavesThatTurnIntoCameras; #MicroWaveGate:
During an interview with columnist Mike Kelly on 12 March 2017 Kellyanne Conway attempted to clarify Donald Trump's false claims that Obama

wiretapped him at Trump Tower. She made the following comment about microwaves during this exchange:

Mike Kelly: Do you know whether Trump Tower was wiretapped?

Kellyanne Conway: What I can say is that there are many ways to surveil each other now unfortunately. =There was-=

Mike Kelly: =Do you believe-=

Kellyanne Conway: There was an article this week that talked about how you can surveil someone through their phones, through their - certainly through their television sets - any number of different ways and **microwaves** that turn into cameras etc. So we know that that is just a fact of- =of modern life=.

Mike Kelly: =Sure.=

#NotMyPresident
An anti-Trump tag meaning 'Trump is not my president'. It is also a reference to 'Not My Presidents Day' a series of rallies protesting Donald Trump's presidency that were held on the American federal holiday that is known as Presidents' Day.

#NastyWoman
During the third US presidential debate on 20 October 2017 Trump referred to Hillary Clinton as 'such a nasty woman':

Hillary Clinton: My Social Security payroll contribution will go up, as will Donald's, assuming he can't figure out how to get out of it. But what we want to do is to replenish = the social security trust fund
Donald Trump: =Such a nasty woman.

Hillary Clinton: by making sure that we have sufficient resources and that will come from either raising the cap and or finding other ways to get more money into it.

The phrase was subsequently appropriated by the feminist movement, 'The Nasty Woman Movement'.

#OrangeCheeto
A reference to Trump's orange complexion, apparently the result of fake tanning products. Also a reference to a brand of savoury snack, Cheetos, available in the United States, the consumption of which is associated with low income groups.

#Propagandabarbie
A reference to a meme featuring an image of counsellor to the president, Kellyanne Conway, dressed as a Mattel doll in a Barbie doll box. 'Telling the

truth is HARD' is inscribed on the packaging of the box. Some versions include the additional line, 'Alternative facts sold separately'.

#PutinsPuppet; #PutinsBitch

Reference to alleged ties between Trump and Russian leader, Vladimir Putin, who was accused of interfering in the 2016 presidential election in order to aid Trump's campaign and ensure Hillary Clinton was not elected president. The reference to 'puppets' derives from the following exchange in the final presidential debate on 19 October 2017 in which Clinton refers to Trump as a puppet:

> **Donald Trump:** Now we can talk about Putin. I don't know Putin. He said nice things about me. If we got along well, that would be good. If Russia and the United States got along well and went after ISIS, that would be good. He has no respect for her. He has no respect for our president. And I'll tell you what, we're in very serious trouble, because we have a country with tremendous numbers of nuclear warheads, 1,800, by the way, where they expanded and we didn't, 1,800 nuclear warheads. And she's playing chicken. Look, Putin-

> **Chris Wallace**: Wait, but [inaudible]-

> **Donald Trump::** From everything I see, has no respect for this person.

> **Hillary Clinton**: Well, that's because he'd rather have a puppet =as president of the United States.

> **Donald Trump: =**No puppet. No puppet.

> **Hillary Clinton**: And it's pretty clear- =It's pretty clear-

> **Donald Trump: =**You're the puppet!

> **Hillary Clinton**: you won't admit = that the Russians have engaged

> **Donald Trump:** No, you're the puppet.

> **Hillary Clinton:** in cyberattacks against the United States of America, that you encouraged espionage against our people, that you are willing to spout the Putin line, sign up for his wish list, break up NATO, do whatever he wants to do and that you continue to get help from him because he has a very clear favorite in this race.

#Resistance; #TheResistance; #Resist

A call to 'resist' or marker of resistance to the administration of Donald Trump. The term also invokes the French resistance in the Second World War fighting against fascism.

#SeanSpicerSays; #SpicerSays #SpicerFacts
Used to mock US press secretary Sean Spicer's truthfulness in light of a statement he made during his first White House press briefing on 21 January 2017 about the size of Donald Trump's inauguration crowd:

> We do know a few things so let's go through the facts. We know that from the platform where the President was sworn in to 4th Street holds about 250,000 people. From 4th Street to the media tent is about another 220,000. And from the media tent to the Washington Monument another 250,000 people. All of this space was full when the President took the Oath of Office. We know that 420,000 people used the D.C. Metro public transit yesterday which actually compares to 317,000 that used it for President Obama's last inaugural. This was the largest audience to ever witness an inauguration. Period. Both in person and around the globe. Even the New York Times printed a photog- a photograph showing the- the- a- a misrepresentation of the crowd in the original Tweet in their paper which showed the full extent of the support, depth in crowd and intensity that existed. These attempts to lessen the enthusiasm of the inauguration are shameful and wrong …

See also #AlternativeFacts.

#TinyTrump; #TinyHands; #TinyPresident
A reference to Trump's apparent small hand size. Part of ongoing ridicule of Trump traceable to references in *Spy* magazine which described him as a 'short fingered vulgarian' (Carter, 2015).

#ToddlerTrump; #ToddlerInChief
Used to critique Trump as behaving as if he is a tempestuous child. Often used as part of visual memes in which Trump is depicted as a child or infant (see also #TinyTrump).

#Trumps7WordWireTapLeaks
A meme mocking Trump's claim that Obama had surveiled him, seen in the following Tweet by Trump:

```
Terrible! Just found out that Obama had my 'wires tapped' in
Trump Tower just before the victory. Nothing found. This is
McCarthyism!
```

The meme invites users to compose humorous posts that imagine what secrets about Trump might be leaked.

#TrumpCare
A term mocking Trump's failed attempt to create a replacement for 'Obamacare' (the Affordable Care Act).

#TrumpTaxReturns

A reference to Trump's failure to release his tax return to the general public, up until this point a convention amongst US presidential candidates and presidents.

#TrumpTrain

A marker of participation in general pro-Trump communication.

#TrumpRussia

A reference to the Trump campaign's alleged ties with Russia. Russia appears to have interfered in the US presidential election in order to prevent Clinton from winning and to undermine US democratic processes.

#VeryLimitedRole

The claim that Paul Manafort, a Trump campaign manager, played a 'very limited role' during his association with the campaign. This claim was made in light of apparent connections between Manafort and Russia.

#WomensMarch; #IMarchFor; #WhyIMarch

An international protest aimed at Donald Trump that was held on 21 January 2017 to advocate for women's rights. The protest attracted larger crowds than Trump's inauguration the day before. Many women wore pink knitted 'pussy hats', a reference to Trump's comments about grabbing women by 'the pussy' in a recorded conversation with TV host Billy Bush in 2005 in which Trump stated:

> **Donald Trump**: I moved on her, actually. You know, she was down on Palm Beach. I moved on her, and I failed. I'll admit it.
>
> **Unknown**: Whoa.
>
> **Donald Trump**: I did try and fuck her. She was married.
>
> **Unknown:** That's huge news there.
>
> **Donald Trump**: No, no, Nancy. No, this was [unintelligible] and I moved on her very heavily. In fact, I took her out furniture shopping. She wanted to get some furniture. I said, "I'll show you where they have some nice furniture." I took her out furniture. I moved on her like a bitch. But I couldn't get there. And she was married. Then all of a sudden I see her, she's now got the big phony tits and everything. She's totally changed her look.
>
> **Billy Bush**: Geez, your girl's hot as shit. In the purple.
>
> **Donald Trump**: Whoa!
>
> **Billy Bush**: Yes!

Billy Bush: Whoa!

[further exchanges]

Donald Trump: Yeah, that's her. With the gold. I better use some Tic Tacs just in case I start kissing her. You know, I'm automatically attracted to beautiful — I just start kissing them. It's like a magnet. Just kiss. I don't even wait. And when you're a star, they let you do it. You can do anything.

Bush: Whatever you want.

Donald Trump: Grab them by the pussy. You can do anything.

Bush: Uh, look at those legs, all I can see is the legs.

Donald Trump: Oh, it looks good.

Bush: Come on shorty.

Trump: Ooh, nice legs, huh?

This recording was released during his presidential campaign and Trump's statement received widespread condemnation.

#Yuge
Aimed at mocking Trump's pronunciation of 'huge' as 'yuge', possibly a feature of New York City dialect.

Notes

Chapter 1

1 'Brexit' is a portmanteau combining 'Britain' and 'exit'.

2 Social tagging is the practice of appending metadata (data about data) to social media texts. Most definitions of social metadata imply that it is 'social' because it is embedded in some form of social media (often termed *social platform*) and can be 'easily exploited for a social search task' (Bouadjenek, Hacid, & Bouzeghoub, 2016).

3 The Word of the Year proceedings itself introduced a hashtag category in 2014, with *#blacklivesmatter* the first winner in this category (Zimmer & Solomon, 2015).

4 I will hereon employ the term 'user' to simultaneously refer to the idea of a social media user (i.e. someone who makes use of a social media service) and a language user (someone who construes meaning with language).

5 The 'alt-right' or 'alternative right' is a term used to refer to far-right ideologies in US politics. It is associated with White Supremacism.

6 For instance as associated with being 'white trash', 'a cultural figure and rhetorical identity… a means of inscribing social distance and insisting upon a contempt-laden social divide, particularly (though not exclusively) between whites' (Newitz & Wray, 2013, p. 50).

7 The 'social stream' is a term used to describe social streaming services (such as Twitter and Instagram) in which posts are presented to the user in reverse chronological sequence (hence the stream metaphor). This is also termed 'real-time' media.

8 Examples include a study of #bully in education (Calvin, Bellmore, Xu, & Zhu, 2015), #addiction/#addict/#addicted in drug addiction research (Dwyer & Fraser, 2016), and #supplychain in supply chain research (Chae, 2015). These are just a few example from a very broad range of research.

9 It should be noted that collections of social media texts used in domains outside linguistics are not necessarily 'corpora' since they may not have been collected with the intent of being representative of some form of discourse. As always, it is important to inspect the selection criteria used to create a potential corpus.

10 The Twitter API is the language that software tools made by third party developers used to communicate with Twitter's infrastructure.

11 Interestingly some preliminary research has found that the presence of hashtags (along with links and @user mentions) decreases likes and retweets by reportedly increasing cognitive disfluency in the audience (Pancer & Poole, 2016).

12 Hashtag activism has been criticized as being a form 'slacktivism' with little consequence in the material world (Christensen, 2011).

13 A forthcoming special issue of the journal *Social Semiotics* considers social media in relation to semiotic technologies and semiotic resources.

14 The focus on meaning in context is a perspective that arises out of the 'functional tradition' of Firthian systemics (Firth, 1957). SFL initially drew its ideas about context from the work of the anthropologist, Malinowski, who introduced the notion of an ethnographic theory of language.

Chapter 2

1 Depending on the service, metadata may be more or less directly generated. For example, by liking/favouriting a post a heart or thumbs up icon will appear, however the user does not have control over how the system stores this information.

2 For a study of the Twitter heart/star button for liking/favouriting, see Bucher & Helmond (2017, in press).

3 SFL has drawn its ideas about context from the work of the anthropologist, Malinowski, who introduced the notion of an ethnographic theory of language. Malinowski argued that 'the real linguistic fact is the full utterance within its context of situation' (Malinowski, 1935, p. 11).

4 For channels that were password protected.

5 A reference to Trump's comments about grabbing women by 'the pussy' in a recorded conversation with TV host Billy Bush in 2005 (see hashtag glossary entry #WomensMarch).

6 Sometimes referred to as hashtag coalescence (Maity, Ghuku, Upmanyu, & Mukherjee, 2015) or hashtag compounds (Maity, Saraf, & Mukherjee, 2016).

7 By 'body post of a post', I mean the untagged part of a post. For instance, in HTML the <body> element defines the content of an HTML document.

8 There has also been dispute regarding whether *meta-* is a problematic prefix since it would seem to imply that metadiscourse operates 'beyond' or 'outside' the text. For instance, Hyland argues that metadiscourse is not a 'different level of meaning' since 'the meaning of a text depends on the integration of its component elements, both propositional and metadiscoursal, and these do not work independently of each other' (Hyland, 2005, p. 23).

9 The exact nature of this algorithm is proprietary knowledge but Twitter does indicate that it 'identifies topics that are popular now, rather than topics that have been popular for a while or on a daily basis' and that '[t]he number of Tweets that are related to the trends is just one of the factors the algorithm looks at when ranking and determining trends' (Twitter, 2017).

Chapter 3

1 Bastos, Puschmann, and Travitzki (2013, p. 164) note a clustering of hashtags in these domains within languages, with the exception of activism-related hashtags which are used across language as part of 'globalized political debate'.

2 Joffrey Baratheon is a sadistic King in the *Song of Ice and Fire* series by George R.R. Martin. This character is part of popular consciousness as a villain icon due to the popularity of the televised version of this book series, *Game of Thrones*.

3 Black Mirror is a British TV anthology series that examines the potentially dark consequences of new technologies such as social media on society.

4 Interestingly, despite social tagging being widely associated with information retrieval (when used in collaborative tagging systems), some studies have suggested that social tags are not typically employed by users to find annotated items at a later date (Lorince, Joseph, & Todd, 2015).

5 A reference to the address of the US Presidential Whitehouse: 1600 Pennsylvania Avenue, Washington, DC.

6 For work on semiotic goods and services, see Ventola (1987).

7 For instance, Pullum (2010) traces how the / symbol has entered spoken communication as a 'coordinator' as in the following example:

> At the top of the stairs on the left is a sort of spare bedroom slash boxroom slash clothes-drying room slash sewing room. (Pullum, 2010)

Chapter 4

1 This systemic orientation arose out of the Firthian tradition in linguistics (Firth, 1957). Firth asserted that a distinction needed to be made between structure and system, that is, between syntagmatic and paradigmatic relations in language.

2 It should be noted at this point that I am not arguing that hashtags should be interpreted without taking into account both co-textual and contextual meanings (as they are realized in a post and within a culture). We will return to a more comprehensive analysis of how hashtags enter into these relationships later in this chapter.

3 There are of course a range of other dimensions that might be considered, depending on the particular aspect of meaning requiring illumination.

Chapter 5

1 For example, 'promoted' tweets where users pay for their post to achieve prominence in the social stream.

2 Research into hashtags also been interested in how hashtags function as a reflexive signal of a user's 'metapragmatic awareness' of their own voice. For example there has been research considering this in relation to self-promotion practices (e.g. hashtags by politicians featuring their own name (Coesemans & De Cock, 2017 in press)) and how hashtag use differs across different types of voices (e.g. ordinary versus corporate tweeters (Page, 2012)).

3 This has been of particular interest to quantitative studies of 'information diffusion', concerned with how topics proliferate on social networking services, as well as in professional domains such as marketing. The information diffusion approach has, due to the difficulties of automating linguistic analysis of large datasets, however, tended to background dimensions of communication such as how 'meaning, values, and norms' are construed in texts (Rieder, 2012, p. 1).

4 This is related to Voloshinov's (1929/1973/1986, p. 103) suggestion that all utterances are necessarily construed with an 'evaluative accent', that is, they invoke value judgements implicated in particular ideological systems. The idea that speakers and writers 'encode their point of view' in any utterance they produce is also seen in corpus-based approaches to stance (Stubbs, 1986, p. 1).

5 A 'vlog' (derived from the term 'blog') is a colloquial term for a video in which a user narrates or shows some form of personal activity (e.g. a 'day in the life' vlog where the user shows highlights of their activity over a day).

6 Halliday and Matthiessen (2004, p. 315) define, according to Systemic Functional Grammar, a circumstance of extent as construing 'the extent of the unfolding of the process in space-time: the distance in space over which the process unfolds or the duration in time during which the process unfolds'.

7 I am indebted to Sumin Zhao for making clear this relation in our work on social media images.

Chapter 6

1 The *t*- notation indicates that the item is a 'token' of judgement.

2 Here 'fake' is negative appreciation of the news (-valuation); however, 'fake news' also evokes negative judgement regarding the news makers and so can be considered a token of judgement, hence the *t*- notation.

3 This post is mimicking Trump's tweet on 4/3/17: 'How low has President Obama gone to tapp my phones during the very sacred election process. This is Nixon/Watergate. Bad (or sick) guy!'

4 SFL initially drew its ideas about context from the work of the anthropologist Malinowski, who introduced the notion of an ethnographic theory of language. Malinowski (1935, p. 11) argued that 'the real linguistic fact is the full utterance within its context of situation'. By *context*, Malinowski means phenomena that the anthropologist must describe in order to understand, for example, the meaning of a word in a different culture. Translation of a word that has no equivalent in the language of the anthropologist is made possible by description of its context.

5 The ideation affords positive attitude (i.e. reading is a positive activity).

6 *Tabling* is used as a term to suggest that a coupling is offered as a potential bond that can be shared or rejected.

7 Martin notes that Saussure's notion of the sign is often subject to the common sense misinterpretation that it is a symbol standing for a concept. This is an interpretation which Saussure hoped to guard against by employing analogies such as likening 'the sign to a piece of paper – where neither side can be said to stand for the other, and with respect to which you cannot cut one side without at the same time cutting the other' (Martin, 2013, p. 2).

Chapter 7

1 This variation can occur across phonology, grammar, and semantics and has been seen as characterizing different personae and groups (Martin, 2010).

2 More generally, the idea of 'virtual community' (Rheingold, 1993) has been prevalent in internet research.

3 This concept is most often traced back to Habermas's (1962/1991) notion of the 'public sphere'.

4 Exactly what is meant by 'community' in a technical sense is problematic with some researchers suggesting that '[other] configurations' such as 'advertising campaigns, political platforms, social movements, smear campaigns, activist protests, harassment crusades, consumer products, and revolutions' are possible and that 'all hashtags have politics, create publics, or maintain communities' (Rambukkana, 2015a, p. 5).

5 Labelling bonds remains a problematic issue and we have not yet adopted a convention.

6 Here, 'fake' is on the one hand functioning to identify the news media (in a reference to Trump's tendency to term them 'the fake news media'), on the other hand it incorporates the coupling [ideation: news/ attitude: -*t*-veracity].

Chapter 8

1 For example, *#BindersFullofWomen* was a prominent hashtag used to mock Mitt Romney's comment that his office received 'whole binders full of women', that is, binders full of women's resumes provided by the governor of Massachusetts. For a study of this hashtag see Zhu (2016).

2 Though it should also be noted that hashtags can themselves be co-opted for alternative/ironic uses. For instance, the hashtag *#notallmen* 'began as a catchphrase among men's rights activists, "not all men are like that" (sometimes

initialized as "NAMALT")' and later 'came to be used in a chiefly ironic fashion, satirizing this defensive reaction' (Zimmer & Solomon, 2015, p. 214).

3   This is shown in brackets since it is the entire original coupling that is coupled with –veracity.

4   The appreciation is general in the sense the type of appreciation is underspecified (i.e. 'great' can construe a wide range of evaluative meanings).

Chapter 9

1   The most popular hashtags (used on the photo-sharing service Instagram at the time of writing) are *#love*, *#instagood*, and *#photooftheday*. *#instagood* is used to tag images of which the user is particularly proud. It originated with the account @instagood which collated impressive images. In practice the tag is used widely, most likely with the intent of increasing the views an image will receive. *#photooftheday* is also related to an account of the same name (@photooftheday) which selects images to feature (that bear the tag). These tags are associated with 'like4like' hashtags where the social expectation is reciprocity in liking/favouriting an image or post.

2   A 'humblebrag' is a form of faux-modesty. Wittels (2012, p. xii) gives the following example of a tweet which would be classed as humblebragging:

    I just got nominated for a damn Grammy. Take that low self-esteem. #fuckyeah.

3   Reddit is a bulletin board-style social news aggregation site where users produce, rate, and discuss web content or content that they have created themselves (such as these Tiny Trump images).

4   Occupy Wall Street, featuring the hashtags *#OccupyWallStreet,* was a protest movement which began in 2011 in New York City's Wall Street financial district aimed at highlighting social and economic inequality. The protest slogan was 'We are the 99%', a reference to uneven wealth distribution in the United States (where 1 per cent of the population hold disproportionate wealth and power).

5   Memes are thought to have originated on sites such as 4-chan that have acted as 'networks of mediated cultural participation – often the epicenter of participatory media artifacts and discourses' (Milner, 2012, p. 10).

6   As hashtag memes evolve, metadiscourse about the hashtag itself can arise. This sometimes means that 'the meme's purpose becomes convoluted, as users mentioned the hashtag in a tweet to mark participation in the discourse rather than personal involvement in the meme' (Leavitt, 2013, p. 144).

7   A 'macroinstruction' in computing is a type of shorthand used to enter large (often repeated) text.

8   Donald Trump was the host of the original US version of *The Apprentice*, a global reality game show franchise. In this show Trump would judge the business acumen of contestants, using the phrase 'You're fired' to dismiss

those who failed the TV show's various challenges. This phase became a well-known popular culture reference.

9 Graydon Carter reflected on his use of this term in an article for *Vanity Fair* (Carter, 2015).

10 Trump made this comment in his recorded conversation with TV host Billy Bush in 2005 (see endnote in Chapter 2).

11 For a linguistic discussion see Liberman (2016).

12 This post engendered many comical replies such as '@realDonaldTrump C'mon man, even your Mexican food has a wall.'

References

Adami, E., & Jewitt, C. (2016). Special issue: Social media and the visual. *Visual Communication, 15*(3), 263–270. doi:10.1177/1470357216644153

Allcott, H., & Gentzkow, M. (2017). *Social Media and Fake News in the 2016 Election*. Retrieved from https://web.stanford.edu/~gentzkow/research/fakenews.pdf

Almutairi, B.A.A. (2013). Visualizing patterns of appraisal in texts and corpora. *Text & Talk, 33*(4–5), 691–723.

Almutairi, B.A.A. (2014). *Visualizing Evaluative Language in Relation to Constructing Identity in English Editorials and Op-Eds*. Doctor of philosophy, University of Sydney, Sydney.

Andrejevic, M. (2014). The big data divide. *2014, 8*, 1673–1689.

Androutsopoulos, J. (2006). Introduction: Sociolinguistics and computer-mediated communication. *Journal of Sociolinguistics, 10*(4), 419–438.

Anstead, N., & O'Loughlin, B. (2015). Social media analysis and public opinion: The 2010 UK general election. *Journal of Computer-Mediated Communication, 20*(2), 204–220. doi:10.1111/jcc4.12102

Baca, M. (2008). *Introduction to metadata*. Los Angeles, CA: Getty Research Institute.

Bagley, P.R. (1968). *Extension of programming language concepts*. Philadelphia, PA: University City Science Centre.

Bakhtin, M. (1935/1981). *The dialogic imagination*. Austin, TX: University of Texas Press.

Bakhtin, M. (1986). *Speech genres and other late essays* (V. McGee, Trans.). Austin, TX: University of Texas Press.

Barton, D. (2015). Tagging on Flickr as a social practice. In R.H. Jones, A. Chik, & C.A. Hafner (Eds.), *Discourse and digital practices: Doing discourse analysis in the digital age* (pp. 48–65). London: Routledge.

Bastos, M.T., Puschmann, C., & Travitzki, R. (2013). Tweeting across hashtags: Overlapping users and the importance of language, topics, and politics. *Proceedings of the 24th ACM Conference on Hypertext and Social Media, Paris, France, 01–03 May 2013* (pp. 164–168). New York, NY: ACM.

Bastos, M.T., Raimundo, R.L.G., & Travitzki, R. (2013). Gatekeeping Twitter: Message diffusion in political hashtags. *Media, Culture & Society, 35*(2), 260–270.

Bateman, J.A., & Wildfeuer, J. (2014). A multimodal discourse theory of visual narrative. *Journal of Pragmatics, 74*, 180–208.

Bateson, G. (1955). A theory of play and fantasy. *Psychiatric Research Reports, 2*, 39–51.

Bateson, G. (1987). *Steps to an ecology of mind*. New Jersey & London: Jason Aronson.

Bauckhage, C. (2011). Insights into Internet Memes. *The Fifth International AAAI Conference on Weblogs and Social Media* (pp. 42–49). Barcelona, Spain, July 17–21: The AAAI Press, Menlo Park, CA.

Bednarek, M., & Martin, J.R. (Eds.). (2010). *New discourse on language: Functional perspectives on multimodality, identity, and affiliation.* London: Continuum.

Berghel, H. (2017). Lies, damn lies, and fake news. *Computer, 50*(2), 80–85. doi:10.1109/MC.2017.56

Berland, L. (2016). #ThisHappened in 2016. Retrieved 21 April 2017 from https:// blog.twitter.com/2016/thishappened-in-2016

Berry, M. (1981). Systemic linguistics and discourse analysis: A multi-layered approach to exchange structure. *Studies in Discourse Analysis, 1*, 20–145.

Bonilla, Y., & Rosa, J. (2015). # Ferguson: Digital protest, hashtag ethnography, and the racial politics of social media in the United States. *American Ethnologist, 42*(1), 4–17.

Bosson, J.K., Johnson, A.B., Niederhoffer, K., & Swann, W.B. (2006). Interpersonal chemistry through negativity: Bonding by sharing negative attitudes about others. *Personal Relationships, 13*(2), 135–150. doi:10.1111/ j.1475–6811.2006.00109.x

Bouadjenek, M.R., Hacid, H., & Bouzeghoub, M. (2016). Social networks and information retrieval, how are they converging? A survey, a taxonomy and an analysis of social information retrieval approaches and platforms. *Information Systems, 56*, 1–18.

Bouma, J., de Groot, M., Adriaanse, M.L., Polak, S., & Zorz, S. (2017). Bottom-up filter bubble mapping based on Trump and Clinton supporters' tweets. Retrieved from https://wiki.digitalmethods.net/Dmi/ WinterSchool2017BeyondTheBubbleInside

Bourlai, E.,Herring, S.,& Abdul-Mageed, M. (2016). Distinguishing functional types of hashtags: A structural approach. In Proceedings of the 3rd International Conference of the American Pragmatics Association (*AMPRA*), 4-6 November (pp. 1–10). Bloomington, IN.

Boxer, D., & Cortés-Conde, F. (1997). From bonding to biting: Conversational joking and identity display. *Journal of Pragmatics, 27*(3), 275–294. doi:http:// dx.doi.org/10.1016/S0378-2166(96)00031-8

boyd, D., Golder, S., & Lotan, G. (2010). *Tweet, Tweet, Retweet: Conversational Aspects of Retweeting on Twitter.* Paper presented at the Proceedings of 43rd Hawaii International Conference on System Sciences (HICSS), 5–8 January 2010, Honolulu, HI, United States of America.

Boyd, S. (2007). Hash Tags = Twitter Groupings.

Bruns, A. (2012). How long is a tweet? Mapping dynamic conversation networks in Twitter using Gawk and Gephi *Information, Communication & Society, 15*(9), 1323–1351. doi:10.1080/1369118X.2011.635214

Bruns, A. (2017). Tweeting to save the furniture: The 2013 Australian election campaign on Twitter. *Media International Australia, 162*(1), 49–64.

Bruns, A., & Burgess, J. (2011a). The use of Twitter hashtags in the formation of ad hoc publics. *Proceedings of the 6th European Consortium for Political Research General Conference, University of Iceland, Reykjavik* (pp. 25–27).

Bruns, A., & Burgess, J. (2011b, 25–27 August 2011). *The use of Twitter hashtags in the formation of ad hoc publics.* Paper presented at the European

Consortium for Political Research Conference, Reykjavik. Retrieved from http://eprints.qut.edu.au/46515/

Bruns, A., & Burgess, J. (2012a). Researching news discussion on Twitter new methodologies. *Journalism Studies, 13*, 801–814. doi:10.1080/146167 0X.2012.664428

Bruns, A., & Burgess, J. (2012b). Researching news discussion on Twitter: New methodologies. *Journalism Studies, 13*(5–6), 801–814.

Bruns, A., & Burgess, J. (2015). Twitter Hashtags from Ad Hoc to Calculated Publics, 13–28.

Bruns, A., Highfield, T., & Burgess, J. (2013). The Arab Spring and social media audiences. *American Behavioral Scientist, 57*(7), 871–898. doi:10.1177/0002764213479374

Bruns, A., & Moe, H. (2014). Structural layers of communication on Twitter. In K. Weller, A. Bruns, J. Burgess, M. Mahrt, & C. Puschmann (Eds.), *Twitter and society* (pp. 15–28). New York, NY: Peter Lang.

Bruns, A., Moon, B., Paul, A., & Münch, F. (2016). Towards a typology of hashtag publics: A large-scale comparative study of user engagement across trending topics. *Communication Research and Practice, 2*(1), 20–46.

Bucher, T., & Helmond, A. (2017 in press). The affordances of social media platforms. In J. Burgess, A.E. Marwick, & T. Poell (Eds.), *SAGE handbook of social media*. London: Sage.

Burgess, J., & Bruns, A. (2012). (Not) the Twitter election: The dynamics of the #ausvotes conversation in relation to the Australian media ecology. *Journalism Practice, 6*(3), 384–402.

Burgess, J., & Bruns, A. (2015). Easy data, hard data: The politics and pragmatics of Twitter research after the computational turn. In G. Langlois, J. Redden, & G. Elmer (Eds.), *From social media to big data* (pp. 93–111). New York, NY: Bloomsbury.

Burgess, J., Galloway, A., & Sauter, T. (2015). Hashtag as hybrid forum: The case of# agchatoz. In N. Rambukkana (Ed.), *Hashtag publics. The power and politics of discursive networks* (pp. 61–76). New York, NY: Peter Lang.

Caldwell, D., & Zappavigna, M. (2011). Visualizing multimodal patterning. In S. Dreyfus, M. Stenglin, & S. Hood (Eds.), *Semiotic margins: Meaning in multimodalities* (pp. 229–243). London: Continuum.

Caleffi, P.-M. (2015). The 'hashtag': A new word or a new rule? *SKASE Journal of Theoretical Linguistics, 12*(2), 46–70.

Callison, C., & Hermida, A. (2015). Dissent and resonance: #Idlenomore as an emergent middle ground. *Canadian Journal of Communication, 40*(4), Retrieved April 2017 from http://cjc-online.ca/index.php/journal/article/view/2958

Calvin, A.J., Bellmore, A., Xu, J.-M., & Zhu, X. (2015). #bully: Uses of hashtags in posts about bullying on Twitter. *Journal of School Violence, 14*, 133–153. doi:10.1080/15388220.2014.966828

Caple, H. (2008a). Intermodal relations in image nuclear news stories. In L. Unsworth (Ed.), *Multimodal semiotics: Functional analysis in contexts of education* (pp. 123–138). London: Continuum.

Caple, H. (2008b). Reconciling the co-articulation of meaning between words and pictures: Exploring instantiation and commitment in image-nuclear news stories. In A. Mahboob & N.K. Knight (Eds.), *Questioning linguistics* (pp. 77–94). Newcastle: Cambridge Scholars Publishing.

Carter, G. (2015). Steel traps and short fingers. *Vanity Fair*. Retrieved 14 May 2017 from http://www.vanityfair.com/culture/2015/10/graydon-carter-donald-trump

Carter, S., Tsagkias, M., & Weerkamp, W. (2011). *Twitter hashtags: Joint Translation and Clustering*. Paper presented at the Proceedings of the ACM WebSci'11, 14–17 June 2011, Koblenz, Germany, 1–3. Retrieved from http://www.websci11.org/fileadmin/websci/Posters/125_paper.pdf

Chae, B. (2015). Insights from hashtag #supplychain and Twitter analytics: Considering Twitter and Twitter data for supply chain practice and research. *International Journal of Production Economics, 165*, 247–259. doi:10.1016/j.ijpe.2014.12.037

Chafe, W.L. (2007). *The importance of not being earnest: The feeling behind laughter and humor*. Amsterdam & Philadelphia, PA: John Benjamins Publishing Company.

Chaudhry, I. (2014). Arab revolutions: Breaking fear| #Hashtags for change: Can Twitter generate social progress in Saudi Arabia. International Journal of Communication,*2014, 8*, 943–961.

Chiluwa, I., & Ifukor, P. (2015). 'War against our children': Stance and evaluation in #BringBackOurGirls campaign discourse on Twitter and Facebook. *Discourse & Society, 26*, 267–296. doi:10.1177/0957926514564735

Christensen, H.S. (2011). Political activities on the Internet: Slacktivism or political participation by other means? *First Monday*. Retrieved 19 April 2017 from http://firstmonday.org/ojs/index.php/fm/article/view/3336/2767

Christie, F., & Derewianka, B. (2008). *School discourse: Learning to write across the years of schooling*. New York, NY: Continuum.

Cislaru, G. (2015). Emotions in tweets: From instantaneity to preconstruction. *Social Science Information, 54*(4), 455–469.

Clark, R. (2016). 'Hope in a hashtag': The discursive activism of #WhyIStayed. *Feminist Media Studies, 16*(5), 788–804. doi:10.1080/14680777.2016.1138235

Coates, J. (2007). Talk in a play frame: More on laughter and intimacy. *Journal of Pragmatics, 39*(1), 29–49.

Coesemans, R., & De Cock, B. (2017 in press). Self-reference by politicians on Twitter: Strategies to adapt to 140 characters. *Journal of Pragmatics*. doi:https://doi.org/10.1016/j.pragma.2016.12.005

Conway, B.A., Kenski, K., & Wang, D. (2015). The rise of Twitter in the political campaign: Searching for intermedia agenda-setting effects in the presidential primary. *Journal of Computer-Mediated Communication, 20*(4), 363–380. doi:10.1111/jcc4.12124

Costello, V. (2016). *Multimedia foundations: Core concepts for digital design*. New York, NY: Routledge.

Crawford, K., & Schultz, J. (2014). Big data and due process: Toward a framework to redress predictive privacy harms. *BCL Review, 55*, 93–128.

Crismore, A. (1989). *Talking with readers: Metadiscourse as rhetorical act*. New York, NY: Peter Lang.

Cunha, E., Magno, G., Comarela, G., Almeida, V., Gonçalves, M.A., & Benevenuto, F. (2011). Analyzing the dynamic evolution of hashtags on Twitter: A language-based approach. *Proceedings of the Workshop on Language in Social Media LSM, 2011*, 58–65.

Curzan, A. (2013). Slash: Not Just a Punctuation Mark Anymore. Retrieved 4 May 2017 from http://chronicle.com/blogs/linguafranca/2013/04/24/slash-not-just-a-punctuation-mark-anymore/

Daer, A.R., Hoffman, R., & Goodman, S. (2014). *Rhetorical functions of hashtag forms across social media applications*. Paper presented at the Proceedings of the 32nd ACM International Conference on The Design of Communication CD-ROM.

Davidov, D., Tsur, O., & Rappoport, A. (2010). Semi-supervised recognition of sarcastic sentences in twitter and amazon. *Proceedings of the Fourteenth Conference on Computational Natural Language Learning, Uppsala, Sweden, 15–16 July 2010* (pp. 107–116). Stroudsburg, PA: Association for Computational Linguistics.

Davis, B. (2013). Hashtag politics: The polyphonic revolution of #Twitter. *Pepperdine Journal of Communication Research*, *1*. Retrieved from http://digitalcommons.pepperdine.edu/pjcr/vol1/iss1/4

Davison, P. (2012). The language of internet memes. In M. Mandiberg (Ed.), *The social media reader* (pp. 120–134). New York, NY: New York University Press.

Dawkins, R. (1989/2006). *The selfish gene* (30th anniversary edn.). Oxford & New York, NY: Oxford University Press.

Dayter, D. (2015). Small stories and extended narratives on Twitter. *Discourse, Context & Media*, *10*, 19–26. doi:http://dx.doi.org/10.1016/j.dcm.2015.05.003

De Choudhury, M., Sundaram, H., John, A., Seligmann, D.D., & Kelliher, A. (2010). 'Birds of a Feather': Does User Homophily Impact Information Diffusion in Social Media? Retrieved 5 May 2017 from http://arxiv.org/abs/1006.1702

Deller, R. (2011). Twittering on: Audience research and participation using Twitter. *Participations*, *8*(1), 216–245.

Desjardins, R. (2016). *Translation and social media: In theory, in training and in professional practice*. London: Palgrave Macmillan.

Dictionary, O.E. *'meta-, prefix'*: Oxford University Press. Retrieved 17 May 2017 from http://www.oed.com/view/Entry/117150?rskey=gJqoMY&result=4

Douglas, K., Ang, C.S., & Deravi, F. (2017 in press). *The Pyschologist*.

Drasovean, A., & Tagg, C. (2015). Evaluative Language and Its Solidarity-Building Role on TED.com: An Appraisal and Corpus Analysis. *Language@ Internet, 12*.

Dreyfus, S., & Tilakaratna, N. (Forthcoming). 'I have a fondness for cadavers...': Issues arising from using Appraisal to analyse a corpus of blog entries. *Text & Talk*.

Drüeke, R., & Zobl, E. (2015). Online feminist protest against sexism: The German-language hashtag #aufschrei. *Feminist Media Studies*, *0777*, 1–20. doi:10.1080/14680777.2015.1093071

DuBois, J.W. (2007). Stancetaking in discourse: Subjectivity, evaluation, interaction. In R. Englebretson (Ed.), *The stance triangle* (pp. 139–182). Amsterdam & Philadelphia, PA: John Benjamins.

Duerringer, C.M. (2016). Who would Jesus bomb? The Republican Jesus meme and the fracturing of ideology. *Social Media + Society*, *2*(1), 1–12. doi:10.1177/2056305116637095

Dunbar, R.I. (2004). Gossip in evolutionary perspective. *Review of General Psychology*, *8*(2), 100–110.

Dwyer, R., & Fraser, S. (2016). Addicting via hashtags: How is Twitter making addiction? *Contemporary Drug Problems*, *43*(1), 79–97.

Dynel, M. (2016). 'I has seen image macros!' Advice animals memes as visual-verbal jokes. *International Journal of Communication*, *10*, 660–688.

Efron, M., & Winget, M. (2010). Questions are content: A taxonomy of questions in a microblogging environment. *Proceedings of the American Society for Information Science and Technology, 47*(1), 1–10. doi:10.1002/meet.14504701208

Eggins, S. (1994). *An introduction to systemic functional linguistics.* London: Pinter Publishers.

Eggins, S., & Slade, D. (1997/2005). *Analysing casual conversation.* London: Equinox.

Enli, G., & Simonsen, C.-A. (2017). 'Social media logic' meets professional norms: Twitter hashtags usage by journalists and politicians. *Information, Communication & Society*, 1–16. doi:10.1080/1369118X.2017.1301515

Evans, A. (2016). Stance and identity in Twitter hashtags. *Language@Internet, 13*(1).

Evans, B.M., & Chi, E.H. (2008). Towards a model of understanding social search. *Proceedings of the 2008 ACM Conference on Computer Supported Cooperative Work, San Diego, CA, 08–12 November 2008* (pp. 485–494). New York, NY: ACM.

Fairclough, N. (1992). *Discourse and social change.* Cambridge: Polity Press.

Fathi, S. (2009). Avoiding hashtag hijacking and other Twitter fouls. *Public Relations Tactics, 16*, 13–22. doi:Article

Ferrara, E., Varol, O., Menczer, F., & Flammini, A. (2016). Early Detection of Promoted Campaigns on Social Media. *Proceedings of the Tenth International AAAI Conference on Web and Social Media* (pp. 563–566). Association for the Advancement of Artificial Intelligence

Firth, J.R. (1957). *Papers in linguistics 1934–1951.* London: Oxford University Press.

Firth, J.R. (1964). *The tongues of men, and speech.* Oxford: Oxford University Press.

Ford, K.C., Veletsianos, G., & Resta, P. (2014). The structure and characteristics of #PhDChat, an emergent online social network. *Journal of Interactive Media in Education, 1*, 1–24.

Fung, I.C.-H., Blankenship, E.B., Goff, M.E., Mullican, L.A., Chan, K.C., Saroha, N.,... Tse, Z.T.H. (2017). Zika-virus-related photo sharing on Pinterest and Instagram. *Disaster Medicine and Public Health Preparedness*, 1–4.

Gagnon, A., & Bourhis, R.Y. (1996). Discrimination in the minimal group paradigm: Social identity or self-interest? *Personality and Social Psychology Bulletin, 22*(12), 1289–1301. doi:10.1177/01461672962212009

Garimella, K., Morales, G.D.F., Gionis, A., & Mathioudakis, M. (2016). Quantifying controversy in social media. In *Proceedings of the Ninth ACM International Conference on Web Search and Data Mining, San Francisco, CA* (pp. 33–42). New York, NY: ACM.

Gawne, L., & Vaughan, J. (2011). I can haz language play: The construction of language and identity in LOLspeak. In M. Ponsonnet, L. Dao, & M. Bowler (Eds.), *Proceedings of the 42nd Australian Linguistic Society Conference* (pp. 97–122). Canberra.

Gerbaudo, P. (2012). *Tweets and the streets: Social media and Contemporary activism.* London: Pluto Press.

Giannoulakis, S., & Tsapatsoulis, N. (in press). Evaluating the descriptive power of Instagram hashtags. *Journal of Innovation in Digital Ecosystems.* doi:http://dx.doi.org/10.1016/j.jides.2016.10.001

Gibbs, M., Meese, J., Arnold, M., Nansen, B., & Carter, M. (2015). # Funeral and Instagram: Death, social media, and platform vernacular. *Information, Communication & Society, 18*, 255–268. doi:10.1080/1369118X2014.987152

Gibson, J.J. (1979). *The ecological approach to perception.* London: Houghton M.

Giglietto, F., & Lee, Y. (2017). A hashtag worth a thousand words: Discursive strategies around #JeNeSuisPasCharlie after the 2015 Charlie Hebdo shooting. *Social Media + Society, 3*(1), 1–15. doi:10.1177/2056305116686992

Gillespie, A., & Cornish, F. (2010). Intersubjectivity: Towards a dialogical analysis. *Journal for the Theory of Social Behaviour, 40*(1), 19–46.

Glasgow, K., & Fink, C. (2013). Hashtag lifespan and social networks during the London riots. In *International conference on social computing, behavioral-cultural modeling, and prediction* (pp. 311–320). Berlin: Springer.

Godin, F., Slavkovikj, V., De Neve, W., Schrauwen, B., & Van de Walle, R. (2013). Using topic models for twitter hashtag recommendation. *Proceedings of the 22nd International Conference on World Wide Web, Rio de Janeiro, Brazil, 13–17 May 2013* (pp. 593–596). New York, NY: ACM.

González-Ibánez, R., Muresan, S., & Wacholder, N. (2011). Identifying sarcasm in Twitter: A closer look. *Proceedings of the 49th Annual Meeting of the Association for Computational Linguistics: Human Language Technologies. Portland, Oregon, 19–24 June 2011* (Vol. 2, pp. 581–586). Association for Computational Linguistics.

Grasso, V., Crisci, A., Morabito, M., Nesi, P., Pantaleo, G., Zaza, I., & Gozzini, B. (2017). Italian codified hashtags for weather warning on Twitter –Who is really using them? *Advances in Science and Research, 14*, 63–69. doi:10.5194/asr-14-63-2017

Group, N.F.W. (2007). A framework of guidance for building good digital collections. Baltimore: National Informations Standards Organization (NISO). Retrieved from http://www.niso.org/publications/rp/framework3.pdf

Guerrero, P., Møller, M.S., Olafsson, A.S., & Snizek, B. (2016). Revealing cultural ecosystem services through Instagram images: The potential of social media volunteered geographic information for urban green infrastructure planning and governance. *Urban Planning 1* (2), S. 1–17.

Habermas, J. (1962/1991). *The structural transformation of the public sphere: An inquiry into a category of bourgeois society.* Cambridge, MA: MIT press.

Halliday, M.A.K. (1973). *Explorations in the functions of language.* London: Edward Arnold.

Halliday, M.A.K. (1978). *Language as social semiotic: The social interpretation of language and meaning.* Baltimore, MD: University Park Press.

Halliday, M.A.K. (1979). Modes of meaning and modes of expression: Types of grammatical structure, and their determination by different semantic functions. In W. Haas, D.J. Allerton, E. Carney, & D. Holdcroft (Eds.), *Function and context in linguistic analysis: A festschrift for William Haas* (pp. 57–79). Cambridge & New York, NY: Cambridge University Press.

Halliday, M.A.K. (1985/1989/1990). *Spoken and written language.* Oxford: Oxford University Press.

Halliday, M.A.K. (1991). Towards probabilistic interpretations. In E. Ventola (Ed.), *Functional and systemic linguistics: Approaches and uses* (pp. 39–62). Berlin & New York, NY: Walter de Gruyter.

Halliday, M.A.K. (1994). *An introduction to functional grammar* (2nd edn.) London: Edward Arnold (Vol. 283).

Halliday, M.A.K. (1996). On grammar and grammatics. In R. Hasan, C. Cloran, & D. Butt (Eds.), *Functional descriptions: Theory in practice* (pp. 1–38). London: Benjamins.

Halliday, M.A.K., & Matthiessen, C.M.I.M (2004). *An introduction to functional grammar* (3rd edn.). London: Arnold.

Han, J. (2015). *'#feminism is not a dirty word': Axiology, ambient affiliation and dialogism in discourses surrounding feminism in microblogging.* Honours thesis, University of Sydney.

Hansen, L.K., Arvidsson, A., Nielsen, F.Å., Colleoni, E., & Etter, M. (2011). Good friends, bad news-affect and virality in twitter. In *Future information technology* (pp. 34–43). Berlin, Heidelberg: Springer.

Hao, J., & Humphrey, S. (2009). The role of 'coupling' in biological experimental reports. *Linguistics & The Human Sciences, 5*(2), 169–194.

Harper, D. (Ed.) (2001) Online etymology dictionary. Retrieved from http://www .etymonline.com/index.php?allowed_in_frame=0&search=meta

Harrington, S. (2013). Tweeting about the Telly: Live TV, audiences, and social media. In K. Weller, A. Bruns, J. Burgess, M. Mahrt, & C. Puschmann (Eds.), *Twitter and society* (pp. 237–248). New York, NY: Peter Lang.

Haugh, M. (2010). Jocular mockery, (dis)affiliation, and face. *Journal of Pragmatics, 42*(8), 2106–2119. doi:http://dx.doi.org/10.1016/j .pragma.2009.12.018

Heyd, T. (2014). Folk-linguistic landscapes: The visual semiotics of digital enregisterment. *Language in Society, 43*(05), 489–514.

Heyd, T., & Puschmann, C. (in press). Hashtagging and functional shift: Adaptation and appropriation of the #. *Journal of Pragmatics.* doi:http://dx.doi. org/10.1016/j.pragma.2016.12.004

Higgins, K. (2016). Post-truth: A guide for the perplexed. *Nature.* Retrieved from http://www.nature.com/news/post-truth-a-guide-for-the-perplexed-1.21054

Highfield, T. (2013). Following the yellow jersey: Tweeting the Tour de France. In K. Weller, A. Bruns, J. Burgess, M. Mahrt, & C. Puschmann (Eds.), *Twitter and society* (pp. 249–262). New York, NY: Peter Lang.

Highfield, T. (2016). *Social media and everyday politics.* Malden, MA: Polity.

Highfield, T., & Leaver, T. (2016). Instagrammatics and digital methods: Studying visual social media, from selfies and GIFs to memes and emoji. *Communication Research and Practice, 2*(1), 47–62. doi:10.1080/22041451. 2016.1155332

Hill, B.M., Monroy-Hernández, A., & Olson, K. (2010). Responses to Remixing on a Social Media Sharing Website. *Fourth International AAAI Conference on Weblogs and Social Media* (pp. 74–81). Washington, DC: The AAAI Press.

Hindman Jr, F.M., Bukowitz, A.E., Reed, B.N., & Mattingly Ii, T.J. (2017). No filter: A characterization of #pharmacist posts on Instagram. *Journal of the American Pharmacists Association.* doi:http://doi.org/10.1016/j.japh.2017.01.009

Hjelmslev, L. (1943/1961). *Prolegomena to a Theory of Language (F.J. Whitfield, Trans.).* Madison, WI: University of Wisconsin.

Hochman, N. (2014). The social media image. *Big Data & Society, 1*(2), 2053951714546645. doi:10.1177/2053951714546645

Honeycutt, C., & Herring, S. (2009). Beyond Microblogging: Conversation and Collaboration in Twitter. *Proceedings of the Forty-Second Hawai'i International Conference on System Sciences* (pp. no page numbers available). Los Alamitos, CA: IEEE Press.

Hood, S. (2010). *Appraising research: Evaluation in academic writing*. London: Palgrave Macmillan.

Hopper, P.J., & Traugott, E.C. (2003). *Grammaticalization*. Cambridge: Cambridge University Press.

Horeck, T. (2014). #AskThicke: 'blurred lines', rape culture, and the feminist hashtag takeover. *Feminist Media Studies, 14*, 1105–1107. doi:10.1080/146807 77.2014.975450

Houston, K. (2013). *Shady characters: The secret life of punctuation, symbols, and other typographical marks*. New York, NY & London: W.W. Norton.

Huang, J., Hornton, K.M., & Efthimiadis, E.N. (2010). *Conversational tagging in twitter*. Paper presented at the Proceedings of the 21st ACM Conference on Hypertext and Hypermedia, Toronto, Ontario, Canada.

Hughes, D. (2015). *Hashtag activism: Well meaning or self promotion dressed up as charity?* Retrieved 26 April 2017 from http://www.smh.com.au/comment/ hashtag-activism-well-meaning-or-self-promotion-dressed-up-as-charity -20150113-12n29r.html

Hundt, M., Nesselhauf, N., & Biewer, C. (2007). *Corpus linguistics and the web*. Amsterdam: Rodopi.

Hunston, S. (2000). Evaluation and the planes of discourse: Status and value in persuasive texts. *Evaluation in text: Authorial stance and the construction of discourse* (pp. 176–207). Oxford: Oxford University Press.

Hutchby, I. (2001). Technologies, texts and affordances. *Sociology, 35*(2), 441–456. doi:10.1177/S0038038501000219

Hyland, K. (2005). *Metadiscourse: Exploring interaction in writing*. London: Bloomsbury.

Jackson, S.J. (2016). (Re)imagining intersectional democracy from black feminism to hashtag activism. *Women's Studies in Communication, 39*(4), 375–379. doi: 10.1080/07491409.2016.1226654

Jackson, S.J., & Foucault Welles, B. (2015). Hijacking #myNYPD: Social media dissent and networked counterpublics. *Journal of Communication, 65*(6), 932–952. doi:10.1111/jcom.12185

Jakobson, R. (1971). *Selected writings. Second expanded edition*. The Hauge: Mouton.

Jaworski, A., & Coupland, J. (2005). Othering in gossip: 'You go out you have a laugh and you can pull yeah okay but like ….' *Language in Society, 34*(5), 667–694. doi:10.1017/S0047404505050256

Jenkins, H., Ford, S., & Green, J. (2013). *Spreadable media: Creating value and meaning in a networked culture*. London & New York, NY: NYU Press.

Jungherr, A., Schoen, H., & Jürgens, P. (2016). The mediation of politics through Twitter: An analysis of messages posted during the campaign for the German Federal Election 2013. *Journal of Computer-Mediated Communication, 21*(1), 50–68. doi:10.1111/jcc4.12143

Jurgens, D., Dimitrov, S., & Ruths, D. (2014). Twitter users# codeswitch hashtags!# moltoimportante# wow. In M. Diab, J. Hirschberg, P. Fung, & S. Thamar (Eds.), *Proceedings of the First Workshop on Computational Approaches to Code Switching* (pp. 51–61). Doha, Qatar: Association for Computational Linguistics.

Kehoe, A., & Gee, M. (2011). Social tagging: A new perspective on textual 'aboutness.' *Methodological and Historical Dimensions of Corpus Linguistics*.

Kennedy, H., & Moss, G. (2015). Known or knowing publics? Social media data mining and the question of public agency. *Big Data & Society*, *2*(2), 1–11. doi:10.1177/2053951715611145

Khattri, A., Joshi, A., Bhattacharyya, P., & Carman, M.J. (2015). Your Sentiment Precedes You: Using an author's historical tweets to predict sarcasm. *Proceedings of the 6th Workshop on Computational Approaches to Subjectivity, Sentiment and Social Media Analysis* (pp. 25–30). Lisboa, Portugal: Association of Computational Linguistics.

Kilgarriff, A., & Grefenstette, G. (2003). Introduction to the special issue on the web as corpus. *Computational Linguistics*, *29*(3), 333–347.

Kilpinen, E. (2008). Memes versus signs: On the use of meaning concepts about nature and culture *Semiotica*, 2008, 215.

Kim, J. (2017). #iamafeminist as the 'mother tag': Feminist identification and activism against misogyny on Twitter in South Korea. *Feminist Media Studies*, 1–17. doi:10.1080/14680777.2017.1283343

Knight, N.K. (2008). 'Still cool…and american too!': An SFL analysis of deferred bonds in internet messaging humour. In N. Nørgaard (Ed.), *Systemic functional linguistics in use, odense working papers in language and communication* (Vol. 29, pp. 481–502). Odense: University of Southern Denmark.

Knight, N.K. (2010a). *Laughing our bonds off: Conversational humour in relation to affiliation*. Doctor of Philosophy, University of Sydney, Sydney.

Knight, N.K. (2010b). Wrinkling complexity: Concepts of identity and affiliation in humour. In M. Bednarek & J.R. Martin (Eds.), *New discourse on language: Functional perspectives on multimodality, identity, and affiliation* (pp. 35–58). London & New York, NY: Continuum.

Knight, N.K. (2013). Evaluating experience in funny ways: How friends bond through conversational humour. *Text & Talk*, *33*(4–5), 553–574.

Knobel, M., & Lankshear, C. (2007). Online memes, affinities, and cultural production. In M. Knobel & C. Lankshear (Eds.), *A new literacies sampler* (pp. 199–227). New York, NY: Peter Lang.

Knox, J.S. (2009). Punctuating the home page: Image as language in an online newspaper. *Discourse & Communication*, *3*(2), 145–172. doi:10.1177/1750481309102450

Kong, S., Mei, Q., Feng, L., Ye, F., & Zhao, Z. (2014). Predicting bursts and popularity of hashtags in real-time. *Proceedings of the 37th International ACM SIGIR Conference on Research and Development in Information Retrieval. Gold Coast, Queensland, Australia, 06–11 July 2014* (pp. 927–930). New York, NY: ACM.

Kovaz, D., Kreuz, R.J., & Riordan, M.A. (2013). Distinguishing sarcasm from literal language: Evidence from books and blogging. *Discourse Processes*, *50*(8), 598–615. doi:10.1080/0163853X.2013.849525

Kristeva, J. (1984). *Word, dialogue, and novel* (S. Hand & L. Roudiez, Trans.). Oxford: Blackwell.

Kroon, Å. (2017). More than a hashtag: Producers' and users' co-creation of a loving 'we' in a second screen TV sports production. *Television & New Media*, 1527476417699708. doi:10.1177/1527476417699708

Kuipers, G. (2002). Media culture and Internet disaster jokes: Bin Laden and the attack on the World Trade Center. *European Journal of Cultural Studies*, *5*(4), 450–470.

Kunneman, F., Liebrecht, C., van Mulken, M., & van den Bosch, A. (2015). Signaling sarcasm: From hyperbole to hashtag. *Information Processing & Management*, *51*(4), 500–509. doi:http://dx.doi.org/10.1016/j.ipm.2014.07.006

Kuo, R. (2016). Racial justice activist hashtags: Counterpublics and discourse circulation. *New Media & Society*, 1461444816663485. doi:10.1177/1461444816663485

Kwak, H., Lee, C., Park, H., & Moon, S. (2010). What is Twitter, a social network or a news media? *Proceedings of the 19th International Conference on World Wide Web, 26–30 April 2010* (pp. 591–600). Raleigh, NC: ACM.

Kytölä, S., & Westinen, E. (2015). 'I be da reel gansta' – A Finnish footballer's Twitter writing and metapragmatic evaluations of authenticity. *Discourse, Context & Media*, *8*, 6–19.

Lachlan, K.A., Spence, P.R., Lin, X., Najarian, K.M., & Greco, M.D. (2014). Twitter use during a weather event: Comparing content associated with localized and nonlocalized hashtags. *Communication Studies*, *65*, 519–534. doi:10.1080/105 10974.2014.956940

Larsson, A.O., & Moe, H. (2012). Studying political microblogging: Twitter users in the 2010 Swedish election campaign. *New Media & Society*, *14*(5), 729–747.

Leavitt, A. (2013). From# FollowFriday to YOLO. In K. Weller, A. Bruns, J. Burgess, M. Mahrt, & C. Puschmann (Eds.), *Twitter and society* (pp. 137–154). New York, NY: Peter Lang

Lee, C. (Ed.) (forthcoming). *Discourse of social tagging*. Special issue of *Discourse, Context and Media*.

Lehmann, J., Gonçalves, B., Ramasco, J.J., & Cattuto, C. (2012). Dynamical classes of collective attention in twitter. *Proceedings of the 21st International Conference on World Wide Web, 16–20 April 2012* (pp. 251–260). Lyon, France: ACM.

Lemke, J.L. (1998). Multiplying meaning: Visual and verbal semiotics in scientific text. *Reading Science: Critical and Functional Perspectives on Discourses of Science*, 87–113.

Lemke, J.L. (2005). *Textual politics: Discourse and social dynamics*. Bristol, PA: Taylor & Francis.

Liberman, M. (2016). Bigly. Language Log. Retrieved 20 May 2017 from http://languagelog.ldc.upenn.edu/nll/?p=24240, http://languagelog.ldc.upenn.edu/nll/?p=29091, http://languagelog.ldc.upenn.edu/nll/?p=28898

Lin, Y.-R., Keegan, B., Margolin, D., & Lazer, D. (2014). Rising tides or rising stars?: Dynamics of shared attention on Twitter during media events. *PloS one*, *9*(5), e94093.

Lin, Y.-R., Margolin, D., Keegan, B., Baronchelli, A., & Lazer, D. (2013). # Bigbirds Never Die: Understanding Social Dynamics of Emergent Hashtag. *Proceedings of the 7th International AAAI Conference on Weblogs and Social Media* (pp. 370–379). Boston, MA: AAAI.

Lindgren, S., & Lundström, R. (2011). Pirate culture and hacktivist mobilization: The cultural and social protocols of #WikiLeaks on Twitter. *New Media & Society*, *13*(6), 999–1018. doi:10.1177/1461444811414833

Litt, E., & Hargittai, E. (2016). The imagined audience on social network sites. *Social Media + Society*, *2*(1). doi:10.1177/2056305116633482

Liu, Y., Kliman-Silver, C., & Mislove, A. (2014). The tweets they are a-changin': Evolution of Twitter users and behavior. *Proceedings of the Eighth*

International AAAI Conference on Weblogs and Social Media, 1–4 June 2014 (pp. 305–314). Ann Arbor: AAAI, University of Michigan.

Lochrie, M., & Coulton, P. (2012). Sharing the viewing experience through second screens. *Proceedings of the 10th European Conference on Interactive TV and Video, Berlin, Germany, 04–06 July 2012* (pp. 199–202). New York, NY: ACM.

Lorince, J., Joseph, K., & Todd, P.M. (2015). Analysis of Music Tagging and Listening Patterns: Do Tags Really Function as Retrieval Aids? In N. Agarwal, K. Xu, & N. Osgood (Eds.), *Social Computing, Behavioral-Cultural Modeling, and Prediction: 8th International Conference, SBP 2015, Washington, DC, USA, 31 March–3 April, 2015. Proceedings* (pp. 141–152). Cham: Springer International Publishing.

Ma, Z., Sun, A., & Cong, G. (2012). Will this #hashtag be popular tomorrow? *Proceedings of the 35th International ACM SIGIR Conference on Research and Development in Information Retrieval* (pp. 1173–1174). Portland, OR: ACM.

Mahajan, D., Kolathur, V., Bansal, C., Parthasarathy, S., Sellamanickam, S., Keerthi, S., & Gehrke, J. (2016). Hashtag Recommendation for Enterprise Applications. *Proceedings of the 25th ACM International on Conference on Information and Knowledge Management, Indianapolis, IN, 24–28 October 2016* (pp. 893–902). New York, NY: ACM.

Maireder, A., & Schlögl, S. (2014). 24 hours of an# outcry: The networked publics of a socio-political debate. *European Journal of Communication, 29*(6), 687–702.

Maity, S.K., Ghuku, B., Upmanyu, A., & Mukherjee, A. (2015). Out of vocabulary words decrease, running texts prevail and hashtags coalesce: Twitter as an evolving sociolinguistic system. *49th Hawaii International Conference on System Sciences* (pp. 1681–1690). DC: IEEE Computer Society Washington.

Maity, S.K., Saraf, R., & Mukherjee, A. (2016). #Bieber + #Blast = #BieberBlast: Early Prediction of Popular Hashtag Compounds. *Proceedings of the 19th ACM Conference on Computer-Supported Cooperative Work & Social Computing* (pp. 50–63). San Francisco, CA: ACM.

Malinowski, B. (1935). *Coral gardens and their magic.* London: Allen & Unwin.

Marlow, C., Naaman, M., boyd, d., & Davis, M. (2006). HT06, Tagging Paper, Taxonomy, Flickr, Academic Article, To Read. *Proceedings of the Seventeenth Conference on Hypertext and Hypermedia, Odense, Denmark, 22–25 August 2006* (pp. 31–40). New York, NY: ACM.

Martin, J.R. (1992). *English text: System and structure.* Philadelphia, PA: John Benjamins Publishing.

Martin, J.R. (2000). Beyond exchange: Appraisal systems in English. In S. Hunston & G. Thompson (Eds.), *Evaluation in text: Authorial stance and the construction of discourse* (pp. 142–175). Oxford: Oxford University Press.

Martin, J.R. (2004). Mourning: How we get aligned. *Discourse & Society, 15*(2–3), 321–344.

Martin, J.R. (2008a). Innocence: Realisation, instantiation and individuation in a Botswanan town. In N.K. Knight & A. Mahboob (Eds.), *Questioning linguistics* (pp. 32–76). Cambridge: Cambridge Scholars Publishing.

Martin, J.R. (2008b). Tenderness: Realisation and instantiation in a Botswanan town. *Odense Working Papers in Language and Communication, 29*, 30–58.

Martin, J.R. (2010). Semantic variation: Modelling system, text and affiliation in social semiosis. In M. Bednarek & J.R. Martin (Eds.), *New discourse on language: Functional perspectives on multimodality, identity, and affiliation* (pp. 1–34). London: Continuum.

Martin, J.R. (2013). *Systemic functional grammar: A next step into the theory-axial relations.* Beijing: Beijing Higher Education Press.

Martin, J.R., & Matthiessen, C. (1991). Systemic typology and topology. In F. Christie (Ed.), *Literacy in social processes: Papers from the inaugural Australian systemic functional linguistics conference, Deakin University* (pp. 345–383). Darwin: Centre for Studies in Linguistics in Education, Northern Territory.

Martin, J.R., & Rose, D. (2008). *Genre relations: Mapping culture.* London: Equinox.

Martin, J.R., & Stenglin, M. (2007). Materializing reconciliation: Negotiating difference in a transcolonial exhibition. In T.D. Royce & W. Bowcher (Eds.), *New directions in the analysis of multimodal discourse* (pp. 215–338). Mahwah, NJ: Erlbaum.

Martin, J.R., & White, P.R.R. (2005). *The language of evaluation: Appraisal in English.* New York, NY: Palgrave Macmillan.

Martin, J.R., Zappavigna, M., Dwyer, P., & Cleirigh, C. (2013). Users in uses of language: Embodied identity in Youth Justice Conferencing. *Text & Talk, 33*(4–5), 467–496.

Marwick, A.E., & boyd, d. (2011). I tweet honestly, I tweet passionately: Twitter users, context collapse, and the imagined audience. *New Media & Society, 13*(1), 114–133.

Matley, D. (in press). 'This is NOT a #humblebrag, this is just a #brag': The pragmatics of self-praise, hashtags and politeness in Instagram posts. *Discourse, Context & Media.*

Matthiessen, C. (1995). *Lexicogrammatical cartography: English systems.* Tokyo: International Language Sciences Publishers.

Matthiessen, C.M.I.M (2006). Frequency profiles of some basic grammatical systems: An interim report. In G. Thompson & S. Hunston (Eds.), *System and corpus: Exploring connections* (pp. 103–142). London: Equinox.

McCosker, A. (2017). Tagging depression: Social media and the segmentation of mental health. In P. Messaris & L. Humphreys (Eds.), *Digital media: Transformations in human communication* (pp. 31–39). New York, NY: Peter Lang.

McGrenere, J., & Ho, W. (2000). Affordances: Clarifying and evolving a concept. In S. Fels & P. Poulin (Eds.), *Proceedings of graphics interface 2000, 15–17 May 2000, Montreal, Quebec, Canada* (pp. 179–186). Montréal: Lawrence Erlbaum Associates.

McNely, B. (2009). Backchannel persistence and collaborative meaning-making. *Proceedings of the 27th ACM International Conference on Design of Communication, Bloomington, IN, 05–07 October 2009* (pp. 297–304). New York, NY: ACM.

Meese, J., Gibbs, M., & Kohn, T. (2015). Selfies at funerals: Mourning and presencing on social media platforms. *International Journal of Communication, 9,* 1818–1831.

Mehrotra, R., Sanner, S., Buntine, W., & Xie, L. (2013). Improving lda topic models for microblogs via tweet pooling and automatic labeling. *Proceedings of the 36th International ACM SIGIR Conference on Research and Development in Information Retrieval, Dublin, Ireland, 28 July–01 August 2013* (pp. 889–892). New York, NY: ACM.

Mendoza, M., Poblete, B., & Castillo, C. (2010). Twitter under crisis: Can we trust what we RT? *Proceedings of the First Workshop on Social Media Analytics, 25 July 2010, Washington, DC* (pp. 71–79). New York: ACM. Retrieved from http://snap.stanford.edu/soma2010/papers/soma2010_11.pdf

Merholz, P. (2004). Metadata for the masses. Retrieved 8 May 2017 from http://adaptivepath.org/ideas/e000361/

Milner, R.M. (2012). *The world made meme: Discourse and identity in participatory media*. Doctor of Philosophy, University of Kansas, Kansas.

Milner, R.M. (2013a). FCJ-156 Hacking the Social: Internet Memes, Identity Antagonism, and the Logic of Lulz. *The Fibreculture Journal* (22), Retrieved 12 April 2017 from http://twentytwo.fibreculturejournal.org/fcj-156-hacking-the-social-internet-memes-identity-antagonism-and-the-logic-of-lulz/

Milner, R.M. (2013b). Pop polyvocality: Internet memes, public participation, and the Occupy Wall Street movement. *International Journal of Communication*, 7, 2357–2390.

Miltner, K.M. (2014). 'There's no place for lulz on LOLCats': The role of genre, gender, and group identity in the interpretation and enjoyment of an Internet meme. *First Monday*, *19*(8).

Mitchell, G., & Clarke, A. (2003). *Videogame art: Remixing, reworking and other interventions*. Utrecht: Utrecht University.

Mohammad, S.M., & Kiritchenko, S. (2015). Using hashtags to capture fine emotion categories from tweets. *Computational Intelligence*, *31*(2), 301–326.

Montemurro, E., & Kamerer, D. (2016). # DearCongress: A public letter. *First Monday*.

Moorley, C.R., & Chinn, T. (2014). Nursing and Twitter: Creating an online community using hashtags. *Collegian*, *21*(2), 103–109. doi:http://dx.doi.org/10.1016/j.colegn.2014.03.003

Moreno, M.A., Ton, A., Selkie, E., & Evans, Y. (2016). Secret society 123: Understanding the language of self-harm on Instagram. *Journal of Adolescent Health*, *58*(1), 78–84.

Murthy, D., Powell, A.B., Tinati, R., Anstead, N., Carr, L., Halford, S.J., & Weal, M. (2016). Automation, algorithms, and political bots and political influence: A sociotechnical investigation of social network capital. *International Journal of Communication*, *10*, 4952–4971.

Myrick, J.G., Holton, A.E., Himelboim, I., & Love, B. (2015). #Stupidcancer: Exploring a typology of social support and the role of emotional expression in a social media community. *Health Communication*, 1–10. doi:10.1080/10410236.2014.981664

Naaman, M., Becker, H., & Gravano, L. (2011). Hip and trendy: Characterizing emerging trends on Twitter. *Journal of the American Society for Information Science and Technology*, *62*(5), 902–918.

Nesbitt, C., & Plum, G. (1988). Probabilities in a systemic-functional grammar: The clause complex in English. In R.P. Fawcett & D. Young (Eds.), *New developments in systemic linguistics, Vol. 2: Theory and applications* (Vol. 2, pp. 6–38). London: Pinter.

Newitz, A., & Wray, M. (2013). *White trash: Race and class in America*. London: Taylor & Francis.

Norman, D.A. (1988). *The psychology of everyday things*. New York, NY: Basic Books.

Norrick, N.R. (1994). Involvement and joking in conversation. *Journal of Pragmatics*, *22*(3), 409–430. doi:http://dx.doi.org/10.1016/0378-2166(94)90117-1

Norrick, N.R. (2003). Issues in conversational joking. *Journal of Pragmatics*, *35*(9), 1333–1359. doi:http://dx.doi.org/10.1016/S0378-2166(02)00180-7

Orwell, G. (1949/1987). *1984*. Boston & New York, NY: Houghton Mifflin Harcourt.

Oulasvirta, A., Lehtonen, E., Kurvinen, E., & Raento, M. (2010). Making the ordinary visible in microblogs. *Personal and Ubiquitous Computing*, *14*(3), 237–249.

Page, R. (2012). The linguistics of self-branding and micro-celebrity in Twitter: The role of hashtags. *Discourse & Communication*, *6*(2), 181–201.

Page, R., Barton, D., Unger, J.W., & Zappavigna, M. (2014). *Researching language and social media: A student guide*. London: Routledge.

Painter, C. (1984). *Into the mother tongue: A case study in early language development*. London: Frances Pinter.

Painter, C., & Martin, J. (2011). Intermodal complementarity: Modelling affordances across image and verbiage in children's picture books. In F. Yan (Ed.), *Studies in functional linguistics and discourse analysis* (pp. 132–148). Beijing: Educational Press of China.

Palen, L., Starbird, K., Vieweg, S., & Hughes, A. (2010). Twitter-based information distribution during the 2009 red river valley flood threat. *Bulletin of the American Society for Information Science and Technology*, *36*(5), 13–17.

Pancer, E., & Poole, M. (2016). The popularity and virality of political social media: Hashtags, mentions, and links predict likes and retweets of 2016 U.S. Presidential nominees' tweets. *Social Influence*, *11*(4), 259–270. doi:10.1080/1 5534510.2016.1265582

Paolillo, J.C. (2001). Language variation on Internet Relay Chat: A social network approach. *Journal of Sociolinguistics*, *5*(2), 180–213.

Papacharissi, Z. (2015). *Affective publics: Sentiment, technology, and politics*. London: Oxford University Press.

Papacharissi, Z. (2016). Affective publics and structures of storytelling: Sentiment, events and mediality. *Information, Communication & Society*, *19*(3), 307–324. doi:10.1080/1369118X.2015.1109697

Paradowski, M.B., & Jonak, Ł. (2012). Diffusion of linguistic innovation as social coordination. *Psychology of Language and Communication*, *16*(2), 131–142.

Pavalanathan, U., & Eisenstein, J. (2015). Audience-modulated variation in online social media. *American Speech*, *90*(2), 187–213.

Pham, M.-H. T. (2015). 'I click and post and breathe, waiting for others to see what i see': On #FeministSelfies, outfit photos, and networked vanity. *Fashion Theory-The Journal of Dress Body & Culture*, *19*, 221–241. doi:10.2752/175174 115X14168357992436

Phillips, W. (2015). *This is why we can't have nice things: Mapping the relationship between online trolling and mainstream culture*. Cambridge, MA: MIT Press.

Posch, L., Wagner, C., Singer, P., & Strohmaier, M. (2013). *Meaning as collective use: Predicting semantic hashtag categories on twitter*. Paper presented at the Proceedings of the 22nd International Conference on World Wide Web Companion, Rio de Janeiro, Brazil.

Potts, A., Simm, W., Whittle, J., & Unger, J.W. (2014). Exploring 'success' in digitally augmented activism: A triangulated approach to analyzing UK activist Twitter use. *Discourse, Context & Media, 6*, 65–76. doi:http://dx.doi.org/10.1016/j.dcm.2014.08.008

Poynton, C. (1984). Names as vocatives: Forms and functions. *Nottingham Linguistic Circular, 13*, 1–34.

Poynton, C. (1991). *Address and the semiotics of social relations: A systemic-functional account of address forms and practices in Australian English.* University of Sydney.

Pullum, G.K. (2010). Part-of-speech classification question. Retrieved 4 May 2017 from http://languagelog.ldc.upenn.edu/nll/?p=2584

Puschmann, C. (2015). The form and function of quoting in digital media. *Discourse, Context & Media, 7*, 28–36.

Qadir, A., & Riloff, E. (2013). Bootstrapped learning of emotion hashtags# hashtags4you. In A. Balahur, E. van der Goot, & A. Montoyo (Eds.), *Proceedings of the 4th Workshop on Computational Approaches to Subjectivity, Sentiment and Social Media Analysis* (pp. 2–11). Atlanta, GA, 14 June 2013: Association for Computational Linguistics.

Rambukanna, N. (2015). From# RaceFail to# Ferguson: The digital intimacies of race-activist hashtag publics. *The Fibreculture Journal* (26), 159–188.

Rambukkana, N. (2015a). *Hashtag publics: The power and politics of discursive networks.* New York, NY: Peter Lang.

Rambukkana, N. (2015b). #Introduction: Hashtags as technosocial events. In N. Rambukkana (Ed.), *Hashtag publics: The power and politics of discursive networks* (pp. 1–10). New York, NY: Peter Lang.

Razer, H. (2016). Who killed the liberal dream? (Spoiler: it wasn't 'fake news'). *Crikey.* Retrieved from https://www.crikey.com.au/2016/12/22/razer-who-killed-the-liberal-dream

Rheingold, H. (1993). *The virtual community: Homesteading on the electronic frontier.* Reading, MA: Addison-Wesley.

Rieder, B. (2012). The refraction chamber: Twitter as sphere and network. *First Monday, 17*(11).

Rightler-McDaniels, J.L., & Hendrickson, E.M. (2014). Hoes and hashtags: Constructions of gender and race in trending topics. *Social Semiotics, 24*, 175–190. doi:10.1080/10350330.2013.859355

Riley, J. (2017). Understanding metadata. What is metadata, and what is it for? Retrieved 30 April 2017 from http://www.niso.org/apps/group_public/download.php/17446/UnderstandingMetadata.pdf

Riley, J., & Shepherd, K. (2009). A brave new world: Archivists and shareable descriptive metadata. *The American Archivist, 72*(1), 91–112.

Riloff, E., Qadir, A., Surve, P., De Silva, L., Gilbert, N., & Huang, R. (2013). Sarcasm as Contrast between a Positive Sentiment and Negative Situation. *Proceedings of the 2013 Conference on Empirical Methods in Natural Language Processing. Seattle, Washington, 18–21 October 2013* (Vol. 13, pp. 704–714).

Rintel, R. (2013). Crisis memes: The importance of templatability to Internet culture and freedom of expression. *Australasian Journal of Popular Culture, 2*(2), 253–271.

Romero, D.M., Galuba, W., Asur, S., & Huberman, B.A. (2011). Influence and passivity in social media. In D. Gunopulos, T. Hofmann, D. Malerba, & M. Vazirgiannis (Eds.), *Machine Learning and Knowledge Discovery in Databases.*

European Conference on Machine Learning and Knowledge Discovery in Databases (ECML PKDD 2011), Lecture Notes in Computer Science (Vol. 6913, pp. 18–33). Berlin & Heidelberg: Springer.

Romero, D.M., Meeder, B., & Kleinberg, J. (2011). Differences in the mechanics of information diffusion across topics: Idioms, political hashtags, and complex contagion on twitter. *Proceedings of the 20th International Conference on World Wide Web* (pp. 695–704). New York, NY: ACM.

Rossi, L., & Giglietto, F. (2016). Twitter use during TV: A full-season analysis of #serviziopubblico hashtag. *Journal of Broadcasting & Electronic Media, 60*(2), 331–346. doi:10.1080/08838151.2016.1164162

Rossi, L., & Magnani, M. (2012). Conversation practices and network structure in Twitter. *Proceedings of the Sixth International AAAI Conference on Weblogs and Social Media* (pp. 563–566). Dublin: The AAAI Press.

Rzeszotarski, J.M., Spiro, E.S., Matias, J.N., Monroy-Hernández, A., & Morris, M.R. (2014). Is anyone out there?: unpacking Q&A hashtags on twitter. *Proceedings of the 32nd Annual ACM Conference on Human Factors in Computing Systems, Toronto, Ontario, Canada, 26 April–01 May* 2014 (pp. 2755–2758). New York, NY: ACM.

Sanderson, J., Barnes, K., Williamson, C., & Kian, E.T. (2016). 'How could anyone have predicted that #AskJameis would go horribly wrong?' Public relations, social media, and hashtag hijacking. *Public Relations Review, 42*(1), 31–37. doi:http://dx.doi.org/10.1016/j.pubrev.2015.11.005

Sauter, T., & Bruns, A. (2014). Tweeting the TV event, creating 'public sphericules': AD HOC engagement with SBS's go back to where you came from – season 2. *Media International Australia, 152*(1), 5–15.

Sauter, T., & Bruns, A. (2015). # auspol: The hashtag as community, event, and material object for engaging with Australian politics. In N. Rambukanna (Ed.), *Hashtag publics: The power and politics of discursive networks* (pp. 47–60). New York, NY: Peter Lang.

Scheible, J. (2015). *Digital shift: The cultural logic of punctuation.* Minneapolis, MN: University of Minnesota Press.

Schirra, S., Sun, H., & Bentley, F. (2014). Together alone: Motivations for live-tweeting a television series. *Proceedings of the 32nd Annual ACM Conference on Human Factors in Computing Systems, Toronto, Ontario, Canada, 26 April–01 May* 2014 (pp. 2441–2450). New York, NY: ACM.

Schlesselman-Tarango, G. (2013). Searchable signatures: Context and the struggle for recognition. *Information Technology and Libraries, 32*, 5–19. doi:10.6017/ital.v32i3.3093

Scott, K. (2015). The pragmatics of hashtags: Inference and conversational style on Twitter. *Journal of Pragmatics, 81*, 8–20. doi:http://dx.doi.org/10.1016/j.pragma.2015.03.015

Scott, K. (in press). The pragmatic functions of spoken hashtags. *Discourse, Context & Media, Special Issue on the Discourse of Social Tagging.*

Scott, S. (2017). #Wheresrey?: Toys, spoilers, and the gender politics of franchise paratexts. *Critical Studies in Media Communication*, 1–10. doi:10.1080/15295036.2017.1286023

Segev, E., Nissenbaum, A., Stolero, N., & Shifman, L. (2015). Families and networks of internet memes: The relationship between cohesiveness, uniqueness, and quiddity concreteness. *Journal of Computer-Mediated Communication, 20*(4), 417–433. doi:10.1111/jcc4.12120

She, J., & Chen, L. (2014). Tomoha: Topic model-based hashtag recommendation on twitter. *Proceedings of the 23rd International Conference on World Wide Web, Seoul, Korea, 07–11 April 2014* (pp. 371–372). New York, NY: ACM.

Shifman, L. (2012). An anatomy of a YouTube meme. *New Media & Society, 14*(2), 187–203.

Shifman, L. (2013a). Memes in a digital world: Reconciling with a conceptual troublemaker. *Journal of Computer-Mediated Communication, 18*(3), 362–377.

Shifman, L. (2013b). *Memes in digital culture*. Boston, MA: MIT Press.

Shifman, L. (2014). The cultural logic of photo-based meme genres. *Journal of Visual Culture, 13*(3), 340–358. doi:10.1177/1470412914546577

Sinclair, J. (2005). Language as a string of beads: Discourse and the M-word. In E. Tognini-Bonelli & G.D.L. Camiciotti (Eds.), *Strategies in Academic Discourse*. London: Benjamins.

Sinclair, J.M. (1988). Mirror for a text. *Journal of English and Foreign Languages, 1*, 15–44.

Skågeby, J. (2009). Exploring qualitative sharing practices of social metadata: Expanding the attention economy. *The Information Society, 25*(1), 60–72.

Skaza, J., & Blais, B. (2017). Modeling the infectiousness of Twitter hashtags. *Physica A: Statistical Mechanics and Its Applications, 465*, 289–296. doi:http://dx.doi.org/10.1016/j.physa.2016.08.038

Small, T.A. (2011). What the Hashtag? A content analysis of Canadian politics on Twitter. *Information, Communication & Society, 14*, 872–895. doi:10.1080/1369118X.2011.554572

Stache, L.C. (2015). Advocacy and political potential at the convergence of hashtag activism and commerce. *Feminist Media Studies, 15*(1), 162–164. doi:10.1080/14680777.2015.987429

Starbird, K., & Stamberger, J. (2010). Tweak the tweet: Leveraging microblogging proliferation with a prescriptive syntax to support citizen reporting. *Proceedings of the 7th International ISCRAM Conference, Seattle, May 2010* (pp. 1–5). Retrieved 2 May 2017 from http://repository.cmu.edu/silicon_valley/41/

Stathopoulou, A., Borel, L., Christodoulides, G., & West, D. (2017). Consumer branded# hashtag engagement: Can creativity in TV advertising influence hashtag engagement? *Psychology & Marketing, 34*(4), 448–462.

Stec, K., Huiskes, M., & Redeker, G. (2016). Multimodal quotation: Role shift practices in spoken narratives. *Journal of Pragmatics, 104*, 1–17.

Stenglin, M. (2008a). Interpersonal meaning in 3D space: How a bonding icon gets its 'charge'. In L. Unsworth (Ed.), *Multimodal semiotics: Functional analysis in contexts of education* (pp. 50–66). London: Continuum.

Stenglin, M. (2008b). Olympism: How a bonding icon gets its 'charge'. In L. Unsworth (Ed.), *Multimodal Semiotics: Functional Analysis in the Contexts of Education* (pp. 50–66). London/New York: continuum.

Stenglin, M. (2012). Transformation & Transcendence: Bonding through ritual. Paper presented at the International Systemic Functional Linguistcs Conference, 16–20 July 2012, University of Technology, Sydney.

Strauss, A., & Corbin, J. (1994). Grounded theory methodology. In N.K. Denzin & Y.S. Lincon (Eds.), *Handbook of qualitative research* (pp. 273–285). Thousand Oaks: Sage.

Stryker, S. (1956). Relationships of married offspring and parent: A test of Mead's theory. *American Journal of Sociology, 62*(3), 308–319.

Stubbs, M. (1986). 'A matter of prolonged field work': Notes towards a modal grammar of English. *Applied Linguistics, 7*(1), 1–25.

Swain, E. (2003). Humour as discordant couplings: An appraisal theory approach. In C. Nocera, G. Persico, & R. Portale (Eds.), *Atti del XX Convegno Nazionale dell'Associazione Italiana di Anglistica, Catania 4/6 ottobre 2001* (pp. 521–532)). Catanzaro: Rubbettino.

Szenes, E. (2016). *The linguistic construction of business reasoning: Towards a language-based model of decision-making in undergraduate business.* Doctor of Philosophy, University of Sydney, Sydney.

Tajfel, H. (1970). Experiments in intergroup discrimination. *Scientific American, 223*, 96–102.

Tann, K. (2010). Imagining communities: A multifunctional approach to identity management in texts. In M. Bednarek & J.R. Martin (Eds.), *New discourse on language: Functional perspectives on multimodality, identity, and affiliation* (pp. 163–194). London: Continuum.

Tann, K. (2013). The language of identity discourse: Introducing a systemic functional framework for iconography. *Linguistics & the Human Sciences, 8*(3), 361–391.

The Tonight Show Starring Jimmy Fallon. (2013). '#Hashtag' with Jimmy Fallon & Justin Timberlake (Late Night with Jimmy Fallon). Retrieved 4 May 2017 from https://www.youtube.com/watch?v=57dzaMaouXA

Trant, J. (2009). Studying social tagging and folksonomy: A review and framework. *Journal of Digital Information, 10*(1), Retrieved 22 April 2017 from https://journals.tdl.org/jodi/index.php/jodi/article/view/269

Tsur, O., & Rappoport, A. (2012). *What's in a hashtag?: Content based prediction of the spread of ideas in microblogging communities.* Paper presented at the Proceedings of the Fifth ACM International Conference on Web Search and Data Mining.

Twitter. (2016). Twitter Text Libraries. Retrieved 29 April 2017 from https://github .com/twitter/twitter-text/blob/master/java/src/com/twitter/Regex.java

Twitter. (2017). FAQs about trends on Twitter. Retrieved 19 April 2017 from https:// support.twitter.com/articles/101125

Urban Dictionary. (2011). Charlie Sheen Winning. Available (posted by Subzero88). Retrieved 8 May 2017 from http://www.urbandictionary.com/define .php?term=Charlie%20Sheen%20Winning.

Vaccari, C., Valeriani, A., Barberá, P., Bonneau, R., Jost, J.T., Nagler, J., & Tucker, J.A. (2015). Political expression and action on social media: Exploring the relationship between lower- and higher-threshold political activities among twitter users in Italy. *Journal of Computer-Mediated Communication, 20*(2), 221–239. doi:10.1111/jcc4.12108

van Dijck, J. (2013). *The culture of connectivity: A critical history of social media.* Oxford: Oxford University Press.

van Leeuwen, T. (2008). New forms of writing, new visual competencies. *Visual Studies, 23*(2), 130–135. doi:10.1080/14725860802276263

Vande Kopple, W.J. (1985). Some exploratory discourse on metadiscourse. *College Composition and Communication, 36*(1), 82–93. doi:10.2307/357609

Vander Wal, T. (2007). Folksonomy Coinage and Definition. Retrieved from http:// vanderwal.net/folksonomy.html

Vásquez, C. (2014). 'Usually not one to complain but ...': Constructing identities in user-generated online reviews. In P. Seargeant & C. Tagg (Eds.), *The language of social media: Identity and community on the internet* (pp. 65–90). London: Palgrave Macmillan UK.

Vats, A. (2015). Cooking up hashtag activism: #PaulasBestDishes and counternarratives of southern food. *Communication and Critical/Cultural Studies, 12*(2), 209–213. doi:10.1080/14791420.2015.1014184

Ventola, E. (1987). *The structure of social interaction: A systemic approach to the semiotics of service encounters.* London: Frances Pinter.

Veszelszki, Á. (2016). #time, #truth, #tradition. An image-text relationship on Instagram: Photo and hashtag. In A. Benedek & Á. Veszelszki (Eds.), *In the beginning was the image: The omnipresence of pictures: Time, truth, tradition* (pp. 139–150). Frankfurt am Main: Peter Lang.

Voloshinov, V.N. (1929/1973/1986). *Marxism and the philosophy of language* (L. Matejka & I.R. Titunik, Trans.). Cambridge, MA: Harvard University Press.

Wang, R., Liu, W., & Gao, S. (2016). Hashtags and information virality in networked social movement. *Online Information Review, 40*(7), 850–866. doi:10.1108/oir-12-2015-0378

Wang, R., Wang, R., Liu, W., Liu, W., Gao, S., & Gao, S. (2016). Hashtags and information virality in networked social movement: Examining hashtag co-occurrence patterns. *Online Information Review, 40*(7), 850–866.

Wang, Y., Liu, J., Huang, Y., & Feng, X. (2016). Using hashtag graph-based topic model to connect semantically-related words without co-occurrence in microblogs. *IEEE Transactions on Knowledge and Data Engineering, 28*(7), 1919–1933.

Wendt, B. (2014). *The allure of the selfie: Instagram and the new self-portrait.* Amsterdam: Institute of Network Cultures, Hogeschool van Amsterdam.

Weng, L., Menczer, F., & Ahn, Y.-Y. (2013). Virality prediction and community structure in social networks. *Scientific Reports, 3*, 2522–2536.

Wert, S.R., & Salovey, P. (2004). A social comparison account of gossip. *Review of General Psychology, 8*(2), 122.

Wesch, M. (2009). YouTube and you: Experiences of self-awareness in the context collapse of the recording webcam. *Explorations in Media Ecology, 8*(2), 19–34.

White, P.R.R. (1998). *Telling media tales: The news story as rhetoric.* Doctoral thesis, University of Sydney, Sydney.

White, P.R.R. (2003). Beyond modality and hedging: A dialogic view of the language of intersubjective stance. *Text & Talk, 23*(2), 259–284.

White, P.R.R. (2012). Exploring the axiological workings of 'reporter voice' news stories – Attribution and attitudinal positioning. *Discourse, Context & Media, 1*(2), 57–67.

Wiggins, B.E., & Bowers, G.B. (2015). Memes as genre: A structurational analysis of the memescape. *New Media & Society, 17*(11), 1886–1906. doi:10.1177/1461444814535194

Wikström, P. (2014). # srynotfunny: Communicative functions of hashtags on Twitter. *SKY Journal of Linguistics, 27*, 127–152.

Williams, J.M. (1981). *Style: Ten lessons in clarity & grace.* Boston, MA: Scott Foresman.

Williams, S. (2015). Digital defense: Black feminists resist violence with hashtag activism. *Feminist Media Studies, 15*, 341–344. doi:10.1080/14680777.2015.1008744

Wittels, H. (2012). *Humblebrag: The art of false modesty.* New York, NY: Grand Central Publishing.

Wu, T. (2017). *The attention merchants: How our time and attention are gathered and sold.* London: Atlantic Books.

Wukich, C., & Steinberg, A. (2013). Nonprofit and public sector participation in self-organizing information networks: Twitter hashtag and trending topic use during disasters. *Risk, Hazards & Crisis in Public Policy, 4*, 83–109. doi:10.1002/rhc3.12036

Yang, L., Sun, T., Zhang, M., & Mei, Q. (2012). We know what @you #tag: Does the dual role affect hashtag adoption? *Proceedings of the 21st International Conference on World Wide Web* (pp. 261–270). New York, NY: ACM.

Zappavigna, M. (2011). Ambient affiliation: A linguistic perspective on Twitter. *New Media & Society, 13*(5), 788–806. doi:10.1177/1461444810385097

Zappavigna, M. (2012a). *Discourse of Twitter and social media.* London: Continuum.

Zappavigna, M. (2012b). Discourse of twitter and social media: How we use language to create affiliation on the web.

Zappavigna, M. (2014a). Ambient affiliation in microblogging: Bonding around the quotidian. *Media International Australia, 151*(1), 97–103.

Zappavigna, M. (2014b). Coffeetweets: Bonding around the bean on Twitter. In P. Seargeant & C. Tagg (Eds.), *The language of social media: Communication and community on the internet* (pp. 139 –160). London: Palgrave.

Zappavigna, M. (2014c). Enacting identity in microblogging through ambient affiliation. *Discourse & Communication, 8*, 209–228. doi:10.1177/1750481313510816

Zappavigna, M. (2014d). Enjoy your snags Australia ... oh and the voting thing too #ausvotes #auspol: Iconisation and affiliation in electoral microblogging. *Global Media Journal: Australian Edition, 8*, 1–18.

Zappavigna, M. (2015). Searchable talk: The linguistic functions of hashtags. *Social Semiotics, 25*, 274–291. doi:10.1080/10350330.2014.996948

Zappavigna, M. (forthcoming). #Convocation and ambient affiliation: Social tagging as a resource for aligning around values in social media. *Discourse, Context & Media* (special issue on the discourse of social tagging).

Zappavigna, M. (2017a). Ambient liveness: Searchable audiences and second screens. In C. Hight & H. Harindranath (Eds.), *Studying digital media audiences: Perspectives from Australasia.* London: Routledge.

Zappavigna, M. (in press-b). 'had enough of experts': Intersubjectivity and quotation in social media In E. Friginal (Ed.), *Studies in corpus-based sociolinguistics.* London: Routledge.

Zappavigna, M. (in press-c). Selfies in 'mommy blogging': An emerging visual genre. *Discourse, Context and Media.*

Zappavigna, M., Cleirigh, C., Dwyer, P., & Martin, J.R. (2010a). The coupling of gesture and phonology. *New Discourse on Language: Functional Perspectives on Multimodality, Identity, and Affiliation*, 219–236.

Zappavigna, M., Cléirigh, C., Dwyer, P., & Martin, J.R. (2010b). Visualizing appraisal prosody. In A. Mahboob & N.K. Knight (Eds.), *Appliable linguistics* (pp. 150–167). London: Continuum.

Zappavigna, M., Dwyer, P., & Martin, J. (2008). Syndromes of meaning: Exploring patterned coupling in a NSW youth justice conference. In A. Mahboob & N.K. Knight (Eds.), *Questioning linguistics. Newcastle: Cambridge scholars publishing* (pp. 103–117). Newcastle: Cambridge Scholars Publishing.

Zhang, L., Zhao, J., & Xu, K. (2016). Who creates trends in online social media: The crowd or opinion leaders? *Journal of Computer-Mediated Communication, 21*(1), 1–16. doi:10.1111/jcc4.12145

Zhao, S. (2010). Intersemiotic relations as logogenetic patterns: The time factor in hypertext description. In M. Bednarek & J.R. Martin (Eds.), *New discourse on language: Functional perspectives on multimodality, identity, and affiliation* (pp. 251–266). London: Continuum.

Zhao, S. (2011). *Learning through multimedia interaction: The construal of primary social science knowledge in web-based digital learning materials.* Doctor of Philosophy, University of Sydney, Sydney.

Zhao, S., Djonov, E., & van Leeuwen, T. (2014). Semiotic technology and practice: A multimodal social semiotic approach to PowerPoint. *Text & Talk*, 349–375, 349.

Zhao, S., & van Leeuwen, T. (2014). Understanding semiotic technology in university classrooms: A social semiotic approach to PowerPoint-assisted cultural studies lectures. *Classroom Discourse, 5*(1), 71–90.

Zhao, S., & Zappavigna, M. (2015). *The recontextualisation of subjective images in three (social) media platforms: A methodological exploration.* Paper presented at MODE Conference – Multimodality: Methodological Explorations, London, 15–16 January.

Zhao, S., & Zappavigna, M. (in press). Beyond the self: Intersubjectivity and the social semiotic interpretation of the selfie. *New Media and Society.* http://journals.sagepub.com/doi/abs/10.1177/1461444817706074#articleCitationDownloadContainer

Zhu, H. (2016). Searchable talk as discourse practice on the internet: The case of '#bindersfullofwomen.' *Discourse, Context & Media, 12*, 87–98. doi:http://dx.doi.org/10.1016/j.dcm.2015.10.001

Zimmer, B., & Carson, C.E. (2013). Among the new words. *American Speech, 88*(1), 81–99.

Zimmer, B., & Solomon, J. (2015). Among the new words. *American Speech, 90*(2), 214–229.

Index